IMAGES
of America

LEHIGH TOWNSHIP

IMAGES
of America

LEHIGH TOWNSHIP

Lehigh Township Historical Society

ARCADIA
PUBLISHING

ISBN 978-0-7385-1021-7

Published by Arcadia Publishing
Charleston, South Carolina

Printed in the United States of America

Library of Congress Catalog Card Number: 2002101511

For all general information contact Arcadia Publishing at:
Telephone 843-853-2070
Fax 843-853-0044
E-mail sales@arcadiapublishing.com
For customer service and orders:
Toll-Free 1-888-313-2665

Visit us on the Internet at www.arcadiapublishing.com

Contents

ACKNOWLEDGMENTS

This book has been written by Beverly Putt, Robert Mentzell, Mary Ann Endy, and Sean Billings on behalf of the Lehigh Township Historical Society on the 250th anniversary of the township. Johanna S. Billings provided editorial support. This book is not intended as a definitive history of the township but as an overview.

The Lehigh Township Historical Society was incorporated as a nonprofit corporation in April 2001. The founding members are J. Clarke Berner, Sean Billings, Mae Bowman, Mary Ann Endy, Darrin Heckman, Daniel Hummel, Robert Mentzell, Peter Pagotto, Sarah Pagotto, Beverly Putt, Wilson Putt, and Nancy Stott.

For contributing materials to be used in this book, thanks go to the Allentown Art Museum, David Altrichter, David Bausch, Norman Borger, Caroline Cook, Cindy Deppe, Vince and Judy Dieter, Shirley Eckhart, Kathy Fogle, Harley Fritz, Paul Gieske, Larry Hillborn, Edgar Jacoby, Alverta and Emily Jones, Carson and Joanne Jones, Florence A. Kline, Margaret Kohler, Mike and Gloria Kravetz, Phaon Kuntz, Virginia Lacko, the Mary Immaculate Center, Elda Miller, Josephine Miller, Metro Myster, Elaine Newhart, Linda Ott, Lester Reimer, Woodrow Reph, Griffith Roberts, Betty Seidel, William Shoemaker, Jean Silfies, Mary Lou Walck, the Walnutport Canal Association, Betty Wattson, Carolyn Werner, Kristin Zarrizski, and Florence Ziegenfuss.

INTRODUCTION

Lehigh Township was surveyed in 1735 by orders of Thomas Penn. It was proposed that 6,500 acres be set aside for Native Americans, but the land became a settlement of immigrants instead. Before October 1752, when the township was officially created, the area had been called Adjacents to Allen, which probably refers to adjacent Allen Township. Although some residents wanted the name Seimsy after an early Moravian Indian convert named Seim, the county court opted for the name Lehigh Township instead.

Originally, Lehigh Township reached from the Lehigh River eastward to the Bushkill Creek. By 1763, however, Moore Township was created out of portions of Allen, Lehigh, and Plainfield Townships. Later, in 1909, Walnutport also broke off as an independent borough.

After the beginning of the colonization of Pennsylvania, settlers began to establish homes in the areas north and west of Philadelphia, even to the foothills of the Blue Mountain. Lehigh Township, located less than 70 miles north of Philadelphia, was directly on the path from Easton and Bethlehem to the wilderness beyond the Lehigh Gap. This area was a place of rolling hills and wooded areas that provided fertile farmland. Creeks and rivers provided ideal places for construction of dams for mills, giving rise to villages in the area.

One of the earliest settlers in the area was Simon Dreisbach, whose family acquired acreage a few miles from Blue Mountain along Indian Creek. Dreisbach's son Jost built a gristmill along Indian Creek, and a German-language Reformed Church congregation began meeting at his home. In 1755, the Dreisbach men filed land patents for the land on which their settlement was located. Although they had already purchased the land from Native Americans, not all the transactions were recognized by the descendants of William Penn, so the Dreisbachs had to repurchase their land. During the Native American attacks of 1755 and 1756, some of the Dreisbachs are said to have fled to Easton. In 1757, Simon Dreisbach was among the Northampton County residents who sent a petition to the governor of Pennsylvania, requesting protection from the Native American raids.

Some other family names appearing on 1761 Lehigh Township tax records are Allemang, Altman, Anderye, Antony, Armstrong, Barron, Barthol, Beck, Becker, Beer, Beninger, Best, Bety, Bossert, Boyd, Brand, Bricker, Brudy, Buchman, Collwell, Creasy, Deater, Diel, Doll, Dorn, Drum, Eberhard, Eckert, Eisonman, Erb, Etmistin, Fassy, Flick, Geissel, Haag, Haring, Hollstein, Hutsheson, Hyl, Kallenbach, Kenedy, Kepple, Kerr, Kester, Klindop, Klingensmith, Koch, Kuntz, Laufert, Leaverman, Lederach, Leyenberger, Luther, Macher, Marsh, Meyer, Miller, Musselman, Naguel, Nyhard, Read, Rearich, Reeb, Remberger, Reph, Rinking, Ris, Road, Roofner, Roushenberger, Ruch, Shantz, Sheeterle, Sherrer, Shlegler, Shnyder, Shup, Shwab, Shyll, Silvius, Singling, Snyder, Sold, Spengler, Steed, Stewert, Stoltz, Straw, Ulrich, Van Deck, Vogel, Walker, Waltman, Wannen, Wertz, William, Young, and Zedel.

The township population was only about 100 people in 1750, but it increased to 350 people by 1770. After the American Revolution, the population increased more rapidly. The 1900 census listed some 1,000 residents, and the 2000 census showed a population of 9,728.

Today, the township is governed by a board of supervisors. Originally a board of three, it was expanded to five supervisors in 1994. The township also has a planning commission, zoning board, recreation commission, and municipal authority. Unfortunately, most of the names of the past supervisors and other officials have been lost to history.

The township's first police force was organized in 1947 by Roland Wieand, who served as the police chief. His son Harold succeeded him, followed by Roland's grandson John. Today, the police force employs 11 officers.

The Lehigh Township Volunteer Fire Company No. 1 was organized on February 3, 1944, at a meeting held at the Indianland Hotel. The 60 people in attendance chose Robert Spangler to be president. The first fire chief was Roland Dieter, who hosted a number of the early meetings at Dieter's Foundry. The foundry machine shop also served as home to the first fire truck, a 1945 Mack. In 1946, the fire company acquired property in Cherryville and, in 1954, built a firehouse.

In 1974, the Lehigh Township Volunteer Fire Company First Aid Squad became the township's first ambulance service. When first organized, the squad stored its vehicles in the fire hall, and first-aid calls were taken at the Reformed parsonage by Rev. George Allen and his wife, Margo. By 1988, the ambulance service changed its name to the Lehigh Township Emergency Squad and operated out of a four-room building owned by the township. In 1997, the squad became part of the Regional Emergency Medical Service, which serves Lehigh Township, North Allen Township, and Catasauqua Borough (in Northampton County), as well as Hanover Township (in Lehigh County).

The Lions Club, which celebrated its 50th anniversary on January 20, 2001, has served the township in many roles. Members help organizations for the blind and seeing-impaired, provide local students with scholarships, and do volunteer work for the fire department. The Lioness Club, founded on October 6, 1977, serves the township in a similar role.

Among the township landmarks is Mary Immaculate Seminary, built between 1935 and 1938 at a cost of $1 million. Located on 569 acres at the highest elevation in the township, it was designed as an interpretation of Romanesque architecture and was made of concrete, cut stone, and limestone. Opened in 1939 to accept an overflow of seminary students, it closed in 1990 with fewer than 20 students. The last ordination service was held for two men in 1990. In 1996, the Catholic Archdiocese of Philadelphia paid $4 million for the seminary and changed its name to the Mary Immaculate Center. It has since become a place for prayerful retreats and study.

One

The Berlinsville Area

The village of Berlinsville was known as Lehighville from the 1830s to the 1850s. Its name was changed in honor of Abraham Berlin III, who settled there after the Revolutionary War.

In 1832, the settlement had seven dwellings, a store, and two taverns. By the 1870s, about 25 houses existed along with several businesses and at least one church. The town was also one of the stops on the Blue Ridge Traction Company's trolley line, built in 1902.

One early business was the hotel, built in 1761 by Richard Peters, who obtained his land from Thomas Penn. The building served initially as a stagecoach stop and then as a farmhouse and a doctor's office. It opened in 1929 as the Berlinsville Hotel, run by Harry and Elizabeth Zellner as a speakeasy until Prohibition ended. It then served as a six-room hotel until 1937, when the Zellners got their restaurant license. On November 1, 1946, the Zellners sold it to Louis and Teresa Filo, who sold it to Anastasia and Steven Kravetz on June 29, 1951. Their son Mike Kravetz managed it until 1964, when he and his wife, Gloria, purchased it from his parents. They still run it today.

The 1856 directory of the Philadelphia diocese lists the St. Nicholas Catholic Church in Berlinsville, but no official record of its founding date is known to exist. The first church building was located on the north side of Blue Mountain Drive, about 150 yards west of Oak Road. In 1872, a second church was built on the east side of Oak Road, about 150 yards north of Mountain View Drive. The current church building, located on the northeast corner of Mountain View Drive and Oak Road, was built in 1967.

Perhaps the most famous landmark in the town is Becky's Drive-In, which is one of the few remaining drive-in theaters in the country. William Beck first started showing movies behind Uncle Charlie's Lunch, a small eatery in the village. Admission was free and Beck charged only for refreshments. He then moved his operation to the area of what is now Bryfogle Park. In 1946, Beck opened the theater at its present-day location, calling it the Route 45 Drive-In. In 1971, the road was renamed Route 248, so Beck changed the name of the theater to Becky's, using his childhood nickname.

As with most drive-ins, sound was a problem at Becky's. Large speakers were used to broadcast the sound before Beck replaced them with individual speakers for each vehicle. The small speaker boxes pumped the sound right into individual cars, so neighbors ceased complaining about lost sleep. The small speaker boxes created other problems, says eldest son, Darrell Beck. He recalls that they were often damaged or stolen when people drove away with them still mounted on their windows.

William Beck died on April 4, 1987. His wife, Alice, and his children, grandchildren, and great-grandchildren continue to operate the drive-in today, showing family films throughout the late spring and summer months. In 1996, Becky's received the Best of the Best Award by the Drive-In Fan Club.

The area known as Apps is located west of Berlinsville, where Hickory Road intersects with Poplar Drive. The area was most likely named after Frederick App and his descendants who owned property there for six generations. The farm was first acquired by Frederick App in 1822. It was then passed down to his son Michael App, to his son Charles App, to his son Thomas App, and then to Charles C. App.

A large rock on the App property is said to have been used by Native Americans for meetings and ceremonial purposes. Stories have it that Benjamin Franklin came up from Philadelphia and met with Native Americans on a hill east of the borough of Walnutport. Known today by many as Council Rock, the stone is located along the north side of West Mountain View Road, which was designed and constructed to carry traffic from Berlinsville to Walnutport without disturbing the location of the important Native American legend.

To the south of Berlinsville and Apps, at the intersection of Maple Drive and Birch Road, is the village of Benningers. This area was named for W.M. Benninger, whose family owned a farm and a creamery nearby. Benninger served as the first postmaster for the Benningers post office, which existed from 1898 until November 30, 1927.

On August 12, 1900, a Lehigh and New England train crashed into an omnibus loaded with people who were returning from a burial service held at the Indianland Cemetery. William Benninger was in his home, located a few yards from the crossing, and he and some hired hands were the first on the scene. Benninger's son rode into town on his bicycle to summon medical help. Fourteen people were killed, 11 of them instantly. Only one person of the 28 people in the vehicle escaped injury.

Walnutport, located to the west of Berlinsville, was founded in the 1830s and was part of Lehigh Township until 1909. The name comes from the walnut trees growing along the Lehigh Canal, which passes through the town. This name appears on maps starting in 1850. In 1874, the town had three hotels, a school, a slate quarry, and about 40 dwellings. The first post office was opened on August 11, 1882, with W.F. Andrews as postmaster.

Just south of Walnutport was the village of Newhartport (also spelled Newhardtport), which existed from 1850 to 1880. It was named after the Newhart family, who ran a village tavern and store in this port on the Lehigh Canal. In 1870, the village contained 12 dwellings. It is now a part of Walnutport Borough.

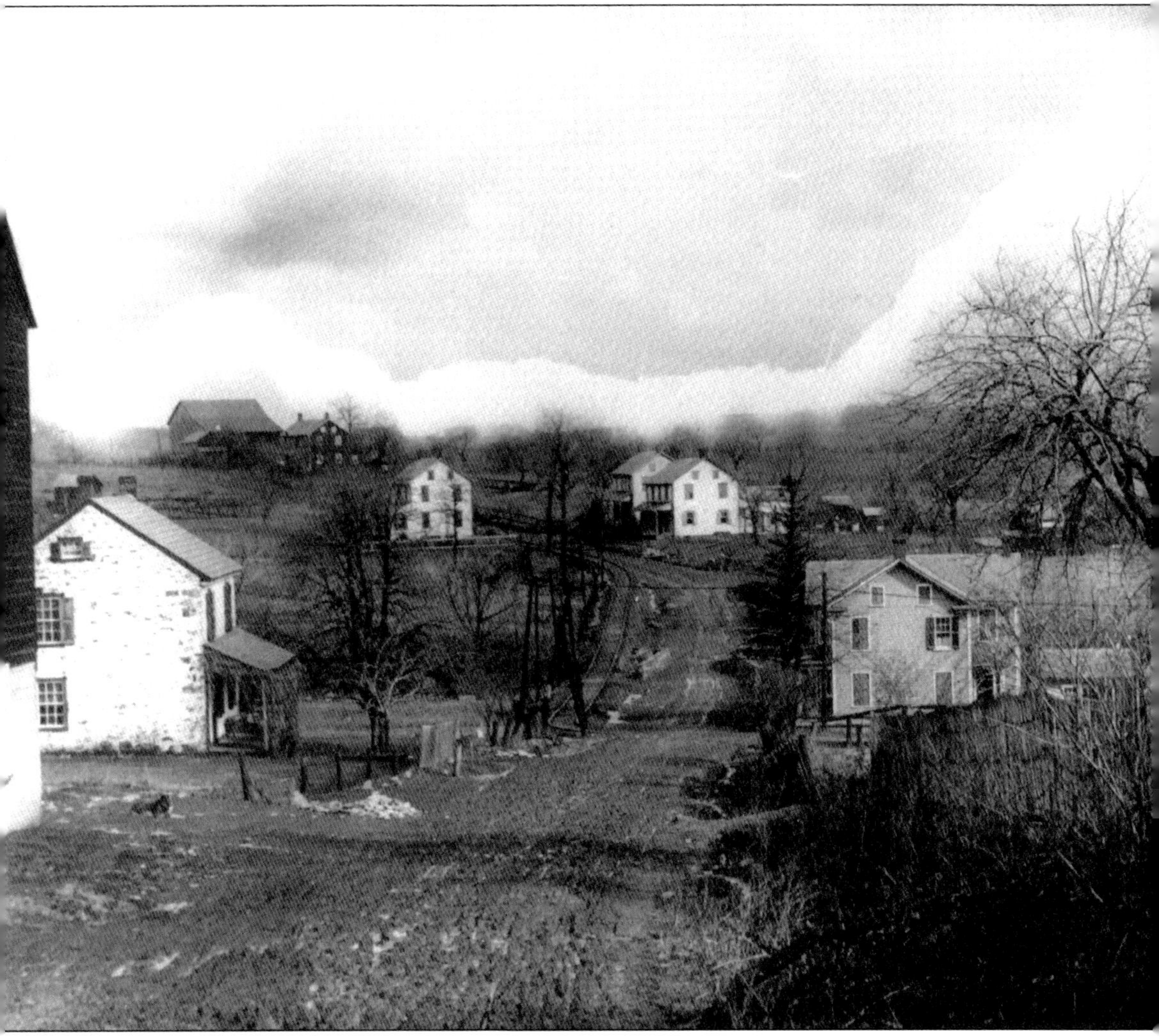

This 1911 view of South Cypress Drive shows the William Benninger and James Stever homes (left) and the homes of Owen Shiner, Arthur Benninger, Louis Reinert, and Ed Daubert (right). The trolley tracks for the Blue Ridge Traction Company can be seen coming down the hill and turning down Alder Drive. (Courtesy Carson and Joanne Jones.)

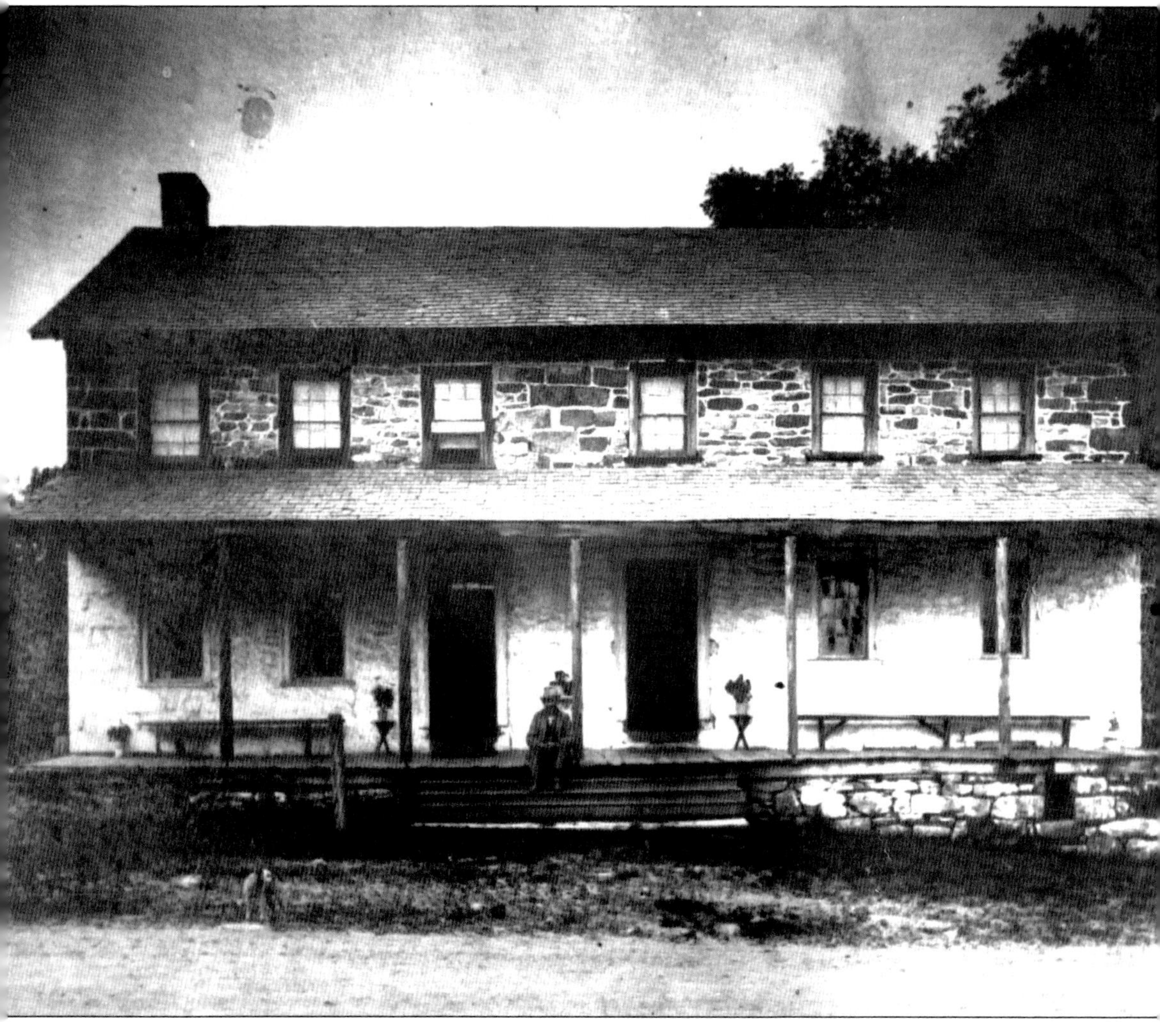

The Berlinsville Hotel was a residence when this photograph was taken *c.* 1900. (Courtesy Mike and Gloria Kravetz.)

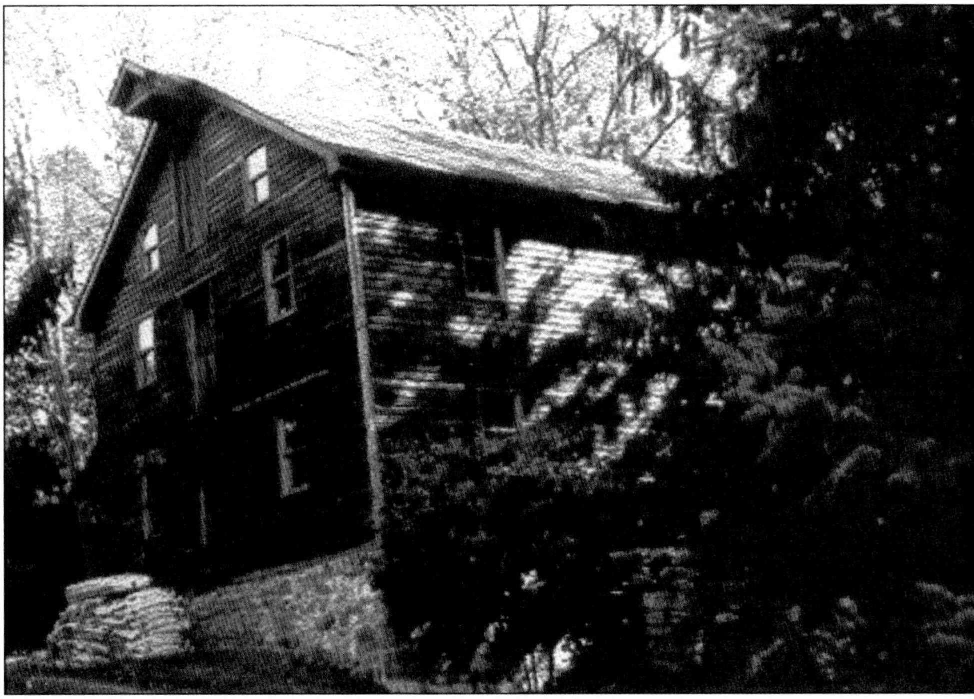

This gristmill, located in Benningers, was built by Peter Anthony in 1760. The waterwheel, gone in this modern photograph, was located on the front left corner of the building. (Courtesy Mike and Gloria Kravetz.)

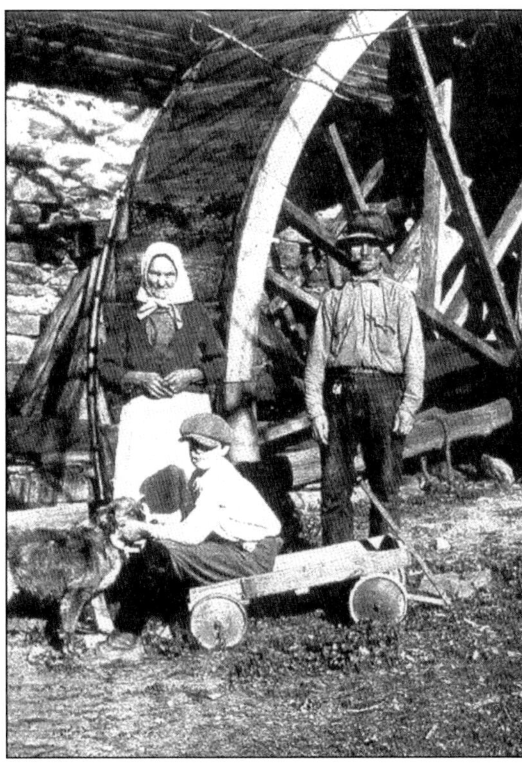

The gristmill waterwheel is shown here with the Petrick family c. 1910. Today, Petrick family descendants live there. (Courtesy Mike and Gloria Kravetz.)

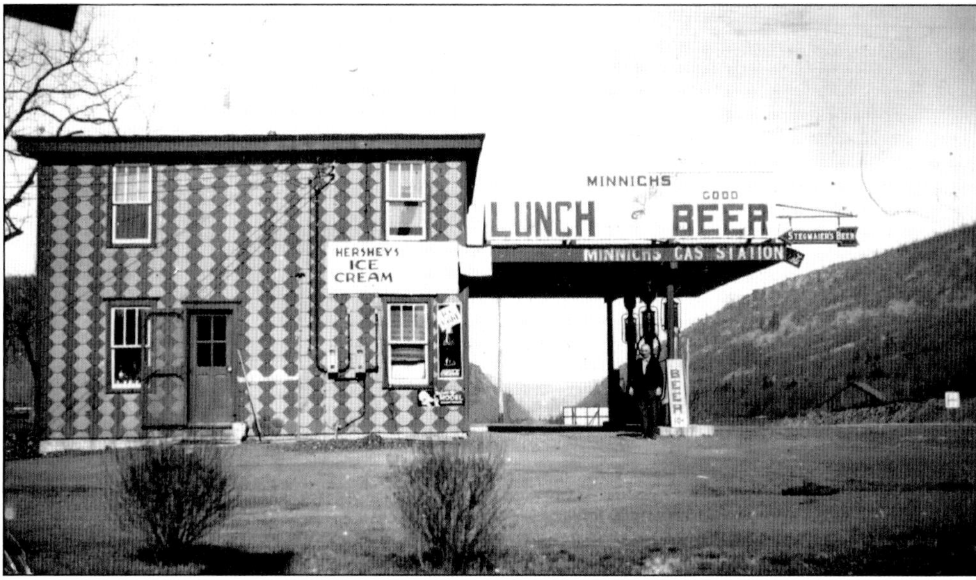

Minnich's Restaurant was located north of Berlinsville on Route 248, across from the current Shell gas station. The Lehigh Gap can be seen in the background in this photograph. (Courtesy Larry Hillborn.)

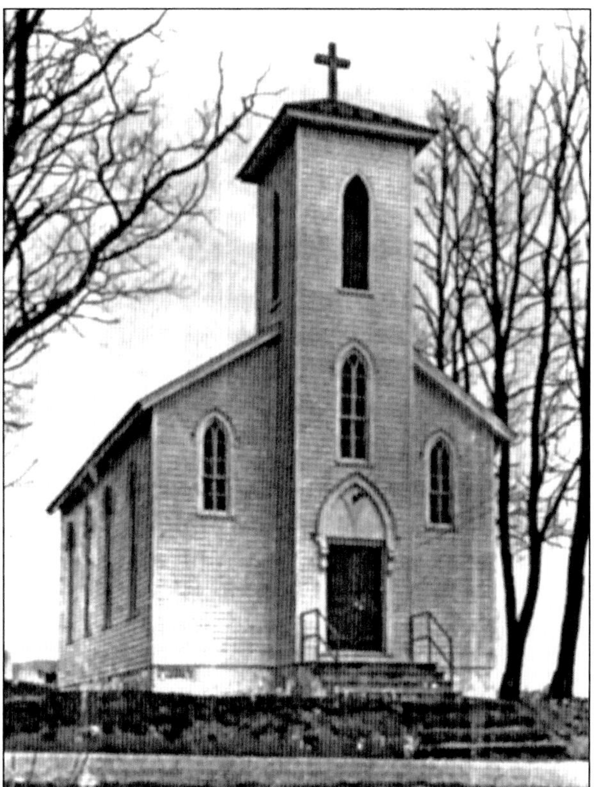

St. Nicholas Church was built in 1872 at a cost of $900. It was named after Nicholas Glasser, who built the first log church in the Berlinsville area in 1840. A larger church has since been built.

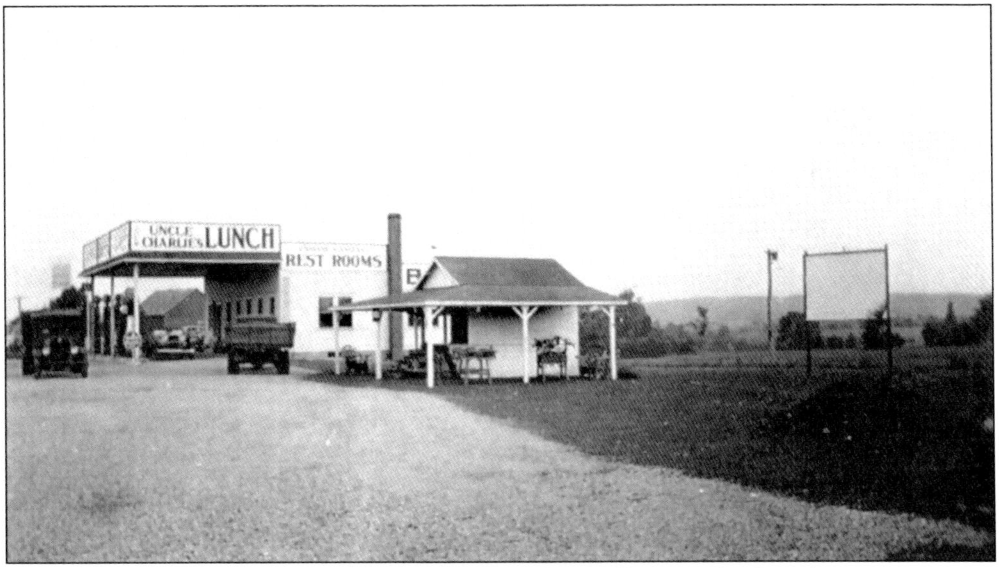

Uncle Charlie's Lunch, shown here in 1936, served as William Beck's first theater. Customers would sit on benches to watch movies on the screen, visible to the right. Beck's income came from selling food. (Courtesy Cindy Deppe.)

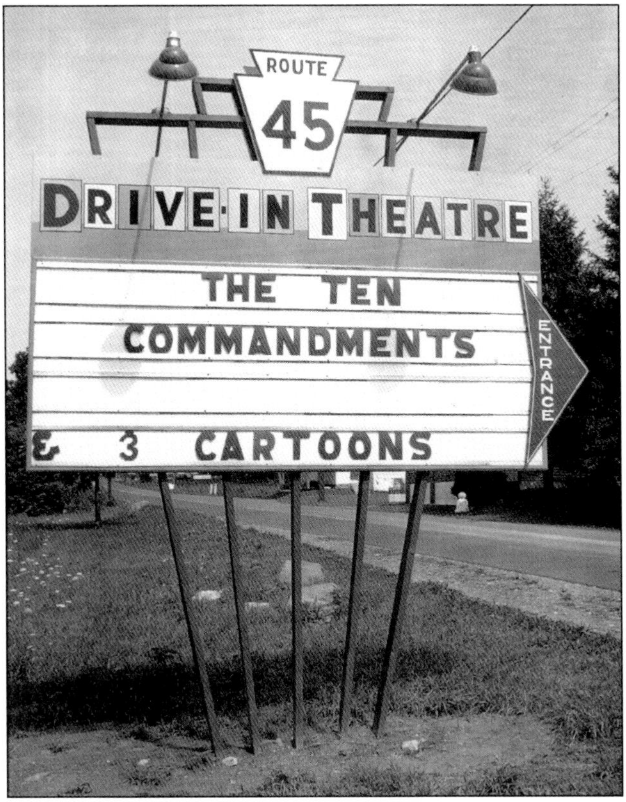

The Route 45 Drive-In sign is shown as it looked in the 1950s. It was situated on the site of what is now Becky's Drive-In. (Courtesy Cindy Deppe.)

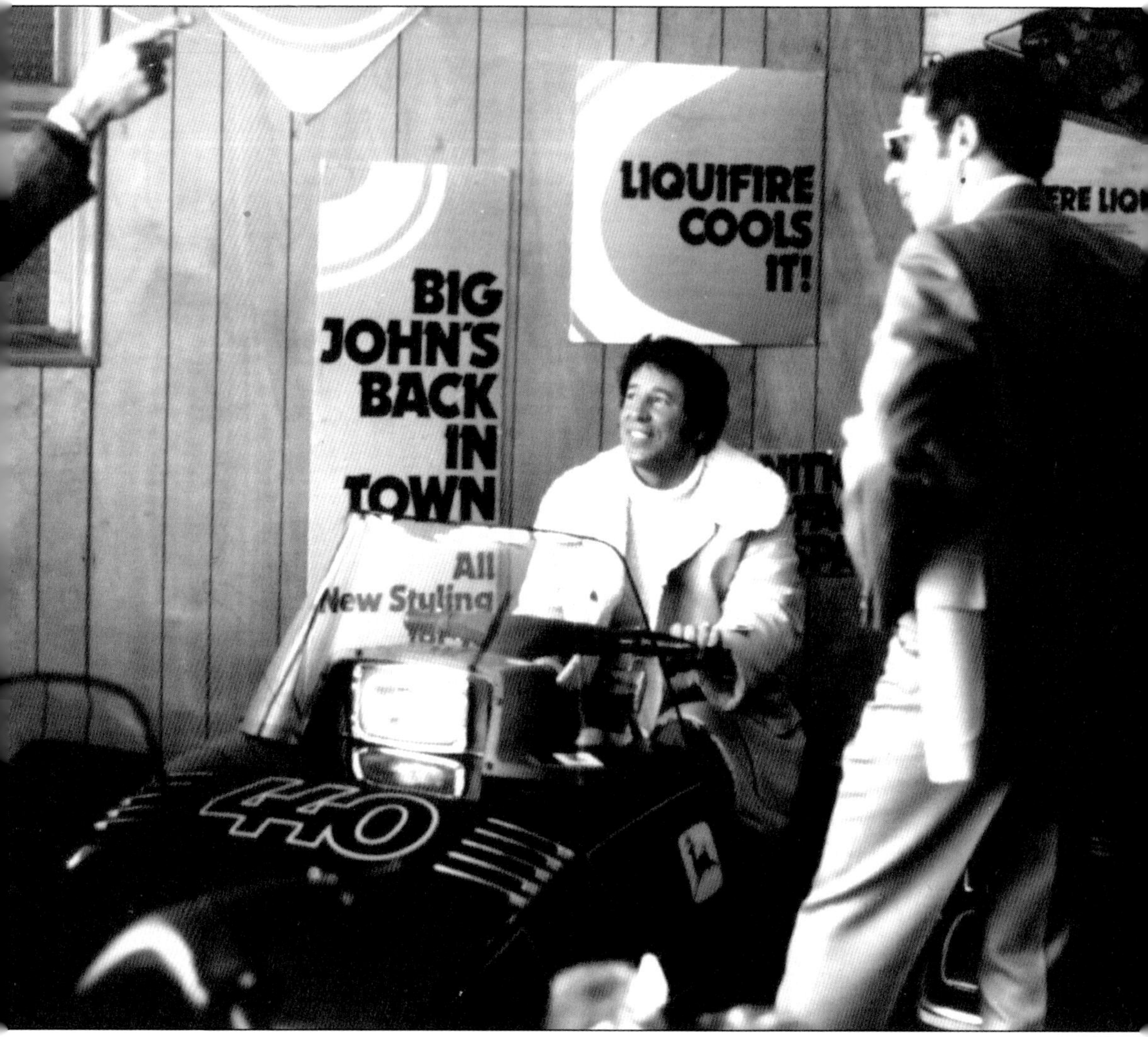

Vince Dieter started a Ski-Mobile center in Berlinsville in 1967 after reading about the new sleds in *Popular Mechanics*. John Deere presented a snowmobile to Mario Andretti (seated) through Dieters' shop in 1980, a year before the shop closed. (Courtesy Vince and Judy Dieter.)

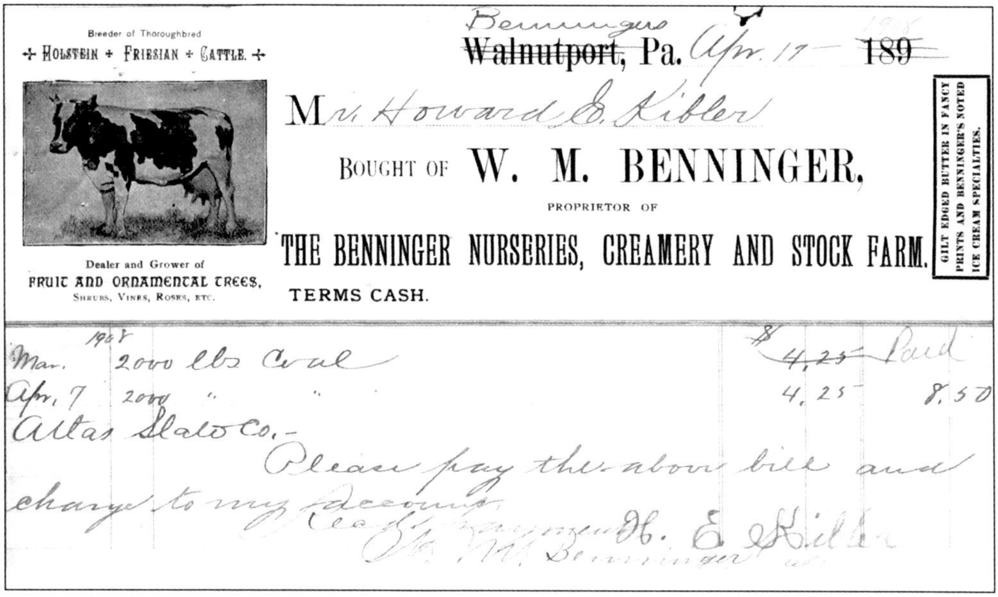

Breeder of Thoroughbred
HOLSTEIN + FRIESIAN + CATTLE.

Dealer and Grower of
FRUIT AND ORNAMENTAL TREES,
SHRUBS, VINES, ROSES, ETC.

~~Walnutport~~, Pa. Apr. 17 ~~189~~ 1908 (Benningers written in above Walnutport)

Mr. Howard E. Kibler

BOUGHT OF W. M. BENNINGER,

PROPRIETOR OF

THE BENNINGER NURSERIES, CREAMERY AND STOCK FARM.

GILT EDGED BUTTER IN FANCY PRINTS AND BENNINGER'S NOTED ICE CREAM SPECIALTIES.

TERMS CASH.

1908 Mar.	2000 lbs Coal	$ ~~4.25~~ Paid	
Apr. 7	2000 " "	4.25	8.50

Atlas Slate Co.-
Please pay the above bill and charge to my account.
H. E. Kibler

Rec'd payment
W. M. Benninger

Pictured is the letterhead from W.M. Benninger, after whom the area known as Benningers was named. Note that the name Walnutport is crossed out and Benningers is written in. (Courtesy David Altrichter.)

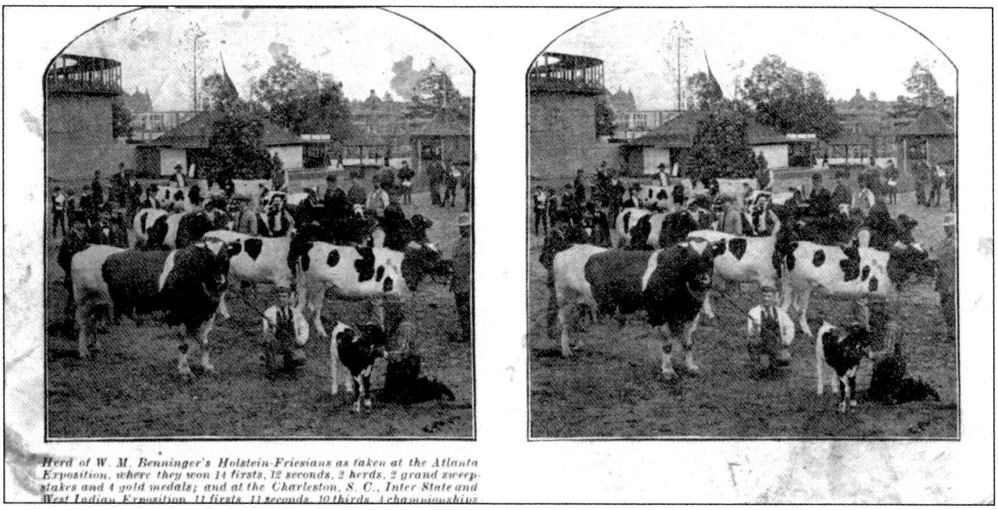

This stereo view shows W.M. Benninger's herd of prized Holsteins at the Atlanta Exposition. Benninger won 14 firsts, 12 seconds, 2 thirds, 2 grand sweepstakes, and 4 gold metals. The back of the stereo view states that the herd had won $35,000 and more than 2,500 ribbons over the previous 20 years.

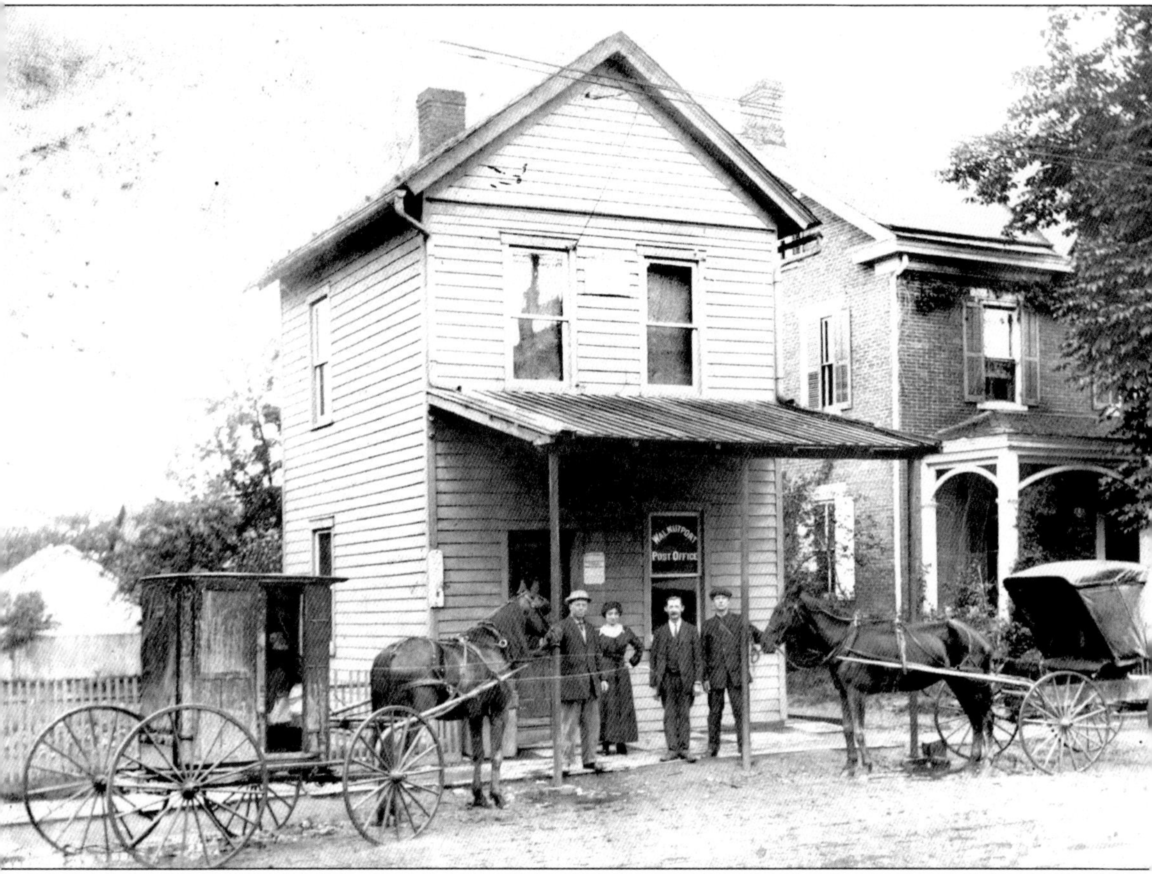

The Walnutport post office used to be located next to the Anchor Inn, at the corner of Main and North Canal Streets. Today, the post office is situated on Route 145. Postmaster Jim Andrews is third from the left. (Courtesy Griffith Roberts.)

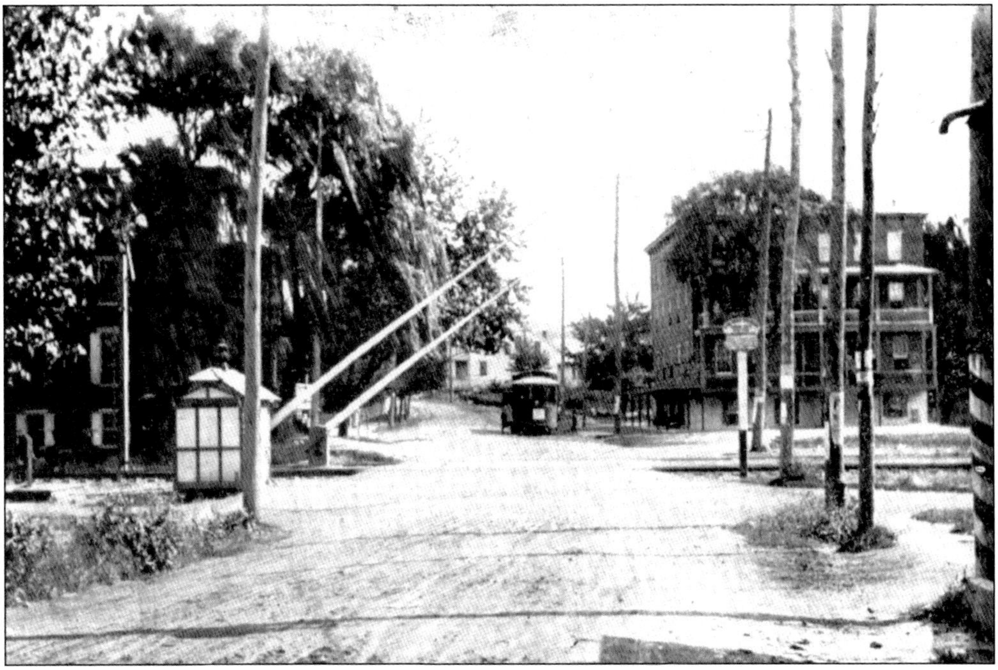

In this *c.* 1907 view of Main Street in Walnutport, the Slate Exchange Hotel can be seen on the right beyond the tracks that represented the end of the Blue Ridge Traction Company trolley line—it could not cross the Central Railroad of New Jersey tracks. (Courtesy Larry Hillborn.)

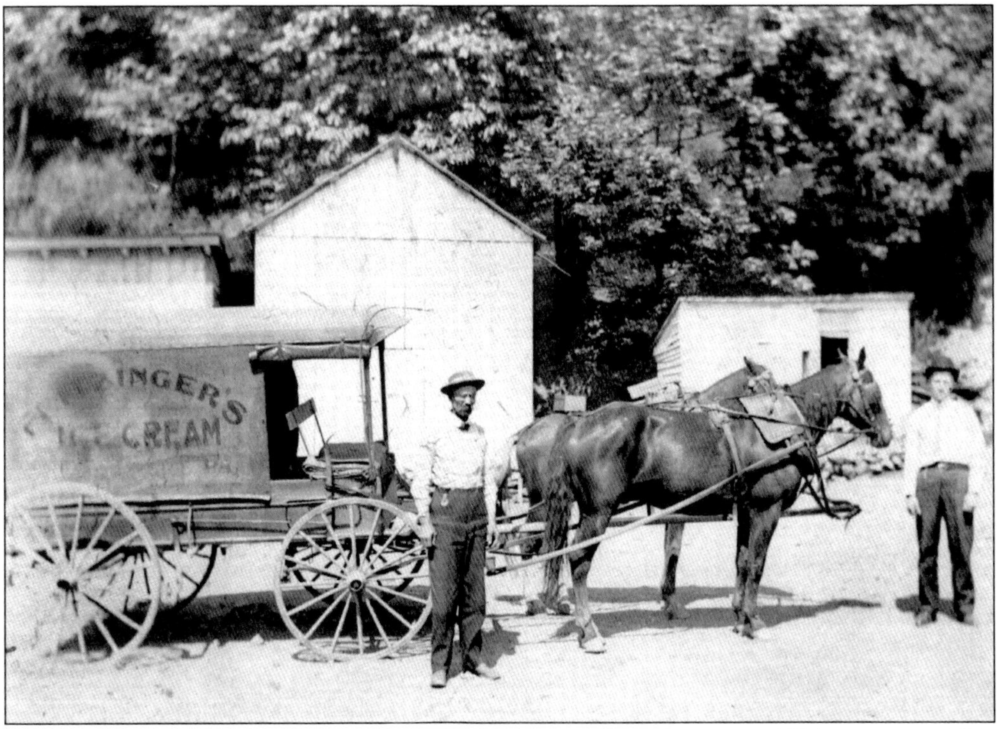

Two men pose with the delivery buggy for Fritzinger's Ice Cream in Walnutport *c.* 1920. (Courtesy Larry Hillborn.)

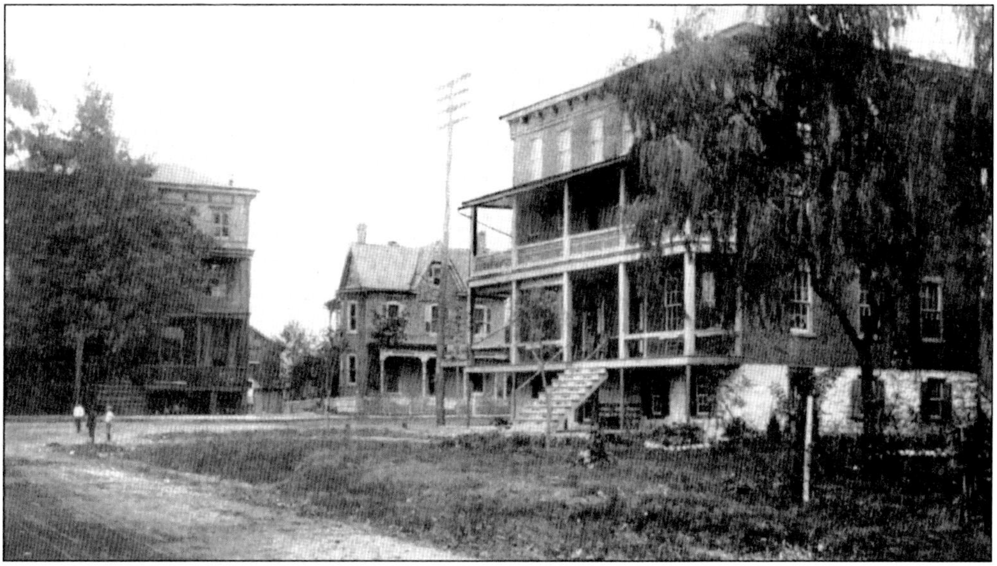

The Slate Exchange Hotel is shown as it looked *c.* 1908. (Courtesy Larry Hillborn.)

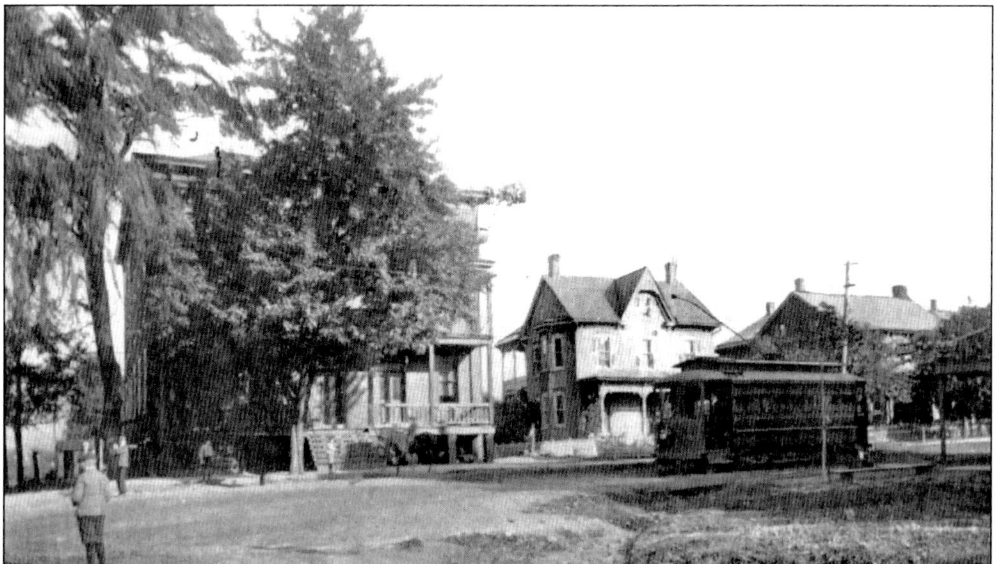

In this *c.* 1912 view of the Pennsylvania Hotel, the Blue Ridge trolley is visible to the right. (Courtesy Larry Hillborn.)

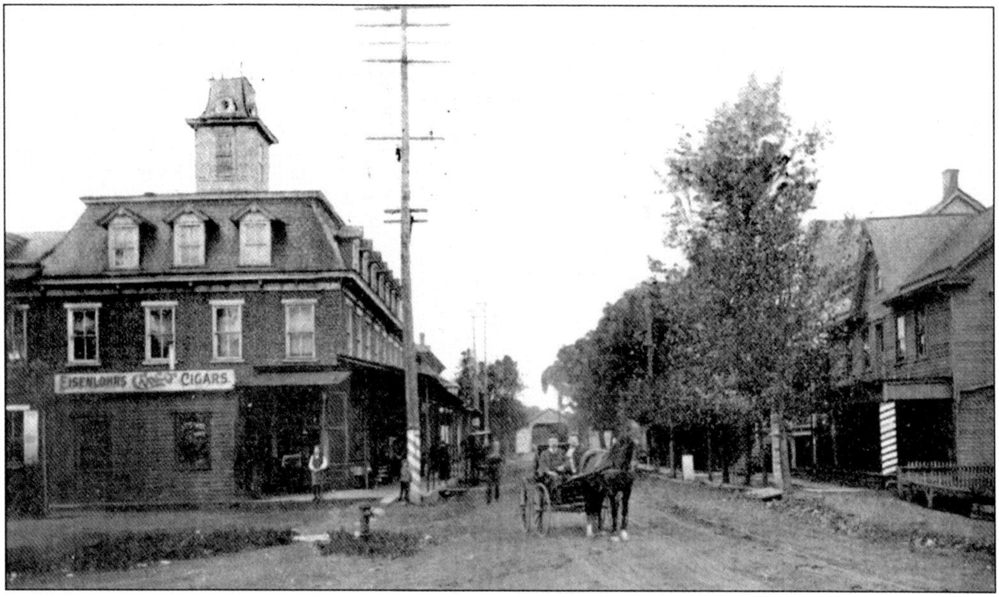

Main Street in Walnutport is pictured in this *c.* 1910 view, which looks toward Slatington from about where the Central Railroad of New Jersey tracks crossed the road. (Courtesy Larry Hillborn.)

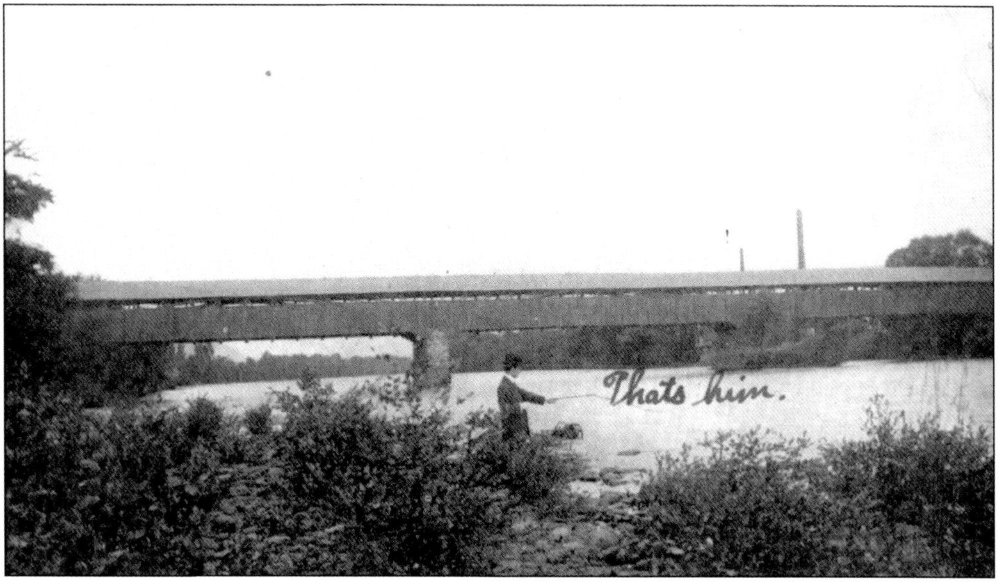

The covered bridge crossing the Lehigh River from Walnutport to Slatington was built in 1854 and was replaced in 1911, when this photograph was taken. A toll was charged to cross the bridge until 1893. The mouth of the bridge in Walnutport can be seen in the previous photograph. The smokestacks visible above the bridge on the right are from the Citizens Electric powerhouse, shown in the next photograph. (Courtesy Larry Hillborn.)

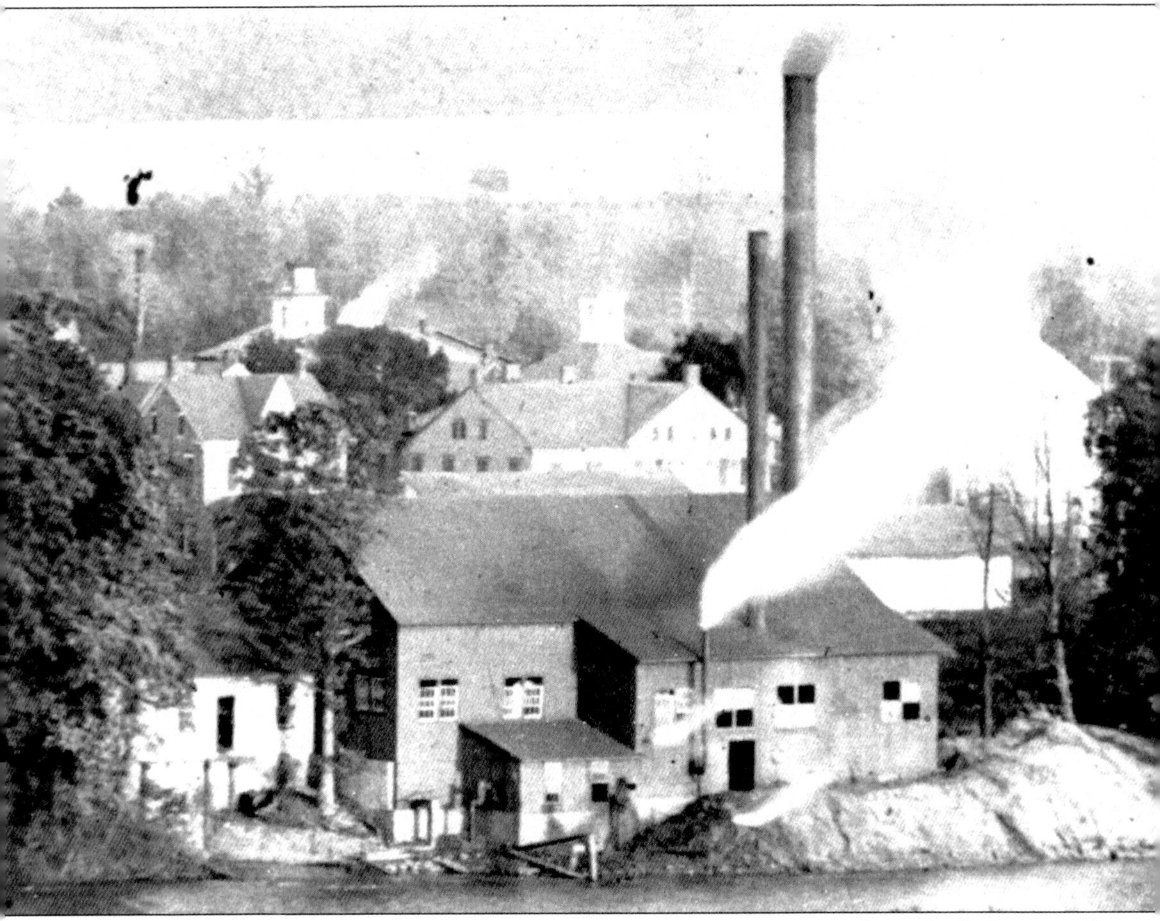

The Citizens Electric powerhouse—located in Walnutport between the Lehigh River and the canal, just north of Main Street—is shown here from the Slatington side of the river c. 1900. The power generated was direct current from two small water-driven generators. When the canal was drained or the river was flooding, there was no electricity. The building was torn down in 1910, and the lumber was used to build the Diamond Fire Company. (Courtesy Walnutport Canal Association.)

Two

THE CHERRYVILLE AREA

Cherryville, located at the intersection of Route 248 and Blue Mountain Drive, was founded c. 1804. Its name is believed to have come from Cherry Row Lane, a road bounded by 100 cherry trees. Prior to the arrival of the railroad in the 1850s, Cherryville was the crossroads of the area.

In 1832, the settlement had a tavern, a store, and several buildings. By 1850, 8 to 10 homes existed along with the Wentz Hotel, Lerch's Store, and the Hower & Kuntz Store. In 1874, Cherryville boasted 25 dwellings, two carriage shops, a wheel shop, a shoe shop, two blacksmiths, three stores, a hotel, and a tailor. Some businesses that existed in Cherryville over the years include the Keystone Attachment Company (1912), George Rehrig Blacksmith (1913), the Frantz Automobile Company (1901), the P.O. Hess General Store (1931), Earl Wentz Bread and Cakes (1931), and the T.T. Matchette Garage (1931).

The original Cherryville post office opened on February 6, 1816, at the corner of Route 248 and Blue Mountain Drive, with J. Applebach as postmaster. For 175 years, it occupied the same building, which also housed a general store owned by Preston O. Hess. Edith Johnson was the postmaster for many years and lived on the other side of the post office. Above the old post office was a meeting place for a men's lodge whose members used the iron steps on the side of the building to reach the second-floor entrance. In 1992, the post office was moved to its present location on Blue Mountain Drive, a few hundred yards north of the intersection.

The Cherryville Chums was an informal organization of residents, many of whom grew up in the village in the 1880s and 1890s. The group was founded one evening in 1904 as a group of residents decided to hold annual reunions of neighbors after saying goodbye to a couple moving to Indiana. Lifelong Cherryville resident Thomas S. Royer was elected secretary. For more than 60 years, gatherings were held at Edgemont Park or in Neff's Park in Lehigh County. In later years, outings were held at Indian Trail Park. A dozen charter members and 400 other people attended the 44th reunion in 1948.

One of the landmarks of Cherryville is the Cherryville Hotel, built in 1767. This stone building was the birthplace of Samuel Henry Kress, who came into the world on July 23, 1863. In 1896, after moving to Memphis, Tennessee, Kress established the S.H. Kress five-and-dime stores. By 1907, he had 51 stores throughout the southeast. He trained J.J. Newberry and William McLellan, who later founded their own chain stores. At the time of his death in 1955, Kress's chain numbered 264 stores. In 1963, the Genesco Corporation bought and liquidated the chain.

During the 1920s, Kress became interested in art and began collecting works by the old masters. When the National Gallery of Art was established in Washington, D.C., in 1937, he saw the opportunity for the public to benefit from his years of collecting. Accordingly, in 1939 and 1945, Kress donated more than 400 paintings and 18 pieces of sculpture and was subsequently elected president of the National Gallery of Art. Kress never married, and his estate (valued at $17.5 million) went largely to the Samuel H. Kress Foundation, which he had established in New York City. He wished to have some of his art collection exhibited close to his birthplace. Therefore, when the Allentown Art Museum was established in 1960, the Samuel H. Kress Foundation donated 63 sculptures and paintings.

In 1932, Harry and Helen Seidel purchased the Cherryville Hotel and ran it as a bar and restaurant until 1960. The hotel had a Hammond organ that provided diners with music. Artwork by the Seidels' daughter Betty was also displayed. After her parents closed the restaurant, Betty Seidel continued to run a gift shop and museum at the inn until her death in 2001. During her heyday, she was most famous for her Pennsylvania Dutch decorations, one of which she used when she designed the birthday plate for Pres. Dwight D. Eisenhower's first birthday in the White House. Eisenhower attended a party in Hershey to celebrate the occasion, and each guest received a commemorative plate.

To the west of Cherryville is an area known as Indianland since the 1700s because it was established as a Native American reservation. Interestingly, Indianland had a couple of other nicknames. From 1850 to 1880, it was known as Poplar Grove because of a large grove of poplar trees. In 1884, it had become known as Lehigh Centre.

In 1859, the Leibenguths ran a tavern in the village. By 1874, Indianland contained a school, about a dozen dwellings, and W.H. Winter's hotel.

William Penn's reservation, called Indian Tract Manor, was established using the natural boundaries of the area—on the east, Indian Creek, which flows from Blue Mountain into the Lehigh River; on the north, the ridge of the Blue Mountain; and on the west and south, the Lehigh River. The reservation covered almost the entire present-day Lehigh Township, an area of about 30 square miles. The Native Americans only sparsely inhabited the territory and never claimed the reservation.

In 1735, when Penn's sons met with tribal representatives in Pennsburg, the result was the infamous Walking Purchase. The Penns "found" an old agreement between the Lenape and William Penn stating that they sold all the land in which a walker could walk in a day and a half. The Lenape agreed, believing the walking would be leisurely the way they traveled along the Delaware River. However, the Penns hired three walkers whose goal was to cover as much land as possible. Only one finished; the other two died from the effort. Although the purchase succeeded in gaining 1,200 square miles of land for the Penns, Lehigh Township paid with attacks from Native Americans antagonized by what they felt was foul play.

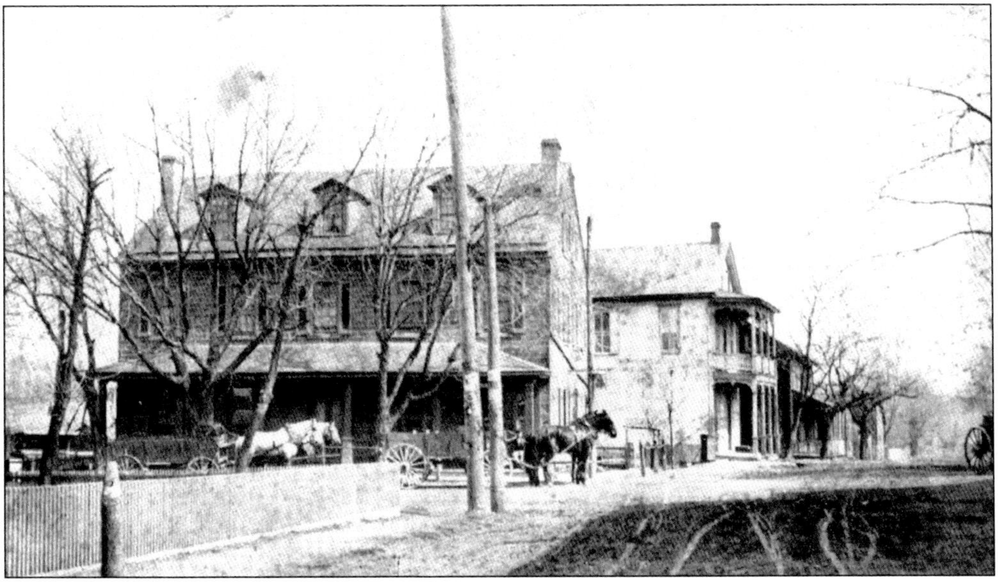

The Cherryville Hotel is shown as it looked *c.* 1900. (Courtesy Larry Hillborn.)

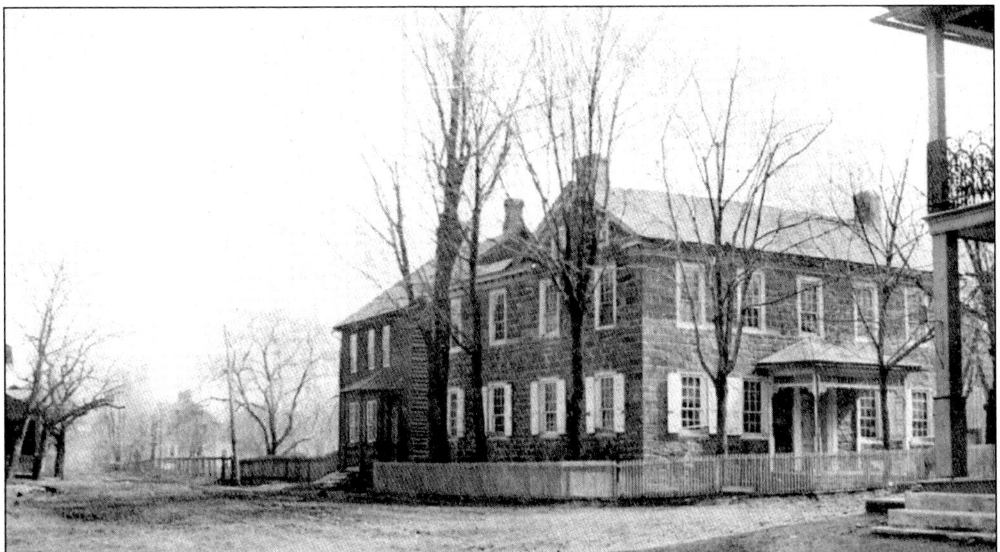

The Newhard Homestead was located on the corner of Route 248 and Blue Mountain Drive, where the Lehigh Township fire hall now stands. This photograph shows the homestead *c.* 1900. (Courtesy Larry Hillborn.)

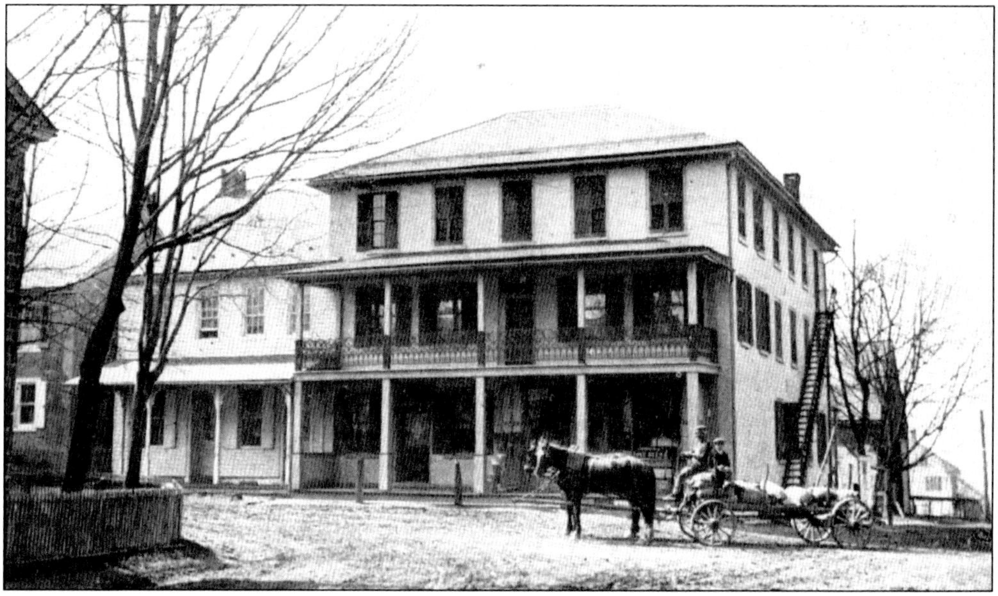

This view shows the Cherryville post office and the store that was later run by Preston O. Hess. (Courtesy Larry Hillborn.)

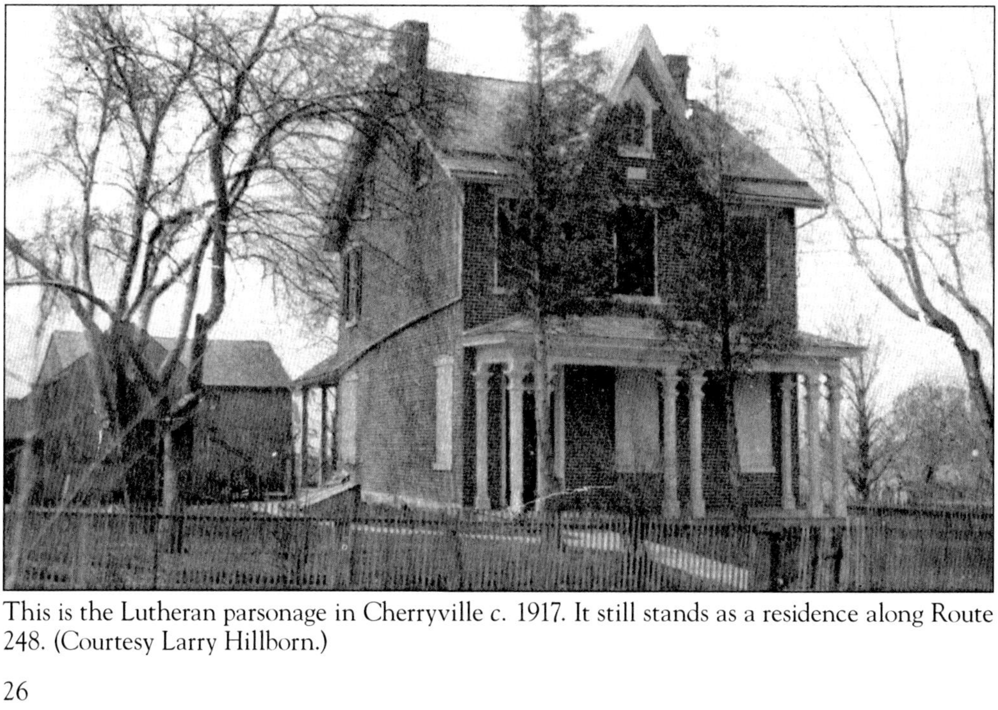

This is the Lutheran parsonage in Cherryville c. 1917. It still stands as a residence along Route 248. (Courtesy Larry Hillborn.)

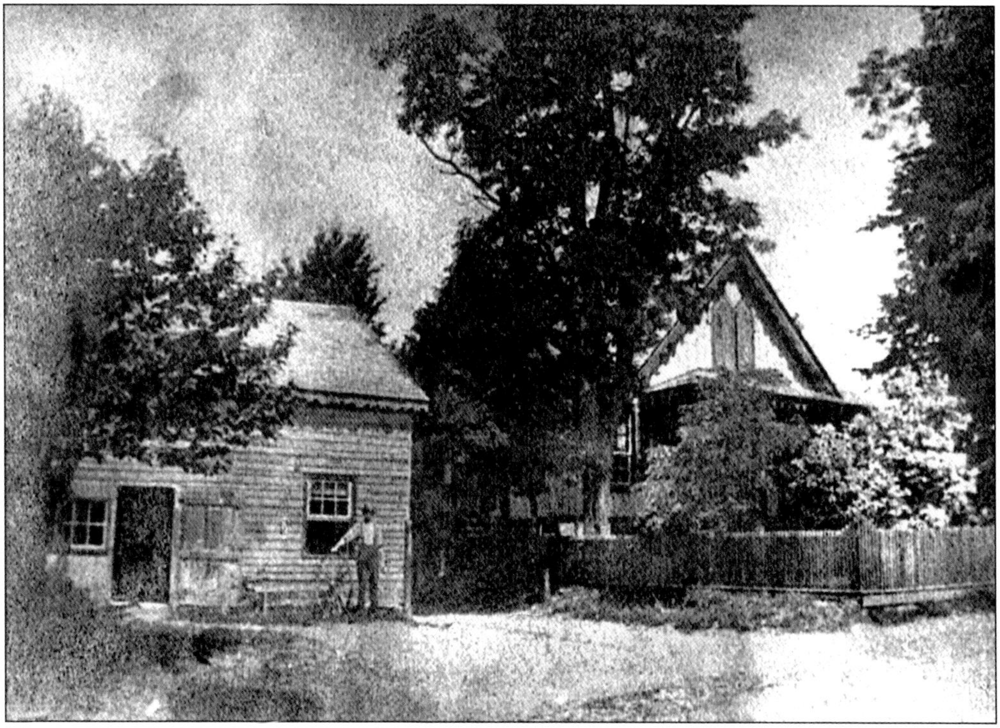

Thomas Royer's home and wagon shop in Cherryville are pictured *c.* 1912.

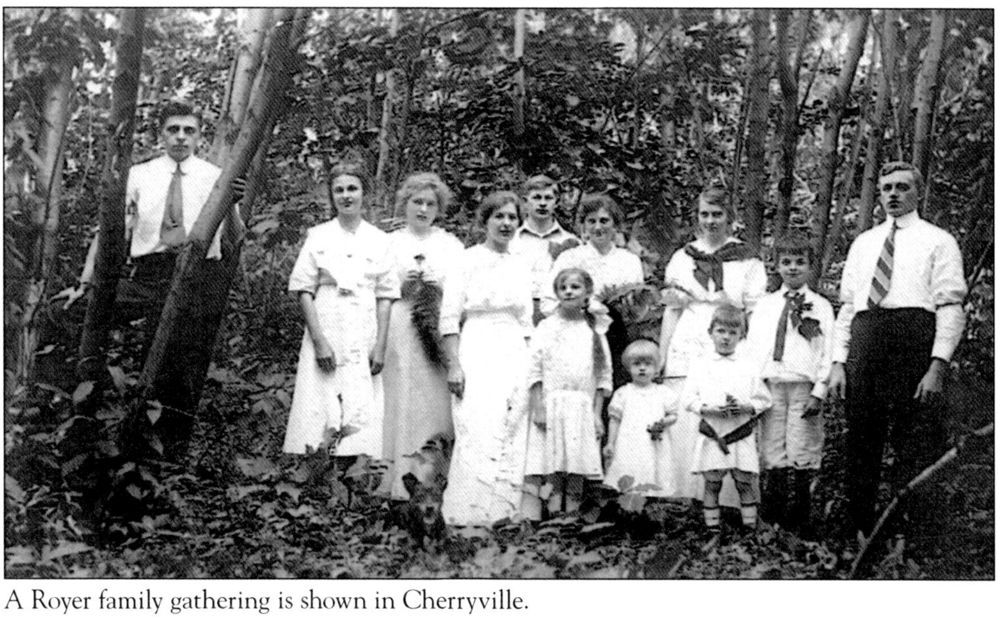

A Royer family gathering is shown in Cherryville.

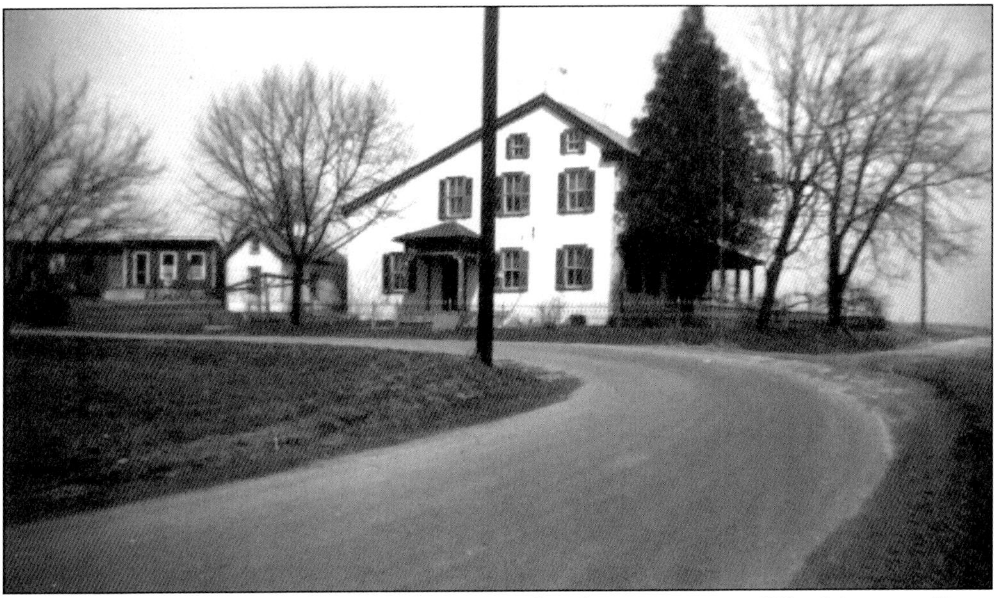

The Ziegenfuss home, shown here *c.* 1940, is located at the intersection of Blue Mountain Drive and South Dogwood Road. The house was built *c.* 1740. (Collection of the Lehigh Township Historical Society.)

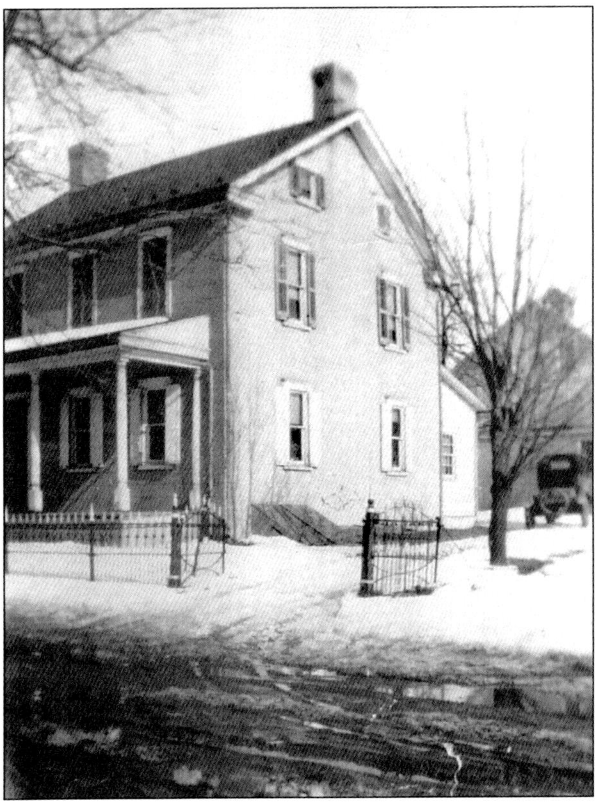

This Cherryville home was used as the parsonage for the Bethany Wesleyan Church during the 1950s. Pictured here in 1920, the house dates from the mid-1800s and is now a private residence. (Courtesy George Alvin Lynn.)

In this 1942 photograph of the Cherryville post office and store, Jack Seidel (brother of Betty Seidel) is leaving for military duty. (Collection of the Lehigh Township Historical Society.)

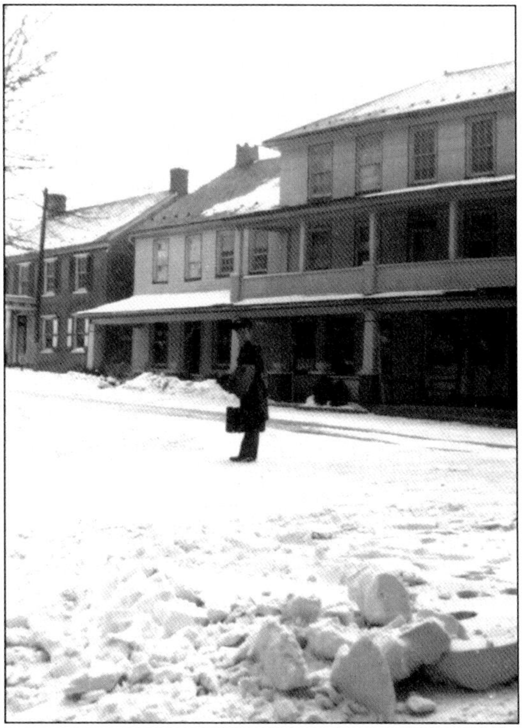

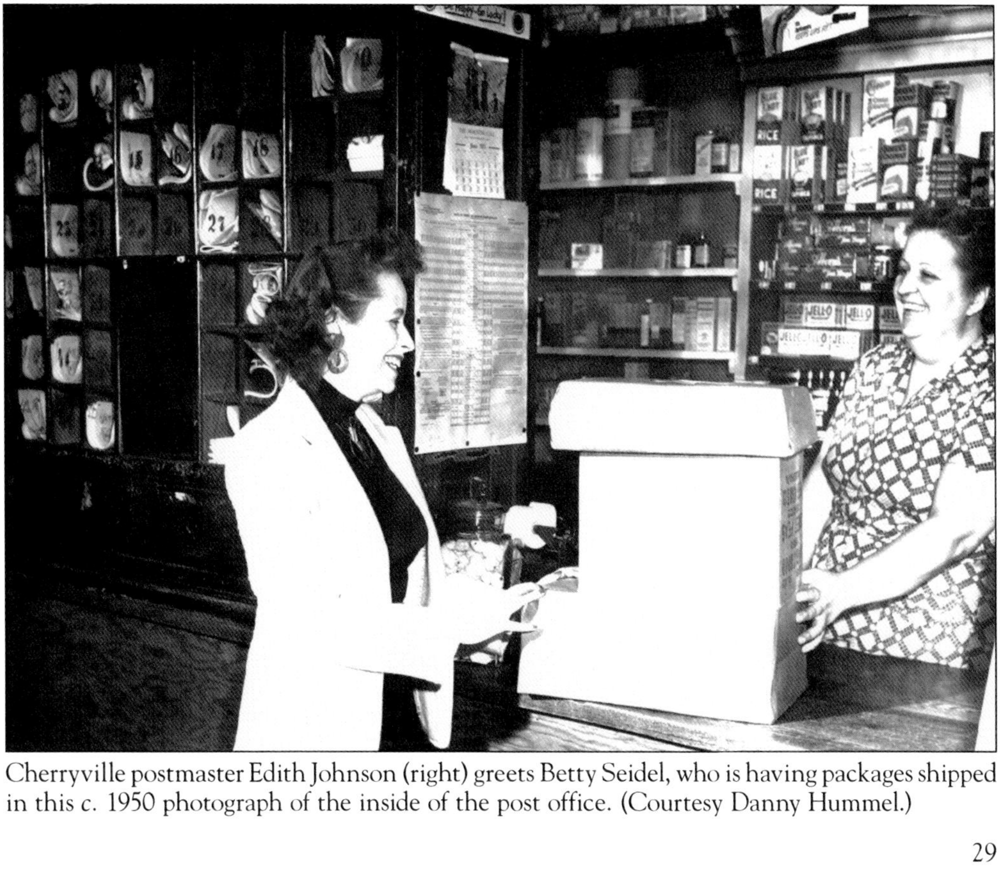

Cherryville postmaster Edith Johnson (right) greets Betty Seidel, who is having packages shipped in this *c.* 1950 photograph of the inside of the post office. (Courtesy Danny Hummel.)

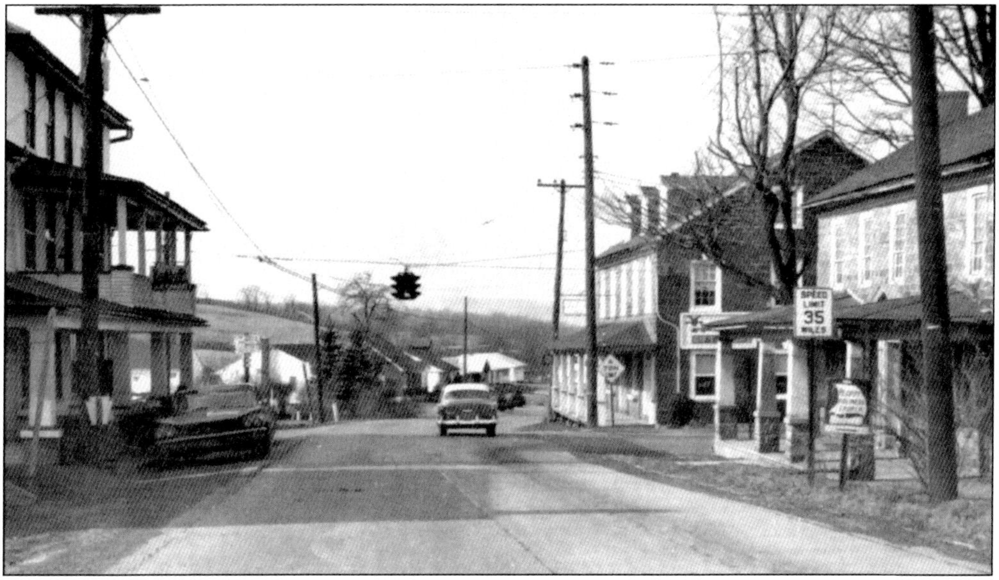

This 1960 photograph postcard shows the intersection of what is now Route 248 and Blue Mountain Drive in Cherryville. The Cherryville Hotel can be seen on the right just past the Newhard Homestead. On the left is the post office. (Courtesy Sean and Johanna Billings.)

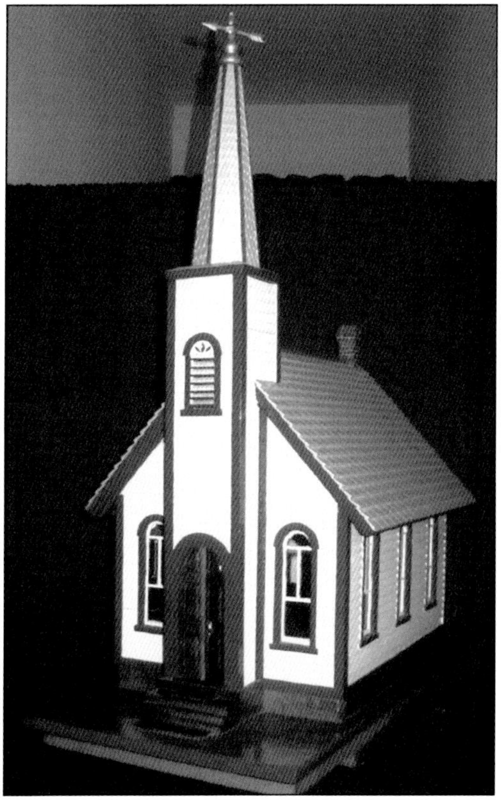

The Cherryville Evangelical Church, located on Route 248, is depicted in this model. The church is currently an apartment building. (Courtesy Paul Dieter.)

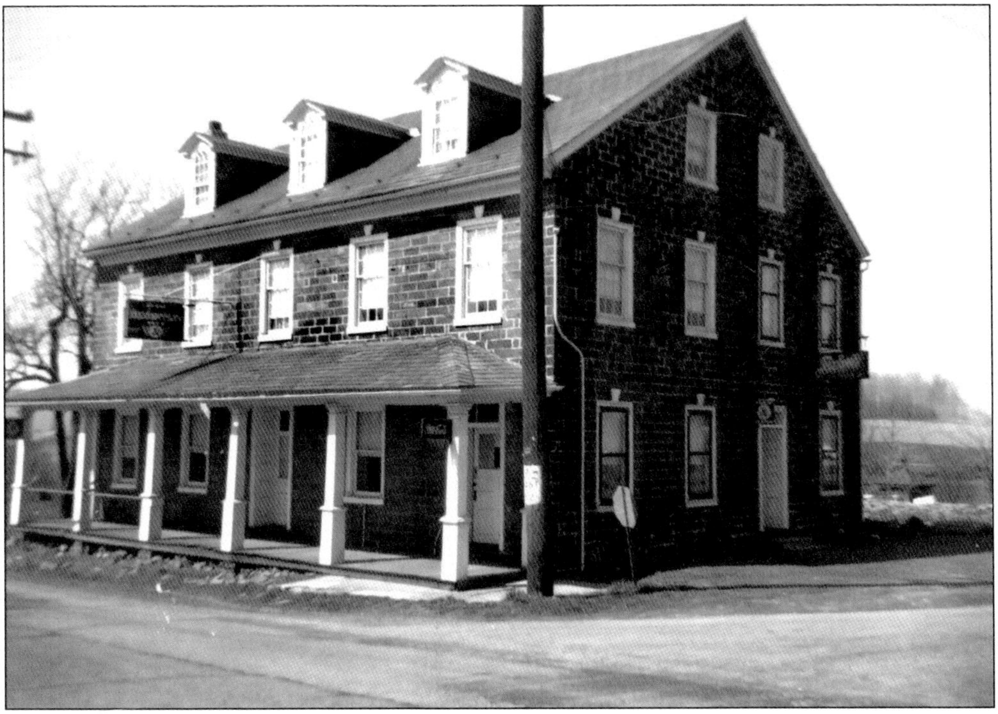

This *c.* 1930 view of the Cherryville Hotel shows the stop sign that was located next to the hotel before the traffic light was installed. (Collection of the Lehigh Township Historical Society.)

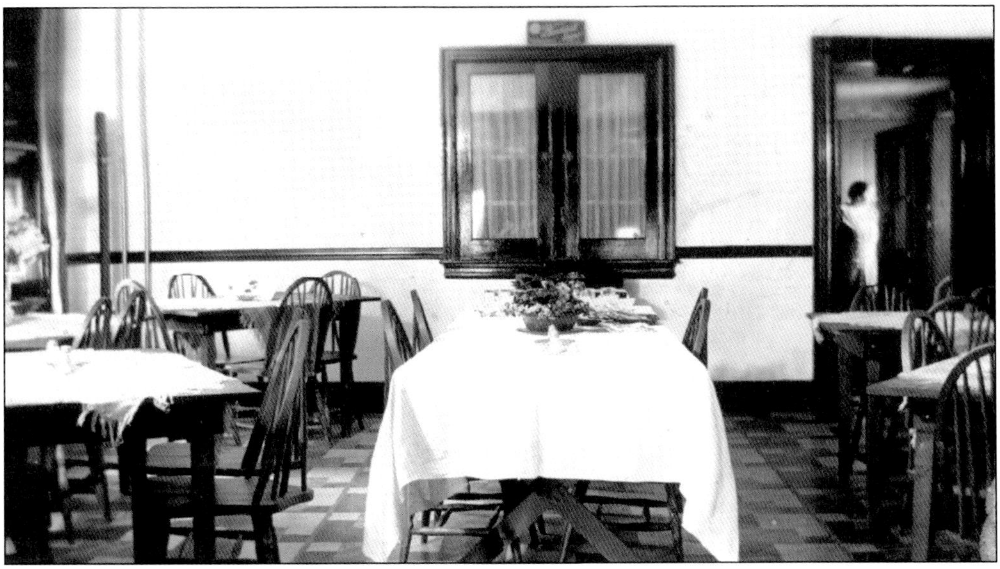

This is what the interior of the Cherryville Hotel looked like on October 20, 1934, shorty after the Seidels bought it. (Courtesy Sean and Johanna Billings.)

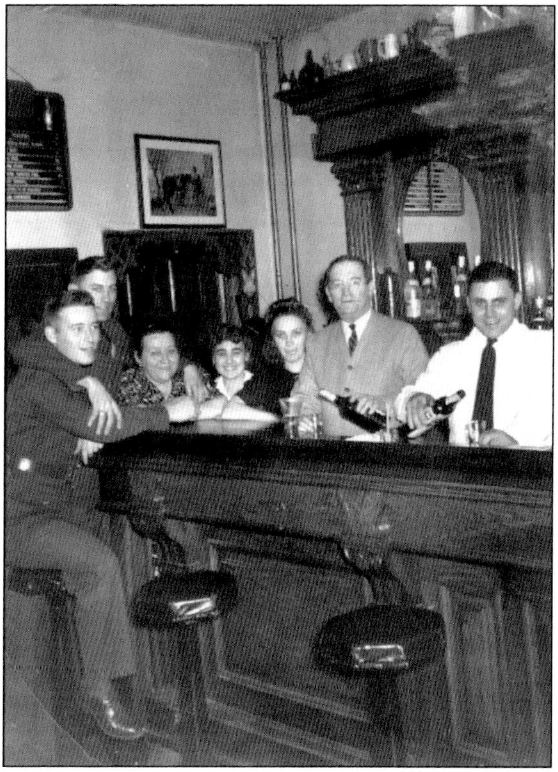

This 1942 photograph of the bar inside the Cherryville Hotel shows Jack Seidel (far left), Helen Seidel (third from left), and Harry Seidel (sixth from left). The others are unidentified. (Collection of the Lehigh Township Historical Society.)

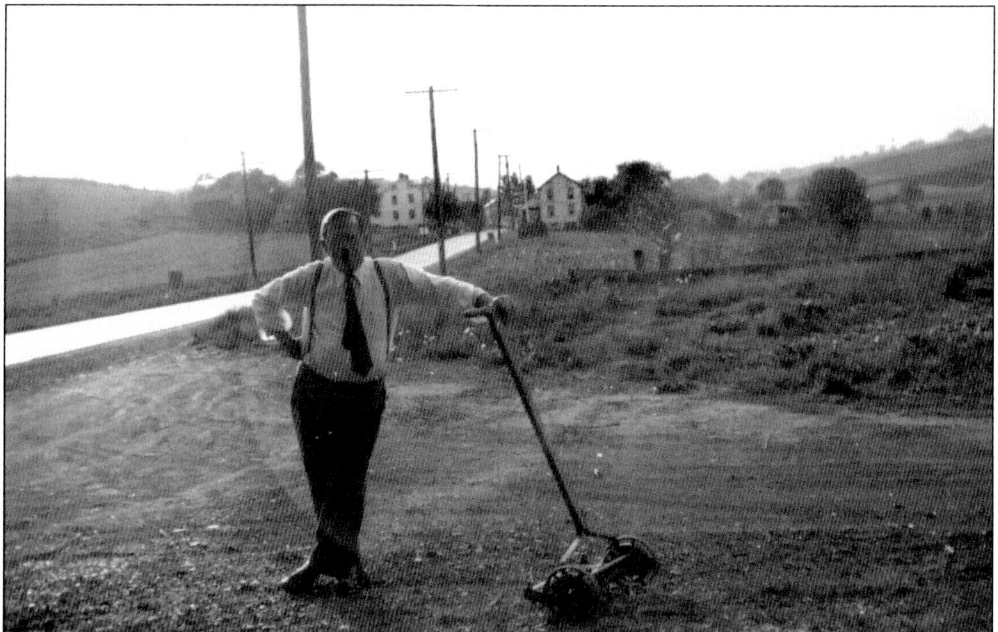

Harry Seidel pauses for a picture while mowing the grass behind the Cherryville Hotel in 1940. Route 45 (now Route 248), leading to Berlinsville, can be seen behind him. Notice all the open space. (Collection of the Lehigh Township Historical Society.)

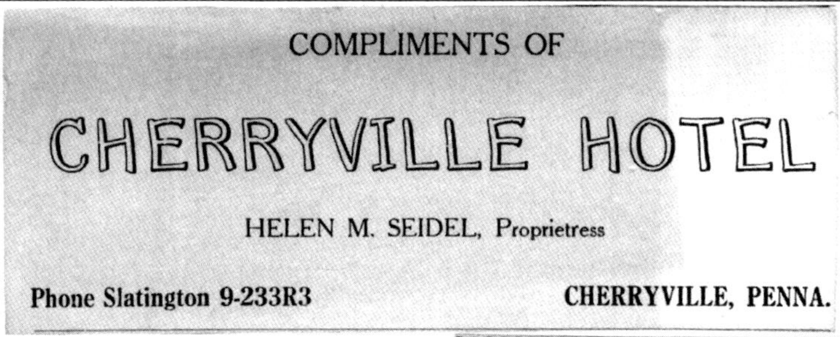

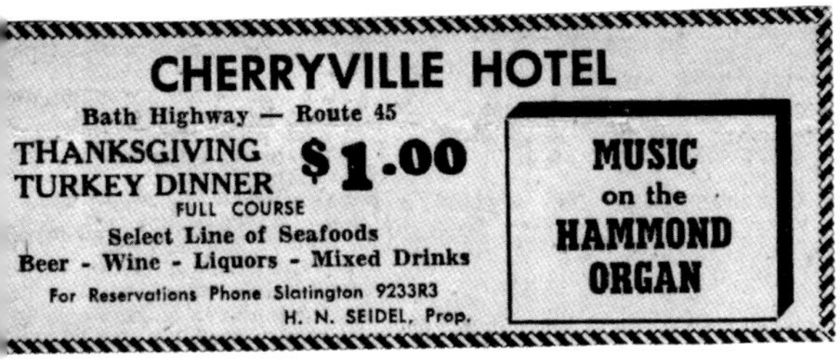

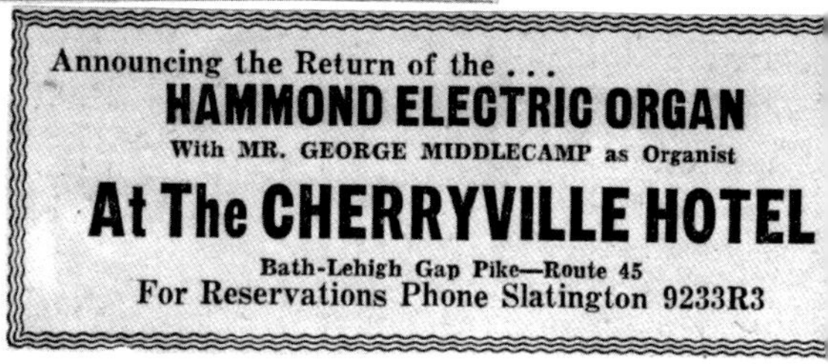

Shown are early advertisements from the Cherryville Hotel. (Collection of the Lehigh Township Historical Society.)

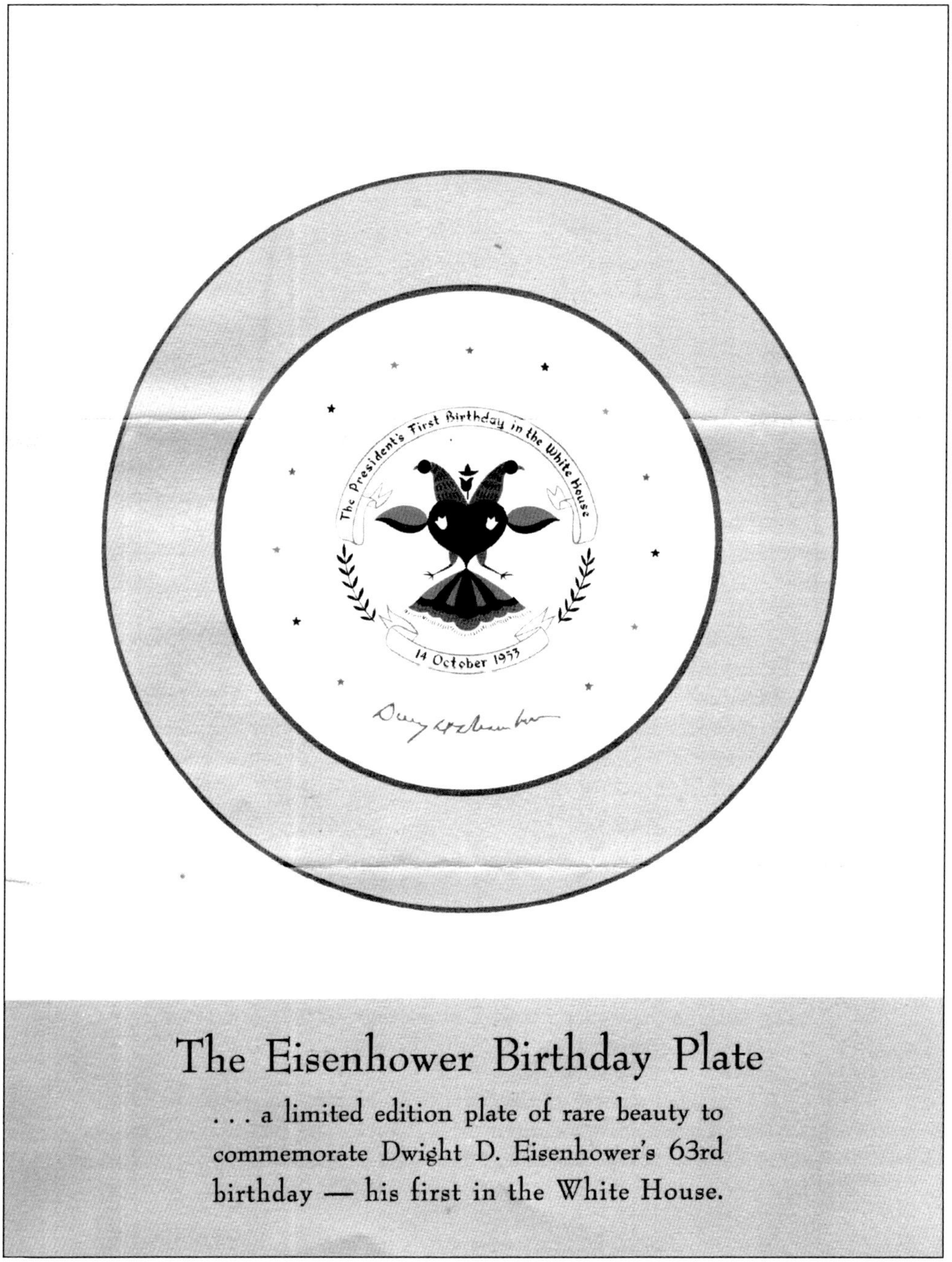

Betty Seidel of Cherryville designed a plate in 1953 to celebrate Pres. Dwight D. Eisenhower's first birthday in the White House. This brochure shows the 12-inch plate, featuring a Pennsylvania Dutch design and Eisenhower's signature. The plates were given to each person attending the October 13, 1953 birthday party in Hershey. Those who did not attend the $100-per-person function could purchase a plate, made by Castletum China, for $10. (Collection of the Lehigh Township Historical Society.)

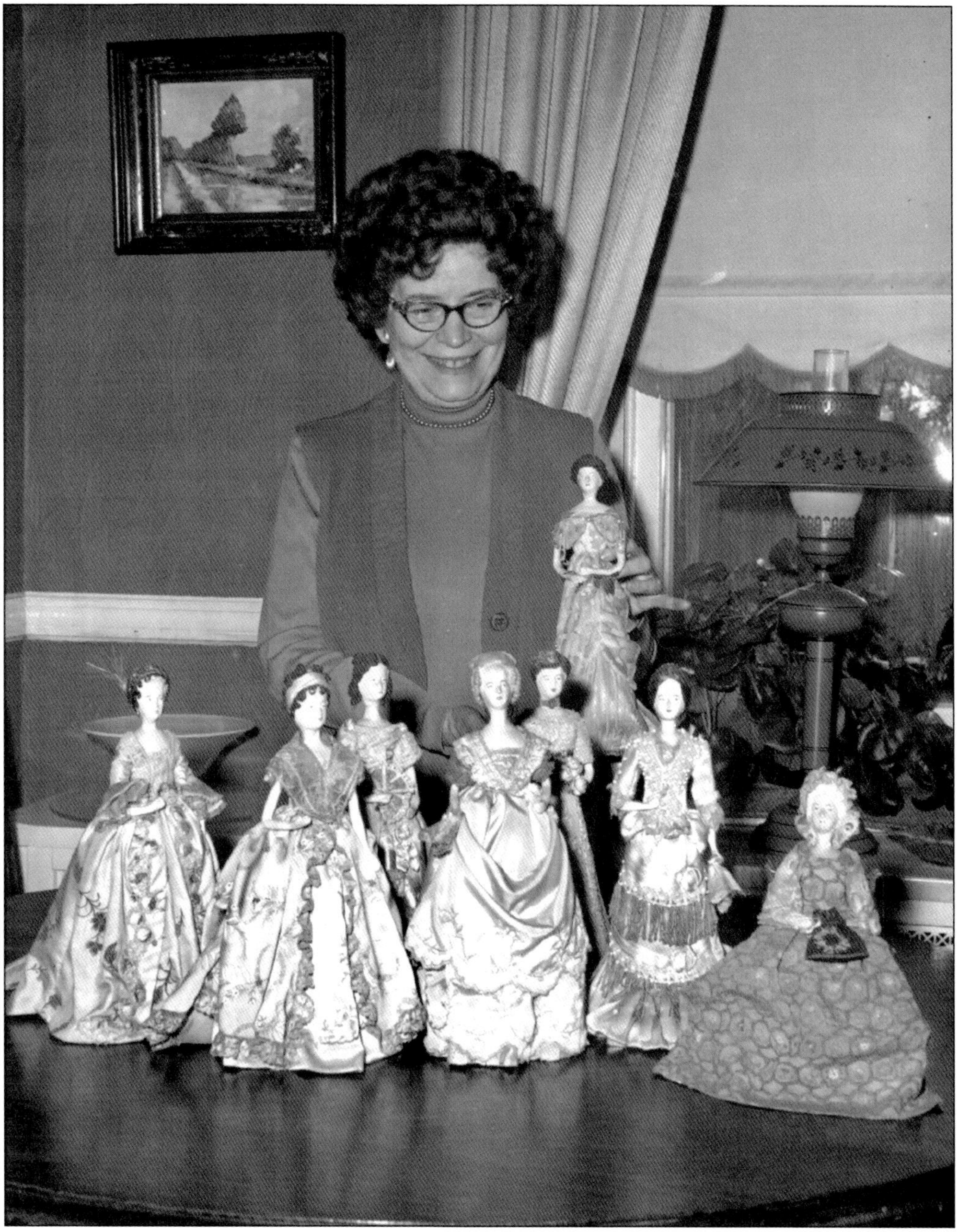

Betty Seidel poses with some of her prized first lady dolls, made to represent the first ladies in their inaugural gowns. (Collection of the Lehigh Township Historical Society.)

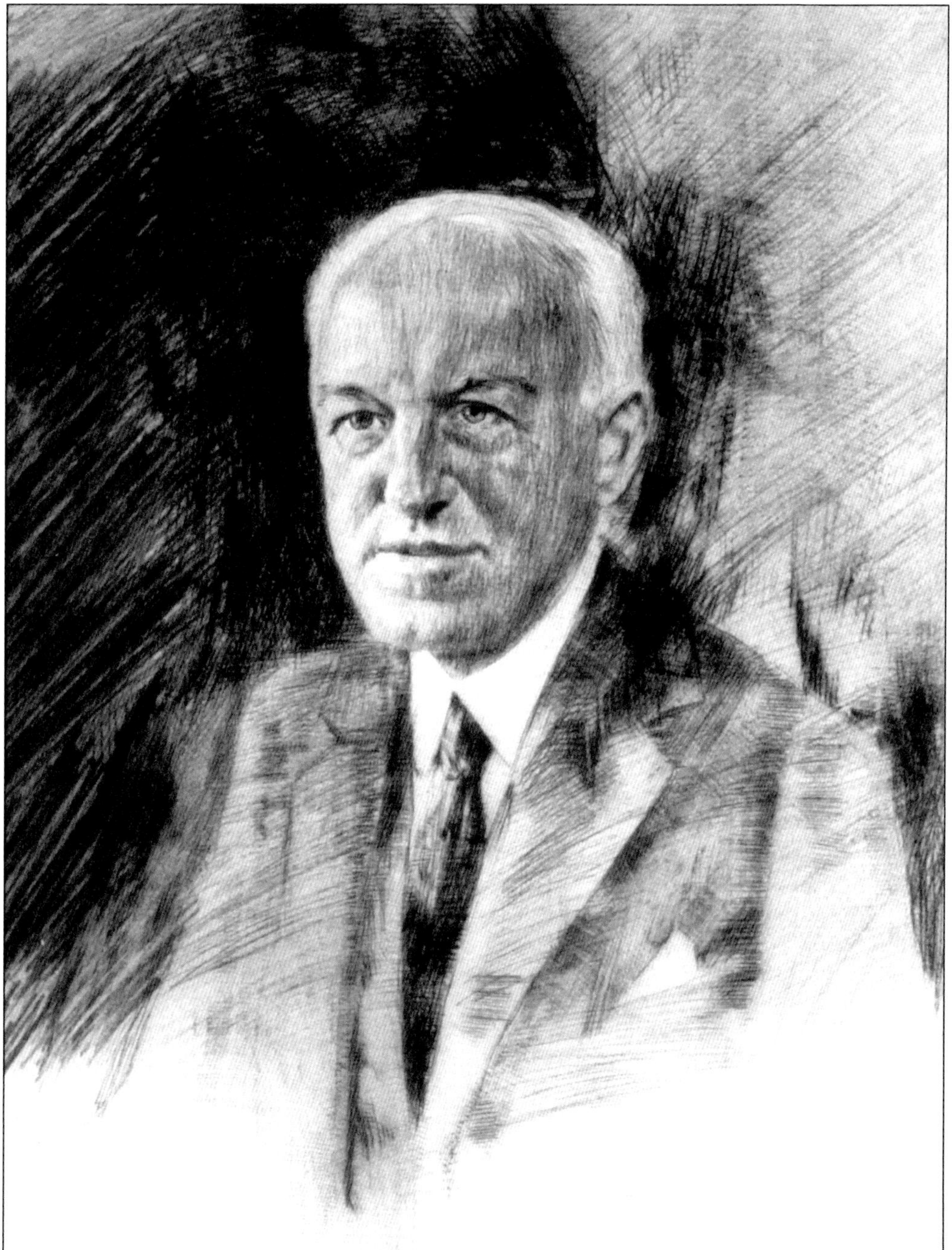

This painting shows Samuel Henry Kress, who was born in the Cherryville Hotel in 1863. Kress, a great art lover, was the first to give pieces to the National Gallery of Art, donating more than 400 paintings and 18 pieces of sculpture in 1937. The Samuel H. Kress Foundation also donated 63 sculptures and paintings to the Allentown Art Museum. (Courtesy the Allentown Art Museum, a gift of Samuel H. Kress Foundation, 1998.)

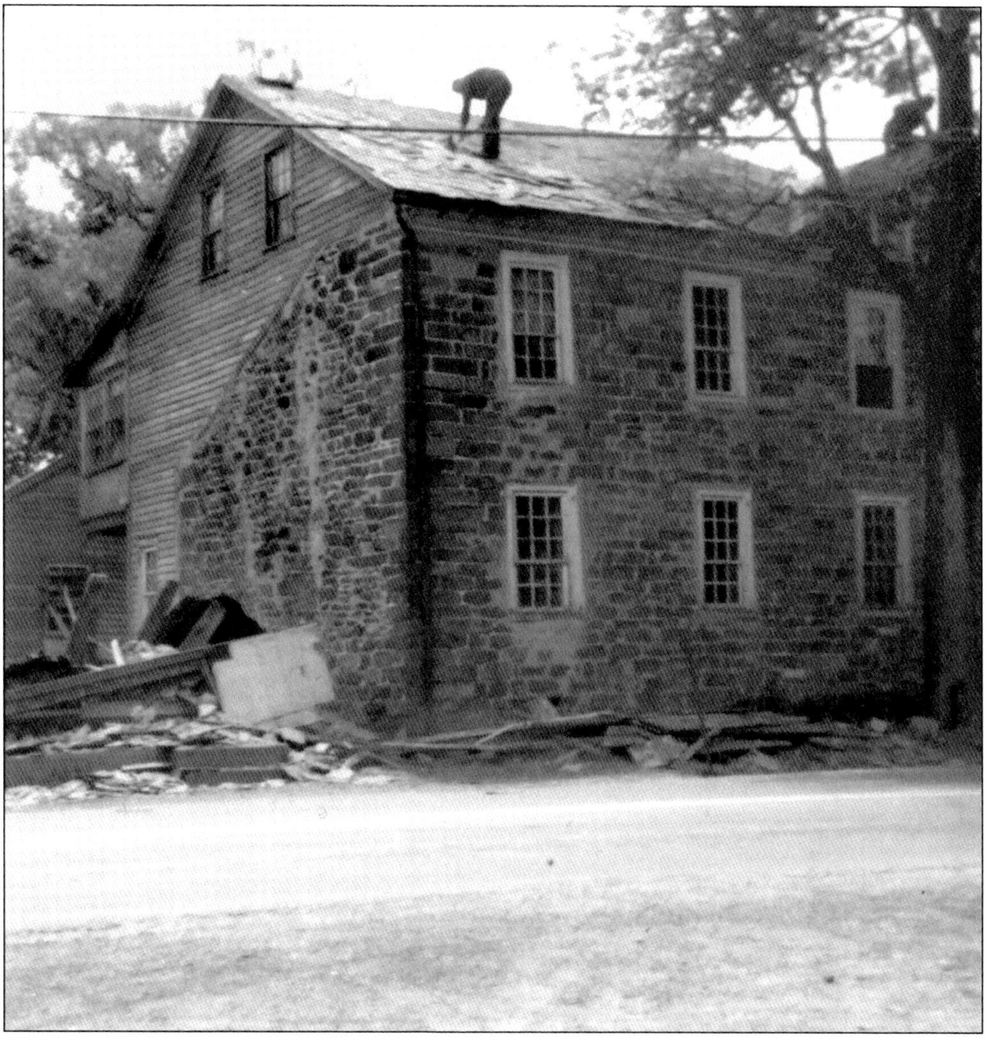

This home, which was removed at the same time as Newhard's home, stood on Blue Mountain Drive behind Newhard's.

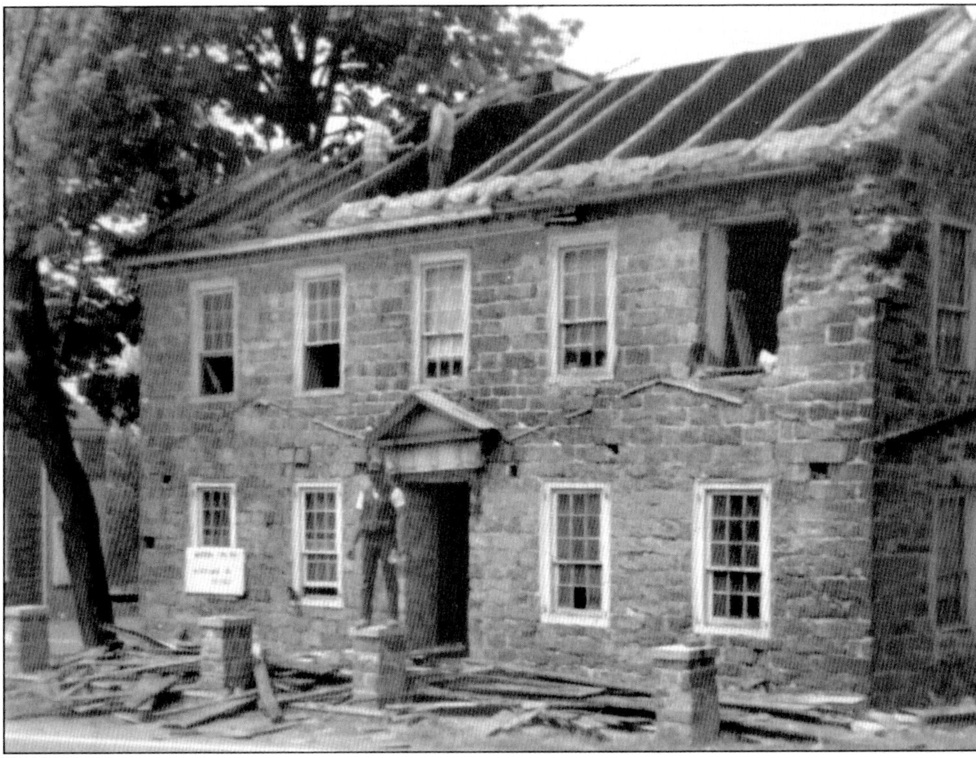

The Newhard Homestead, located where the Lehigh Township fire hall now stands, was torn down in the 1960s. (Collection of the Lehigh Township Historical Society.)

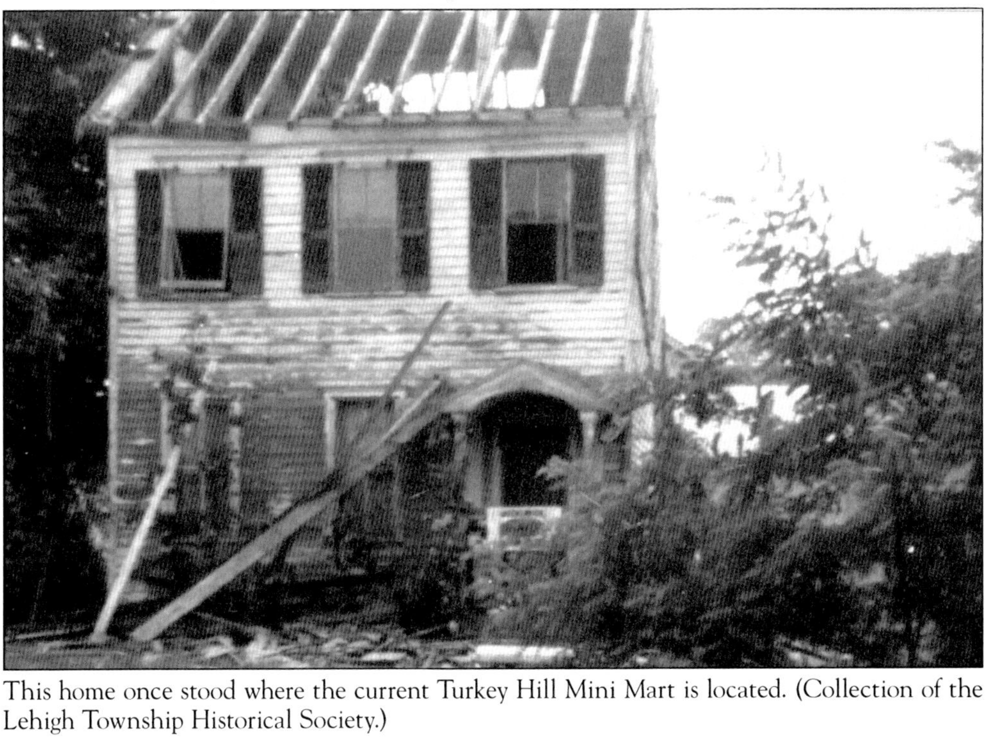

This home once stood where the current Turkey Hill Mini Mart is located. (Collection of the Lehigh Township Historical Society.)

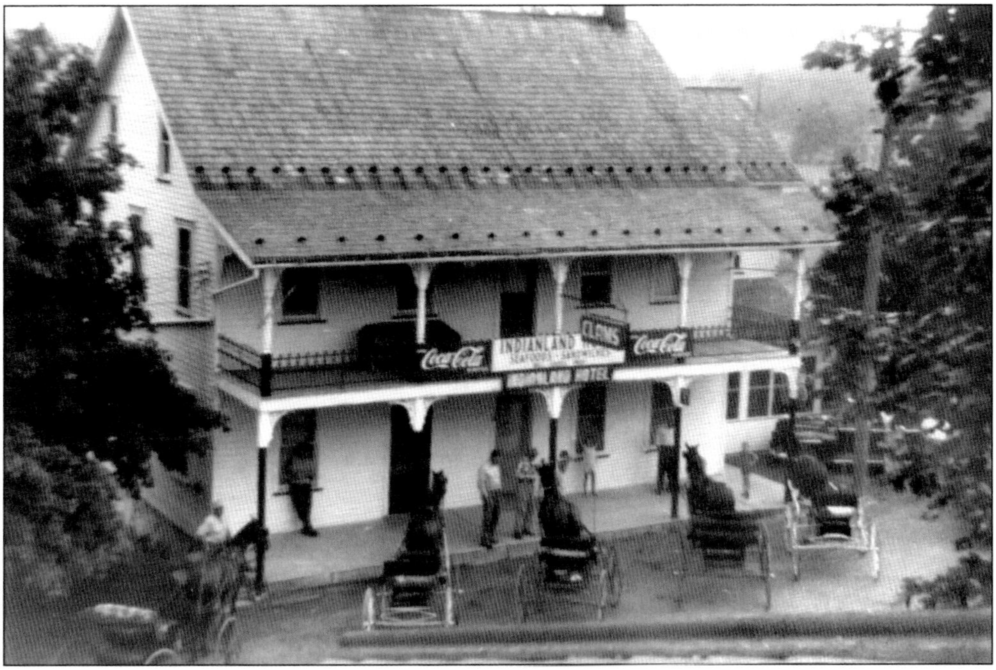

Bill and Irene Gross operated the Indianland Hotel in 1956, when this photograph was taken. They bought it in 1948 from Pete and Lesba Hartzell. The Grosses ran it until 1974. Woodrow and Viola Reph ran it from 1938 to 1941. (Courtesy Brenda Csencsits.)

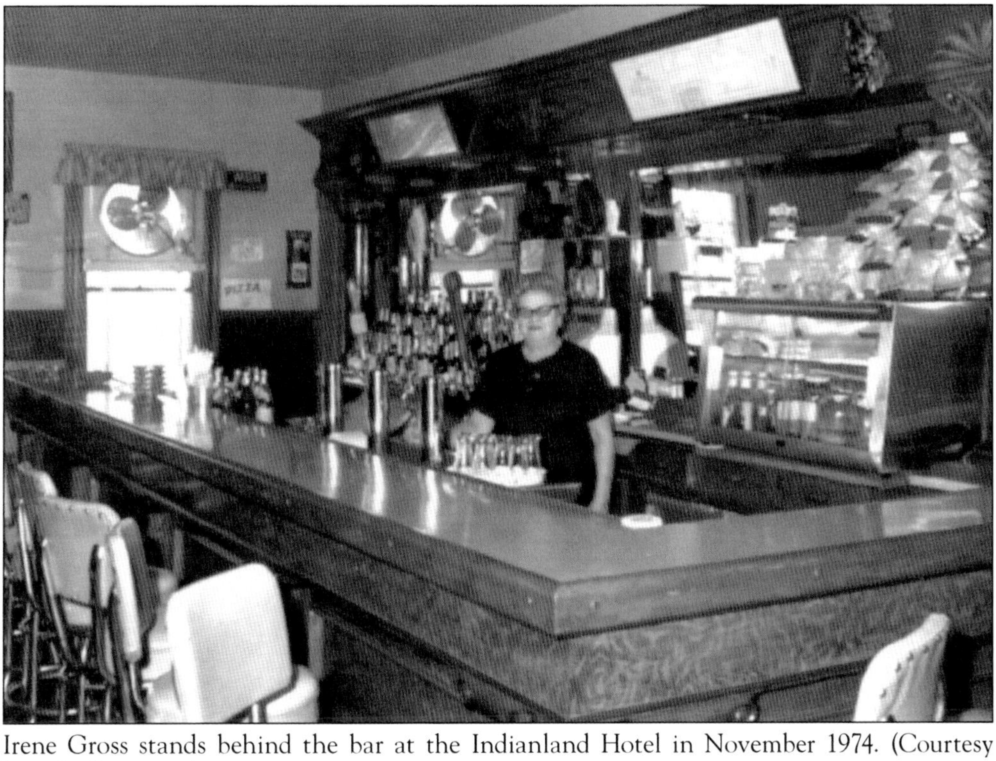

Irene Gross stands behind the bar at the Indianland Hotel in November 1974. (Courtesy Brenda Csencsits.)

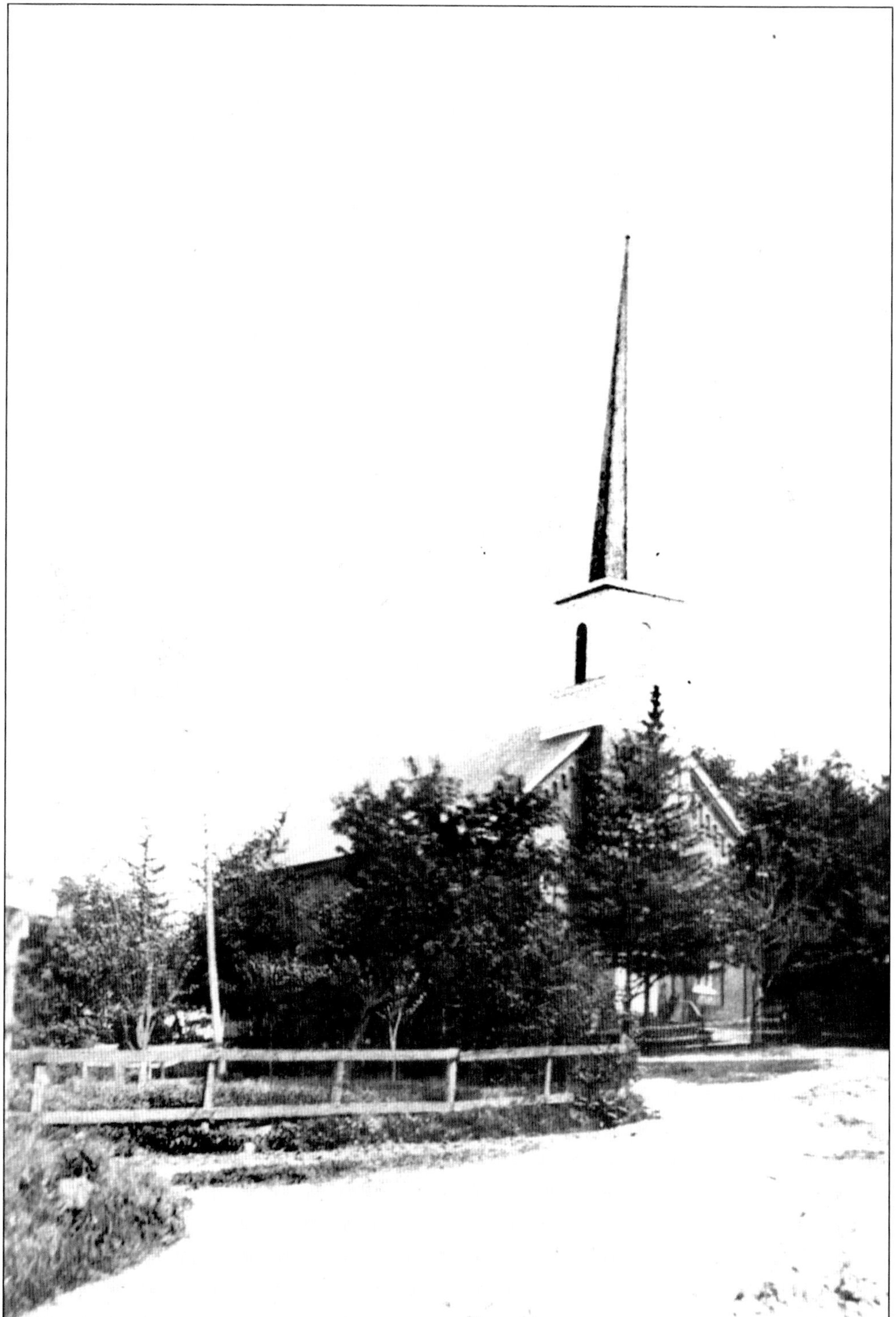

This tall steeple topped St. Paul's Church in Indianland until it was replaced with a much shorter one in 1922. This photograph was taken c. 1910.

Three

THE DANIELSVILLE AREA

Prior to 1850, the village of Danielsville was known as Backman Tavern. It then became known as Wales, and the Wales post office was established on April 9, 1855, with Stinson Hagaman as postmaster. Danielsville obtained its current name on June 7, 1855, in honor of slate quarry owner Charles B. Daniels, who became the postmaster at that time. In 1874, Danielsville contained numerous slate quarries, a hotel, blacksmith shop, and 20 dwellings. The town had two weekly newspapers—the *Danielsville Review*, which was published from 1898 to possibly 1900, and the *Slate Belt Advocate*, published from c. 1912 to 1916.

A good deal of commercial activity in Danielsville can be traced to the Hower family. Franklin M. Hower started as a butcher in Cherryville. By the 1870s, he purchased the six-acre Eagle Slate Quarry. He also operated a lumberyard, a blacksmith shop, and a grain mill, all in the same area. Later, he established the Slate Valley Railroad, the Blue Ridge Traction Company, and Edgemont Park.

Hower was also instrumental in establishing the National Bank of Danielsville, organized in 1905 and opened for business in April 1906. The bank president was Stoken J. Drumheller, and the vice president was Tilghman Henry. Cashiers included Henry H. Hower, Lewis Green, A.W. Hower, H.T. Marsh, and E.E. Vogel. Under its charter, the bank issued its own currency.

On the morning of Friday, November 13, 1931, two armed men entered the bank, yelling, "Stick 'em up!" Bank president Henry Hower, teller William Kromer, and customer Amandeus Reph were ordered to lie on the floor. The bandits made off with $5,000 in cash and fled in a Cadillac parked outside. Local and state police traced the car's license number and found it to be stolen from Lansdale. Within four days, police apprehended Gottfried Adams of Allentown. By January 1932, Adams's younger brother George was caught, and he confessed. Despite his alibis to the contrary, Gottfried Adams was identified by an array of Danielsville residents as being the second bandit. The Adams brothers were found guilty, made to pay $3,000 each in restitution, and were each sentenced to 10–20 years hard labor at Eastern State Penitentiary.

On January 14, 1935, burglars entered the bank and, using an acetylene torch stolen from Allentown, burned an 18- by 30-inch hole in the outer vault. After leaving the torch behind to crawl through the opening, the burglars found themselves unable to open the inner vault to gain access to the paper cash. The heavy manganese-steel door foiled their attempt, despite their success at smashing the combination and handle. They made off with only $430 in coins and the contents of 15 safe-deposit boxes. The vault door was still warm when janitor George Bachman arrived at 7 a.m. to stoke the furnace. Research has not shown whether these burglars were apprehended. These robberies were part of the reason the bank was taken over by the Cement National Bank.

The Danielsville National Bank building became the home of the Roosevelt Democratic Club in 1937, when the club purchased it from the Cement National Bank. The club organized on October 20, 1933, and held meetings at local hotels prior to purchasing this building.

The Salem Evangelical Church in Danielsville (or Brick Church, as it is known) was built in 1867 on the east side of Blue Mountain Drive on land purchased from Peter Becker by Daniel

Oplinger, Stephen Eckert, and Reuben Leibenguth. The building was too small after 20 years, so the current church was built across the street.

To the south of Danielsville, at the intersection of Wood and Blue Mountain Drives, is Bossard's Corner, named after a family who lived in the area. The name appears on early maps, where it is also spelled Bassard and Buzzard.

Also south of Danielsville, along Indian Creek, is Howersville, named for the Hower family. A. Hower operated a store and hotel and, in 1850, ran Hower's Mills and Distillery there. The Eagle Slate Quarry, run by descendants Henry and Jeremiah Hower, employed 80 men at one point.

Harpers, located between Danielsville and Berlinsville, was named for the Harper family who ran slate quarries in that area. A post office opened on September 12, 1890, with G.D. Hall as postmaster. It closed on July 1, 1905. In 1874, the village contained H.W. Harpers Slate Factory, a school, a church, and 10 dwellings. In the 1930s, an area to the northwest was called Harper's Station because it was located on the Lehigh and New England Railroad. The area later became known for Edgemont Park, which sprang up around the Blue Ridge Traction Company's trolley lines.

Rockville, located to the east of Danielsville on Route 946, was named for the nearby slate quarries, but the name did not appear on area maps until the 1870s. In 1874, a hotel and a blacksmith shop were located in the village. The Rockville Hotel was run c. 1900 by Francis O. Marsh and his wife, Ethel. The Marshes also operated a store, an auction house in an adjacent barn, and eventually a gasoline station. From 1904 to 1908, Francis Marsh was the local assessor, recording births, deaths, marriages, and school and voting records for the Rockville-Danielsville area. The Marshes' daughter Irene and her husband, Daniel "Junior" Beers, took over the business and, in 1980, sold it to Ray Tomsic.

From 1945 to 1947, Edwin Smith of Rockville maintained an airstrip for his biplane. It was later taken over by George Kern and came to be known by his name.

Slatefield, located north of Rockville, was bounded generally by Cottonwood Road. The Heffelfinger family was prominent there. The Lehigh and New England Railroad passed through the village, which had its own station.

Slate Valley is located midway between Danielsville and Rockville on Route 946. The village's one-room school still stands along the road. A hotel and about seven slate quarries were also located there. The name Slate Valley fell out of use for the region, and an area near Benningers now goes by this name.

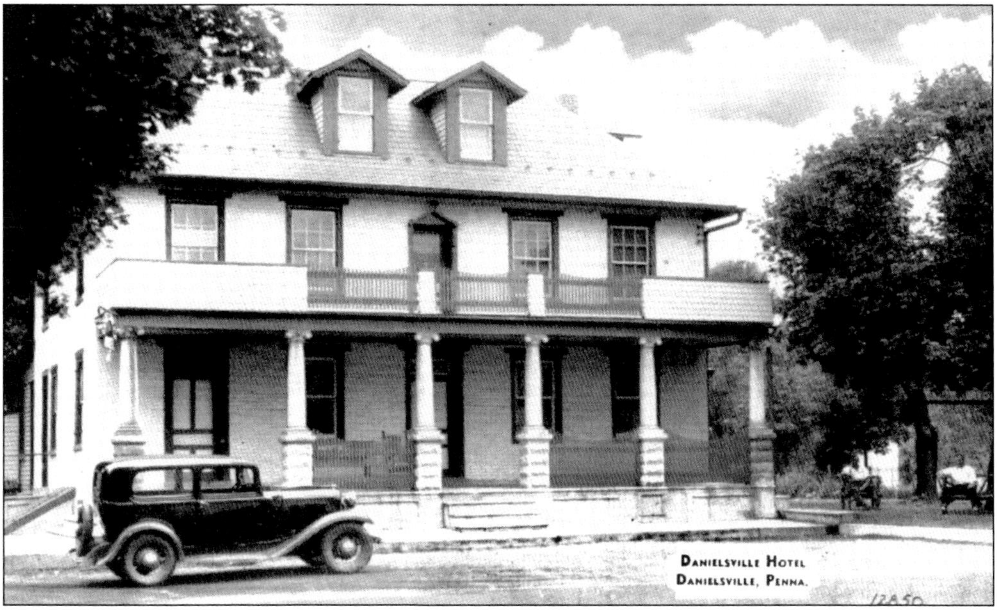

The Danielsville Hotel, shown here in the 1920s, was located next to the Danielsville National Bank. The building is the current site of the Pasta e Vino restaurant. (Courtesy Sean and Johanna Billings.)

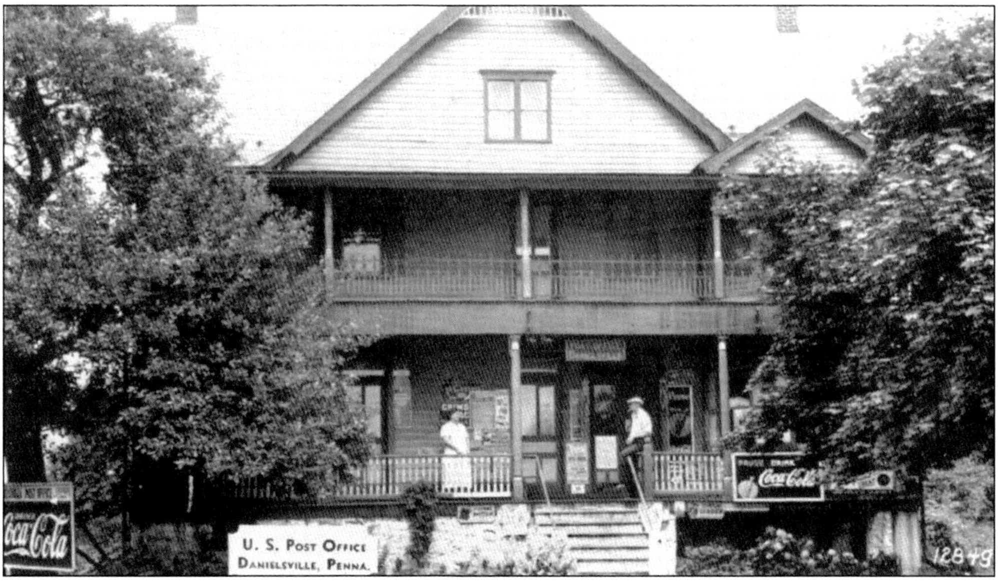

The old Danielsville post office was located across the street from the current one. Originally built by Samuel Longenbach as a 21-room boardinghouse, the building was purchased by Stephen Reph and his wife in 1916, when they moved from Rockville. In 1933, Reph's son John was postmaster here. (Courtesy Sean and Johanna Billings.)

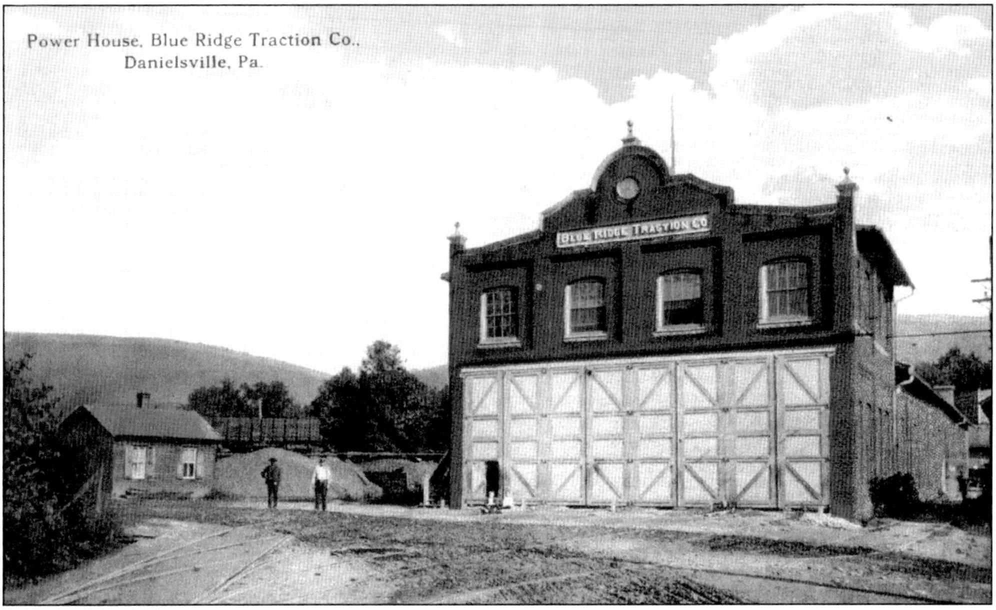

In addition to housing trolleys, the Blue Ridge Traction Company's powerhouse initially produced the power for the trolley line and for public streetlights lining Walnut Drive. (Courtesy Larry Hillborn.)

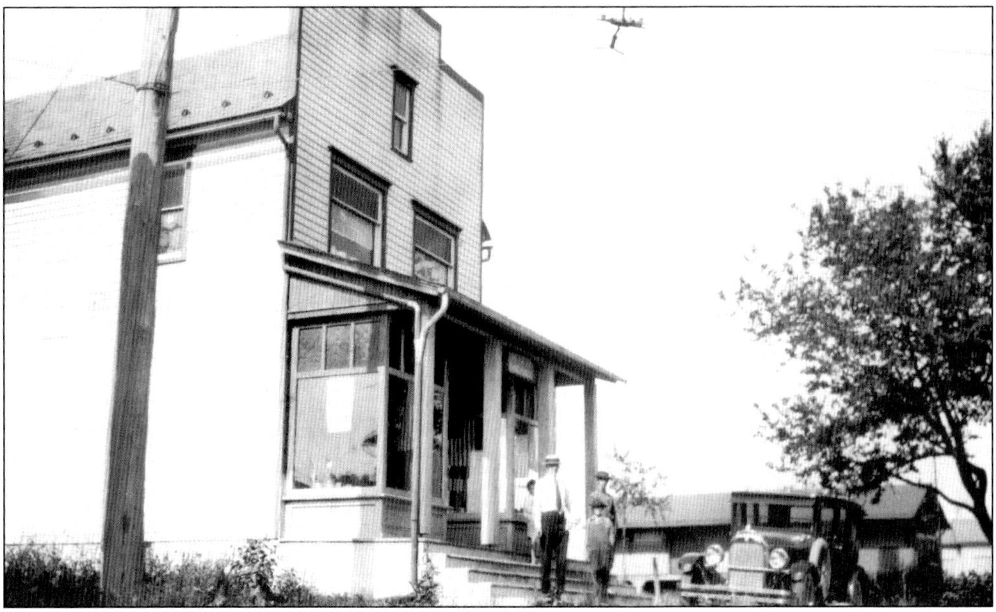

C.A. Herman's store in Danielsville was located across from the powerhouse, next to the train station, in an area that for a short time was known as East Danielsville. C.R. Biechy owned the store before C.A. Herman. (Courtesy Griffith Roberts.)

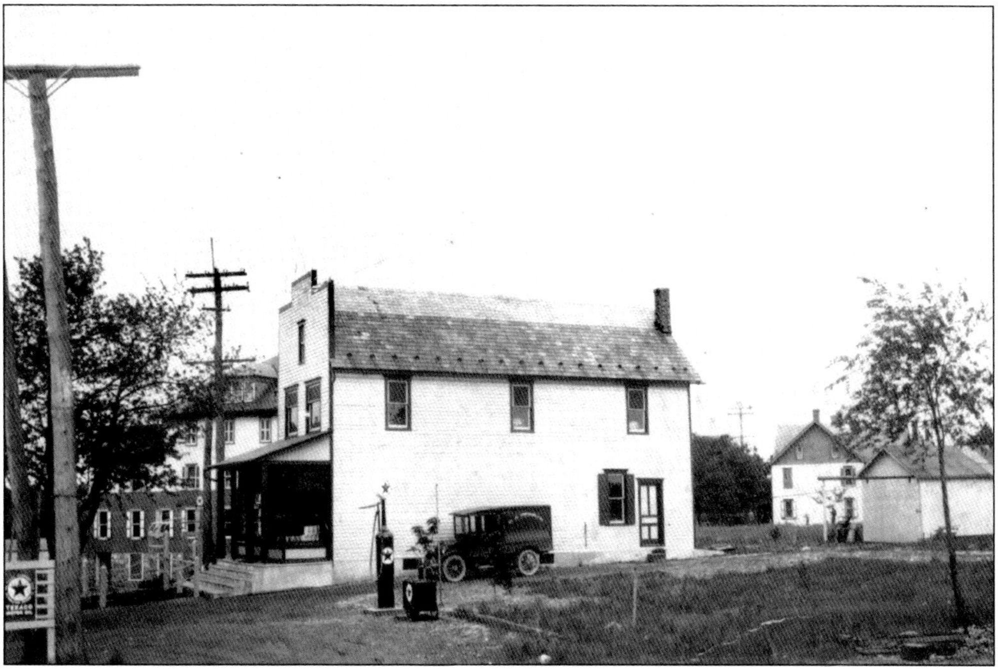

This *c.* 1908 photograph of C.A. Herman's store shows the Texaco gas pumps and Herman's delivery truck. The building is currently vacant. (Courtesy Larry Hillborn.)

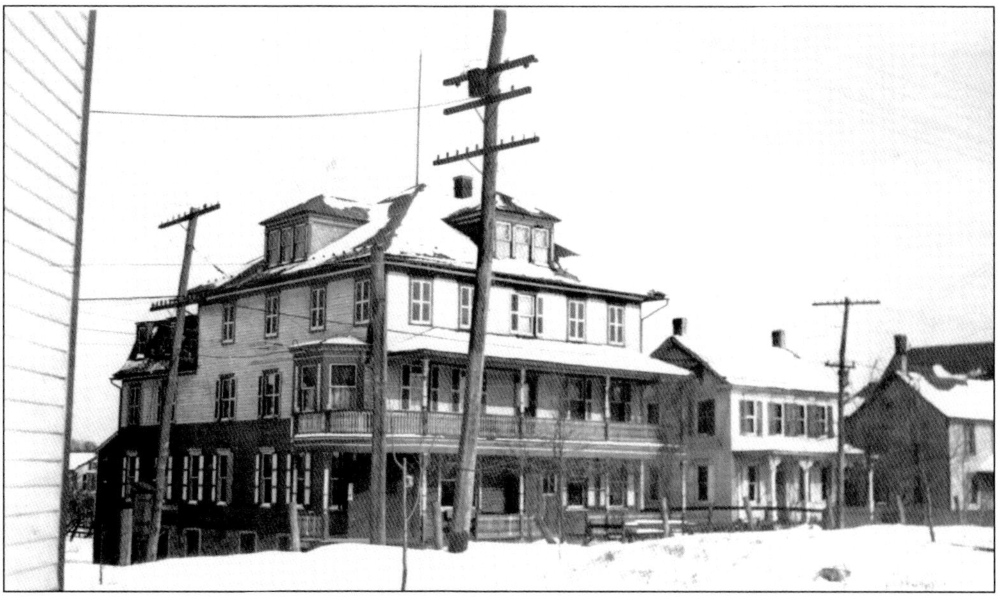

The Hotel Henry, located on the corner of Route 946 and what is now Walnut Drive, was built by A. Henry and was often filled with slate quarry workers. The second owners, Ammon and Laura Redline, continued to use the name Hotel Henry, but the third owners, Harlan and Grant Bossard, changed the name to Bossard's Hotel. The original building was destroyed by fire on March 17, 1945, and was rebuilt by Harvey Dieter as the Mountain House. It is currently vacant. (Courtesy Larry Hillborn.)

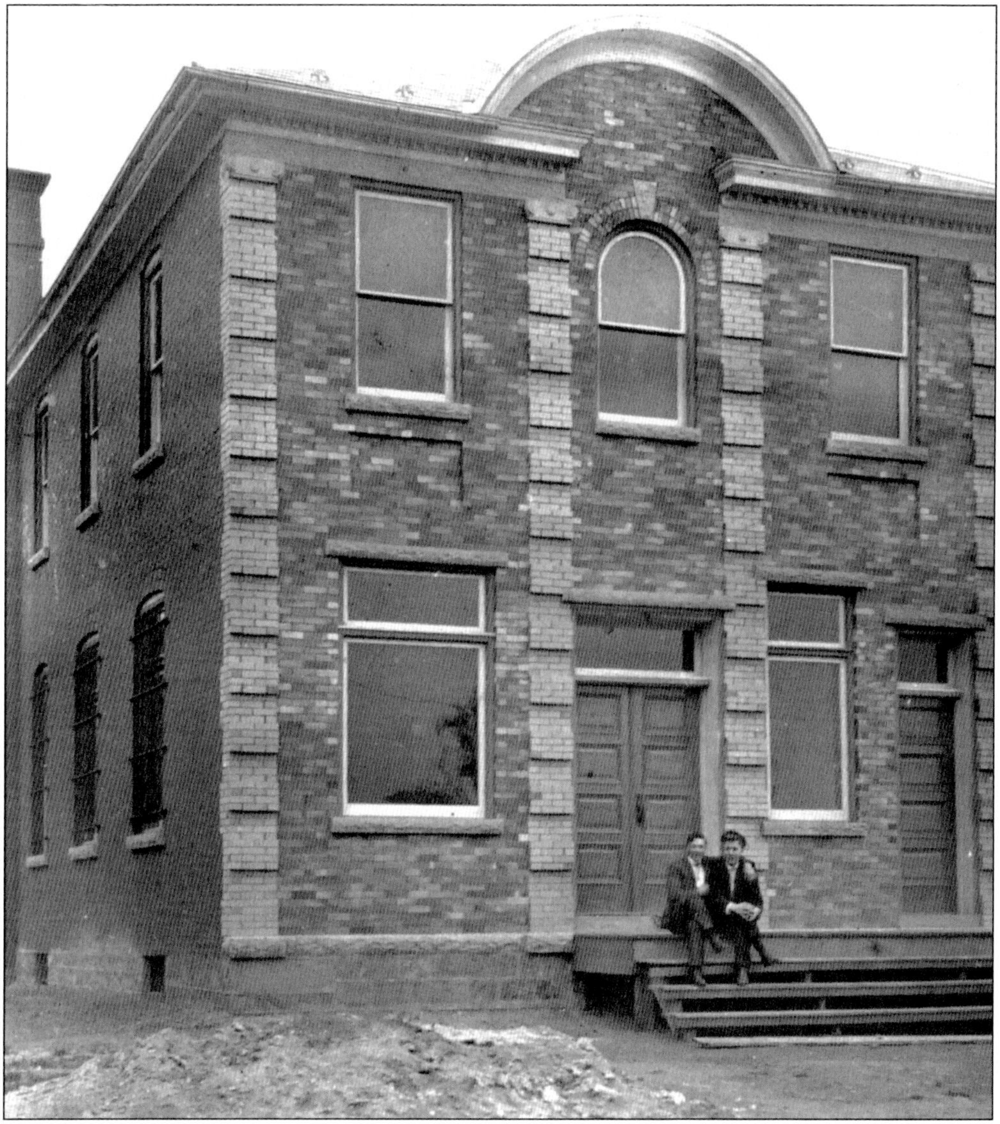

This photograph shows the Danielsville National Bank in 1906, shortly before it opened for business. (Courtesy Edith Sikorsky.)

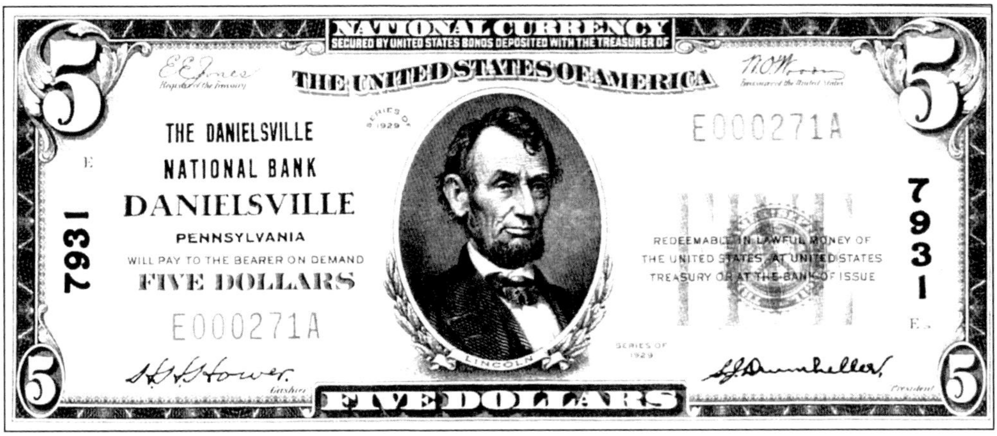

The Danielsville National Bank printed its own currency. Shown here is a $5 bill from 1929. (Courtesy Griffith Roberts.)

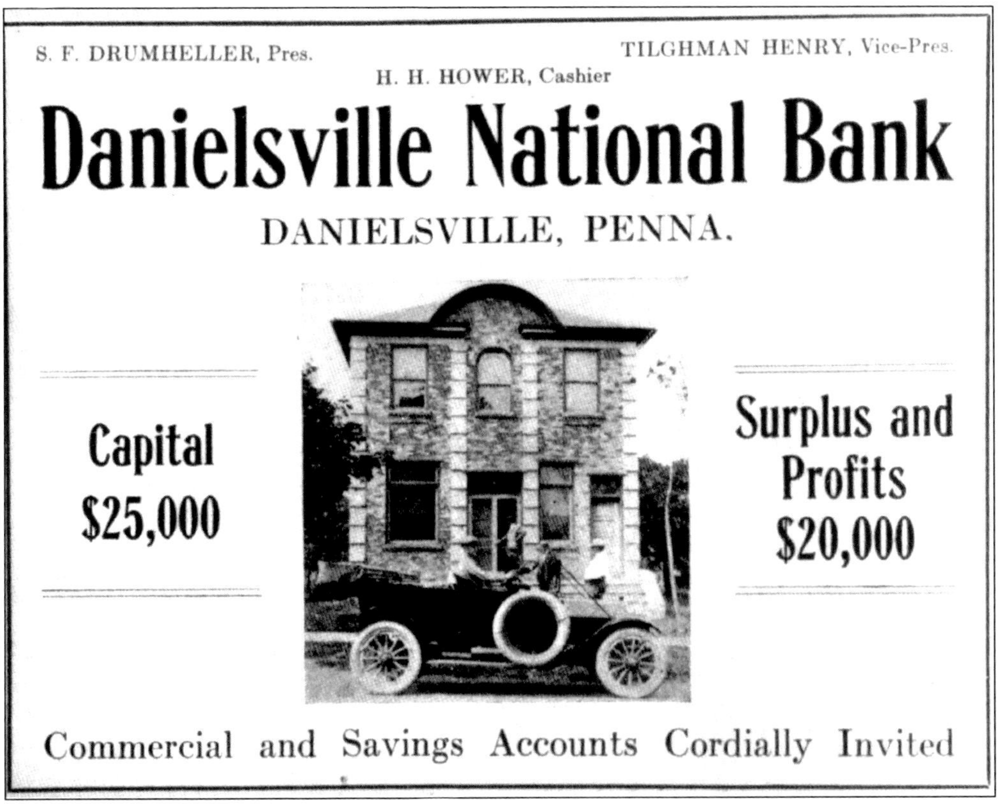

This Danielsville National Bank advertisement appeared in the 1914 *Farmers Directory of Northampton County*. (Courtesy Sarah Pagotto.)

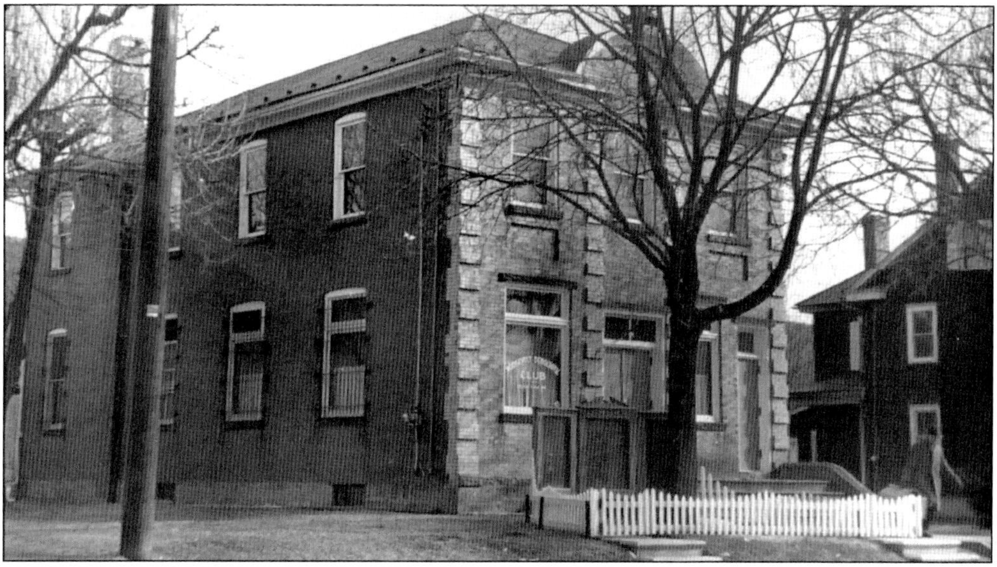

By the 1940s, when this photograph was taken, the Danielsville National Bank building had been converted into the Roosevelt Democratic Club. (Courtesy Sean and Johanna Billings.)

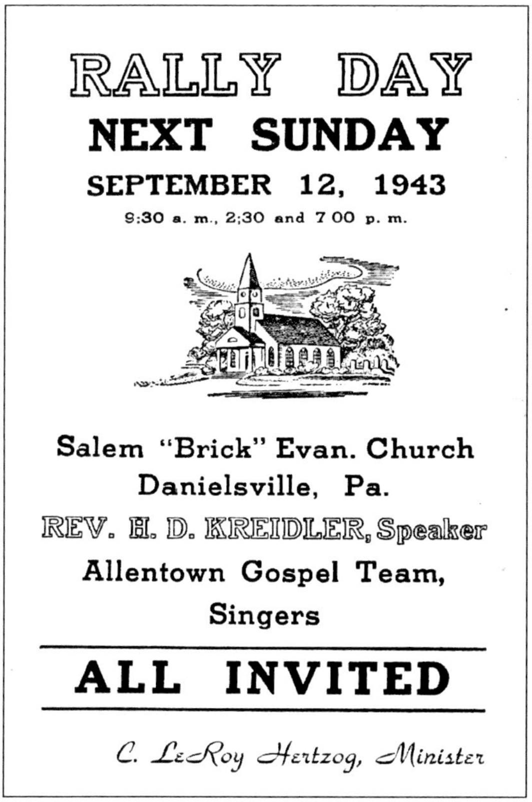

This 1943 postcard advertises Rally Day for the Salem Evangelical Church, also known as Brick Church. (Courtesy Sean and Johanna Billings.)

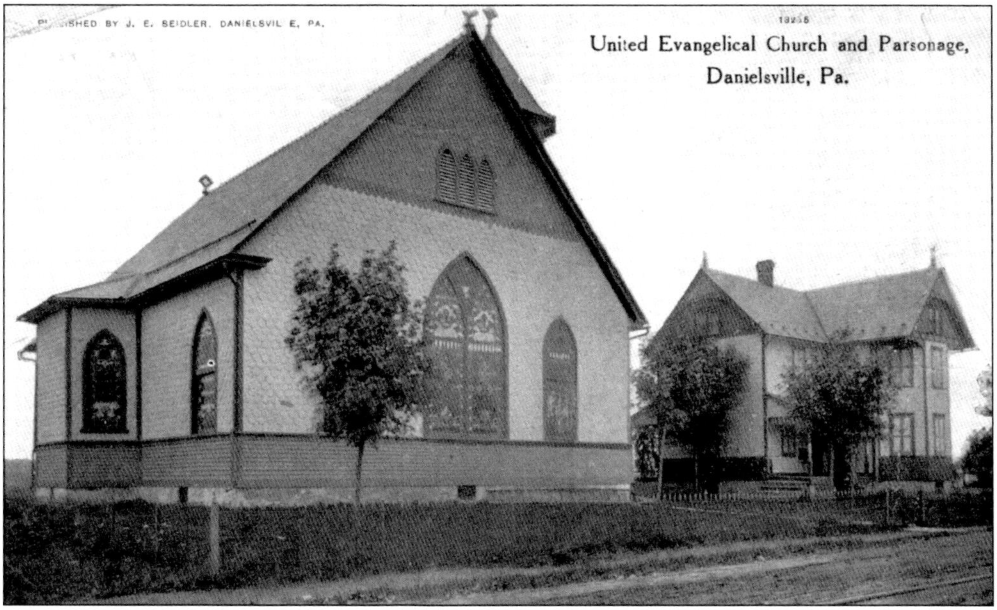

The United Evangelical Church, shown here with the parsonage next door, was built in 1897 after a dispute at the Salem Evangelical Church caused a split in the congregation. The parsonage still stands as a home, but the church was razed in 1998. (Courtesy Sean and Johanna Billings.)

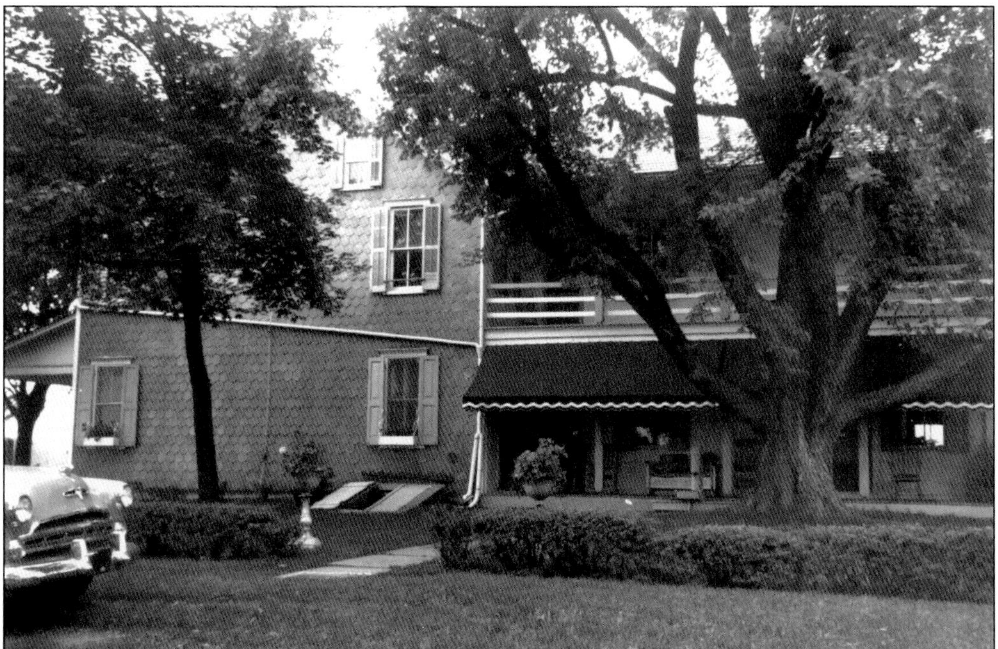

This 1950s view shows the F.M. Hower homestead, which was located in Danielsville in front of the Hower Quarry. The home is sided with slate, a reflection of Hower's involvement in the industry. (Courtesy Edith Sikorsky.)

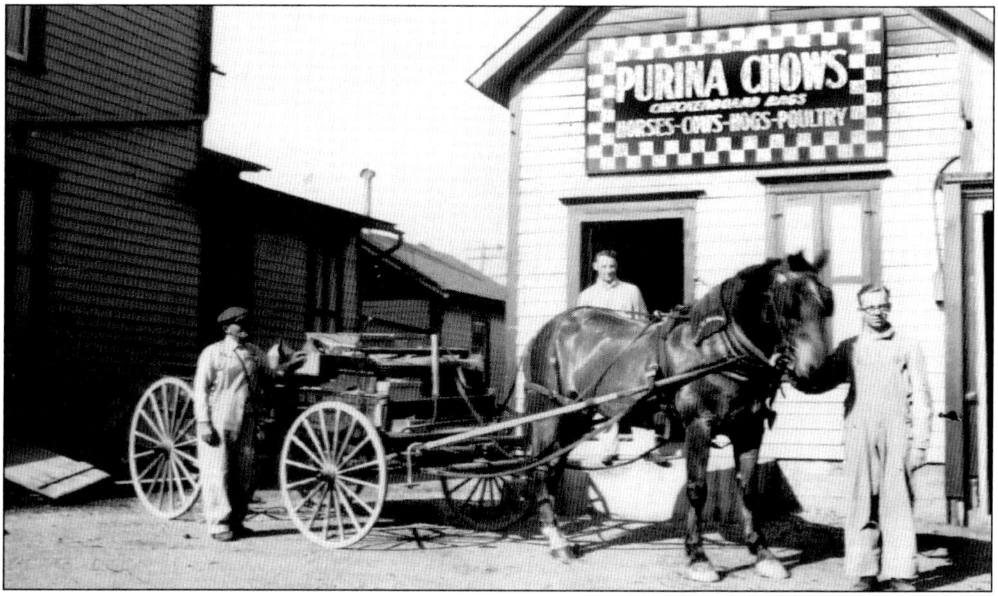

This photograph shows Fred H. Herman's delivery wagon in front of his store in Danielsville. (Courtesy Larry Hillborn.)

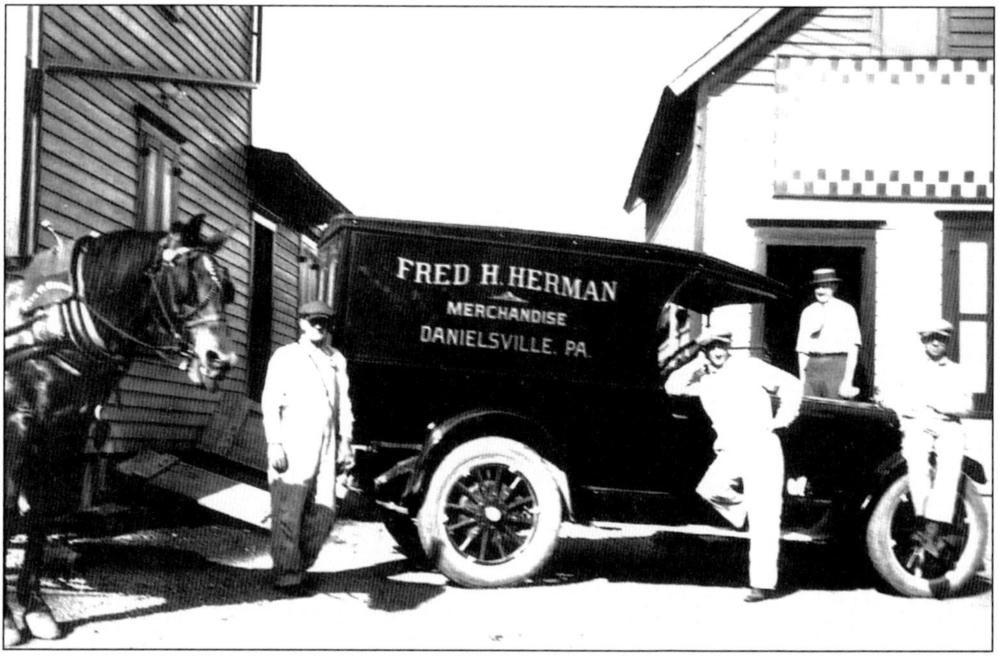

Lewis Bossard delivered orders for Fred H. Herman's store in the Danielsville area with this new Dodge truck. Charles Stoneburner continued deliveries eastward, toward Rockville, using the horse and buggy. In this photograph, Fred Herman stands in the doorway, and Ralph Herman sits on the truck fender. (Courtesy Woodrow Reph.)

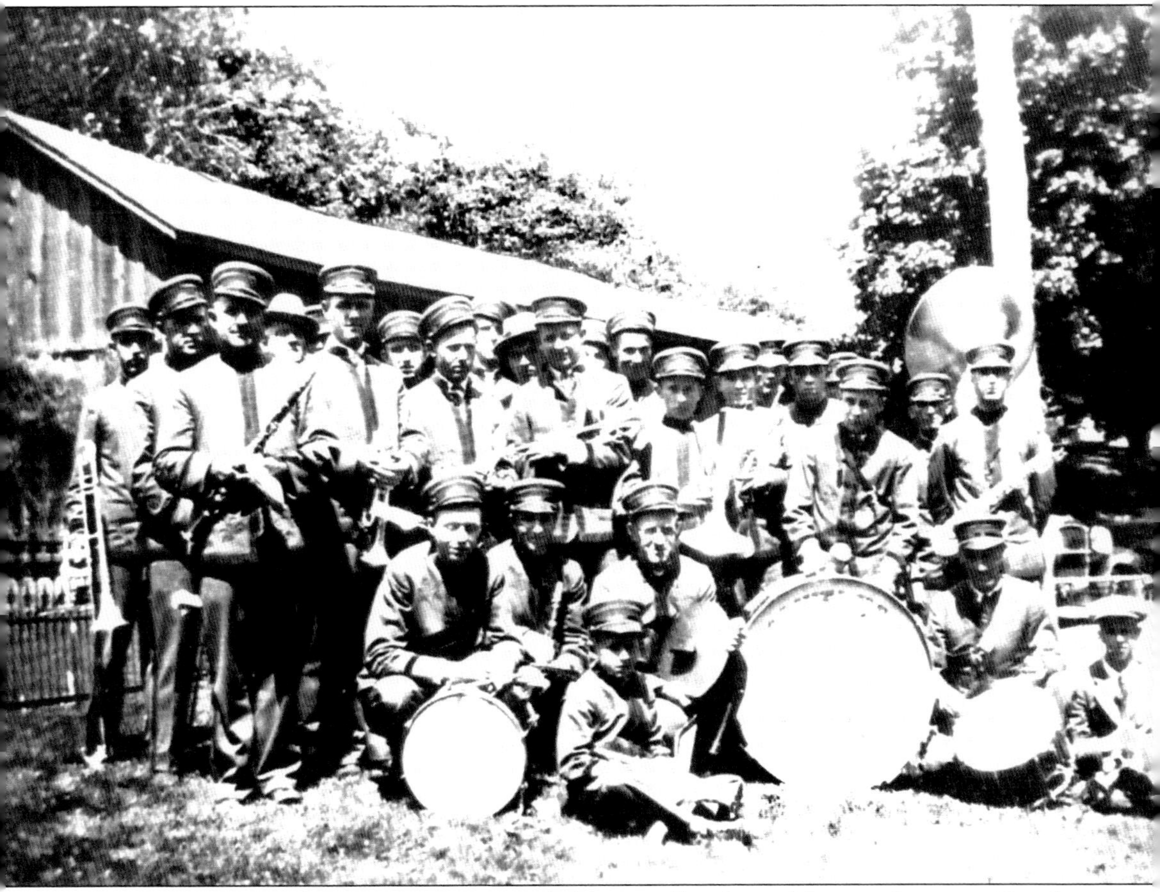

The Danielsville Band, pictured in 1931, was led by Lewellyn Jones. The members were David Anthony, Alvin Vogel, Ralph Vogel, George Vogel, Cubert A. Herman, Quintas Haydt, William Haydt, Howard Althouse, Russell Althouse, Lester Herman, John Spahits, Edward Anthony, Kermit Green, Harold Haydt, Ray Muffly, Alton Muffly, Ray Borger, Allin Binges, Woodrow Reph, Ralph Herman, Eugene Stahley, Ralph Oplinger, Lloyd Knazley, and Grant Vogel. (Courtesy Griffith Roberts.)

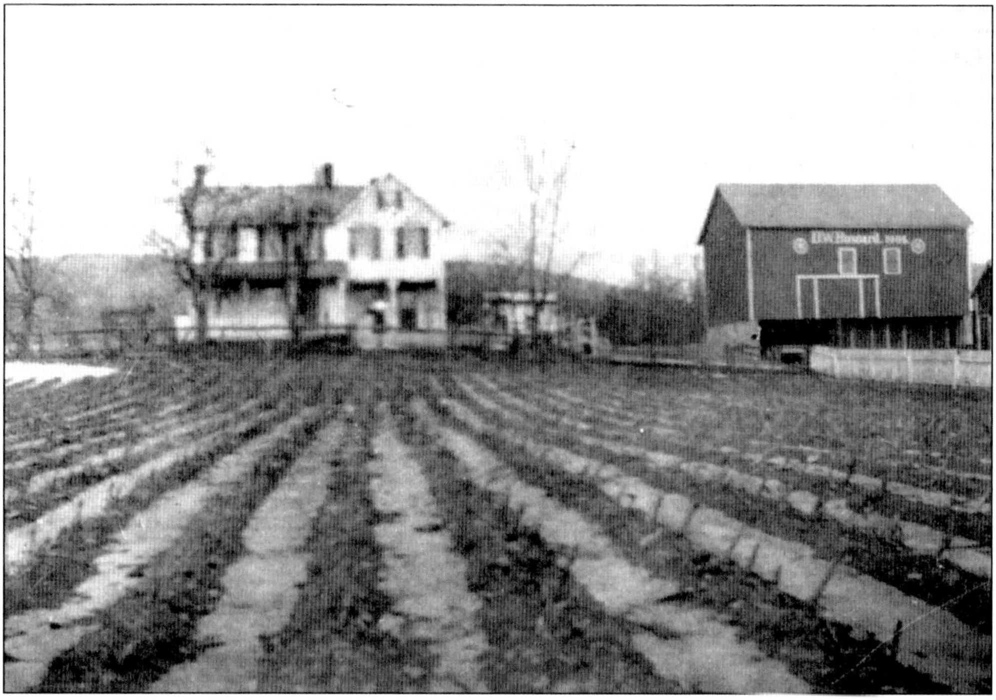

Shown in 1908 is D.W. Bossard's farm, located in Bossard's Corner. (Courtesy Larry Hillborn.)

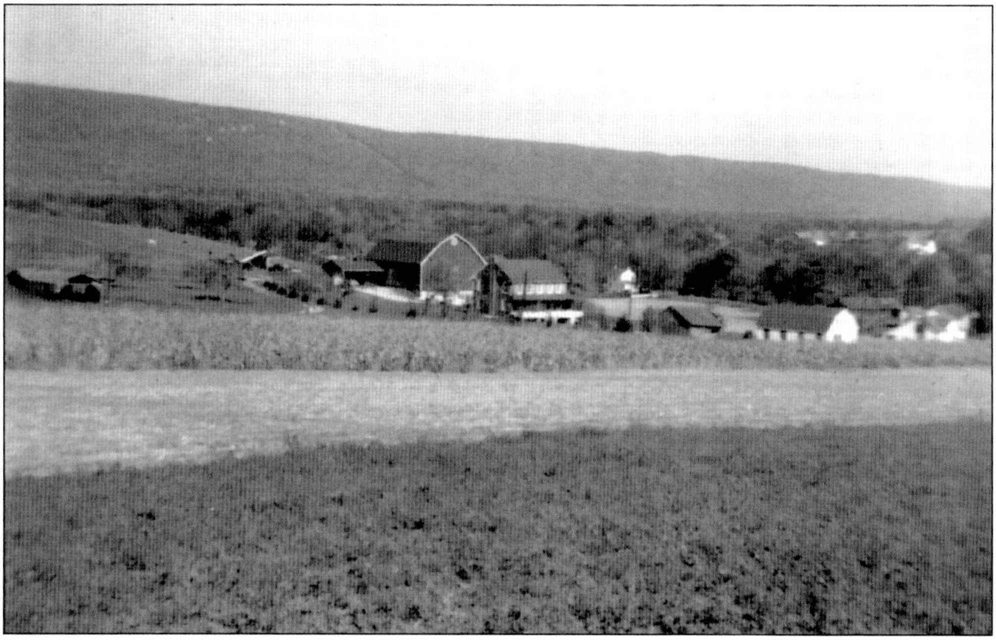

This view shows the Pagotto farm in Rockville, near Cottonwood Road, in 1961. (Courtesy Sarah Pagotto.)

Four

The Pennsville and Petersville Areas

Pennsville was called Newhartsville from 1860 to 1900 for the prominent Newhart family and appears on an 1860 map as "Newhartsville P.O." When the name was changed to Pennsville, it honored William Penn and his family.

The Newhartsville post office was founded on September 8, 1852, with M. Newhart as postmaster. When it closed on June 21, 1875, residents received mail service from Petersville. In 1850, the village had a store, 3 blacksmith shops, 20 dwellings, and a gristmill.

The gristmill was located in the area now known as Indian Trail Park. Powered by water coming down a millrace from a dam, the mill ground corn, oats, and wheat. Resident Metro Myster recalls going down to the old mill as a young boy to grind wheat for flour before the mill ceased operation *c.* 1920. The mill was then used to generate electricity for Indian Trail Park, which hosted dances and roller-skating in the mid-1940s. The gristmill was torn down in the early 1990s because it was structurally unsafe and had become a target for vandals. Although several attempts were made to save the old mill, none of them succeeded.

The Pennsville Hotel was originally one of the stagecoach stops on the King's Highway, which ran through the township on its way from Easton to Gnadenhutten. In 1850, Martin Althouse was the hotel proprietor. Next door lived William Young, who had a blacksmith shop. Another blacksmith shop was owned by the Berlins.

With 23 family-owned farms in the area, a group called the Farmers Institute started meeting in the schoolhouse located between Pennsville and Stone Church. The Harmony Grange No. 1692 purchased the schoolhouse for $300, and in June 1916, 51 members signed a charter. The association was involved in farming and was a social outlet for families.

The United Brethren Church, located near the two-room schoolhouse on Walnut Drive in Pennsville, had an old shed next to it for horses. The church was in existence as early as 1902 and was still in use up until 1922. The pastors of the church included G.W. Hess (1915), R.E. Wiest (1917), J.B. Koons (1918–1920), and W.D. Krick (1921–1922). The church has been gone for many years, but the cemetery that was located with the church is still in existence. Some of the people who attended the church eventually formed the Pilgrim Holiness Church in Cherryville.

Petersville, located east of Pennsville, was also known as Peterfield, Kernville, and Kersville. The village was named after Peter Miller, who along with Nicholas Kern, operated a store and gristmill there *c.* 1805. In 1813, a post office was opened under the name Kernsville, with J. Kearn as postmaster. On September 1, 1836, a post office was opened under the name Petersville, and it closed on November 15, 1908.

In 1845, this village contained seven dwellings and two stores. At one time, it also contained a blacksmith shop; a creamery run by Paul Koch; and the Petersville Hotel, which was located along the creek and was run by J.D. Koons.

The Petersville Store was run by Adam Marsh in the early 1900s. He sold it to Floyd D. Reimer, who ran it with his wife from 1927 to 1929. They sold it to a Mr. Crouthamel from Treichlers and moved to operate a store in Wind Gap. Because Reimer's wife did not like living in Wind Gap, the couple moved back to Petersville and bought the store back in 1933, running it until 1938. The store was then sold to a Mr. Frederick. It sold Atlantic gasoline and general merchandise.

Pomfret was located just northwest of Pennsville. It was named for the Earl of Pomfret, Thomas Penn's father-in-law. It was marked on maps from 1899 to 1901, but the name then passed out of use. The Hower and Kleppinger families were numerous there.

Thomas Werner stands in front of his property, the Pennsville Hotel. (Courtesy Paul Gieske.)

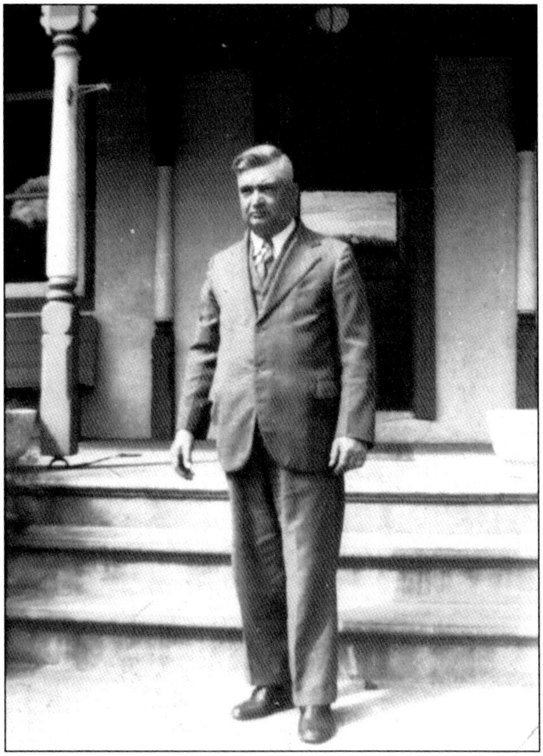

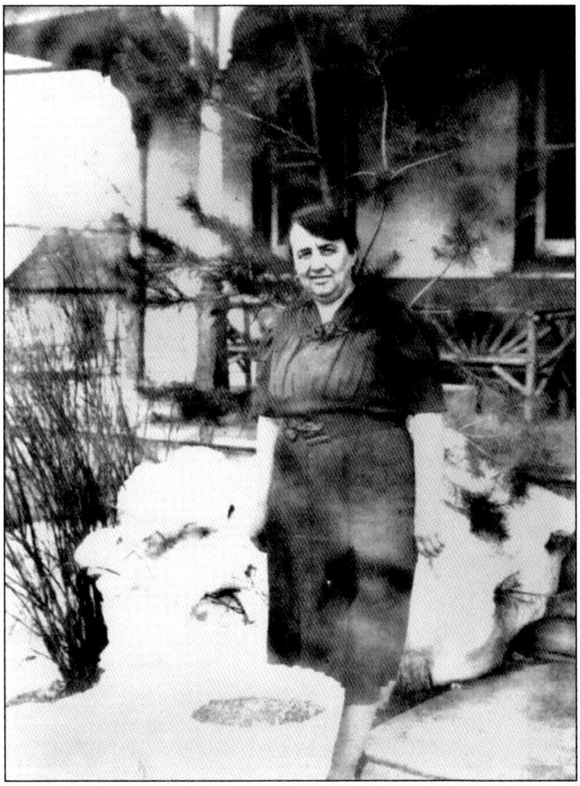

Thomas Werner's wife, Stella, stands in front of the Pennsville Hotel. (Courtesy Paul Gieske.)

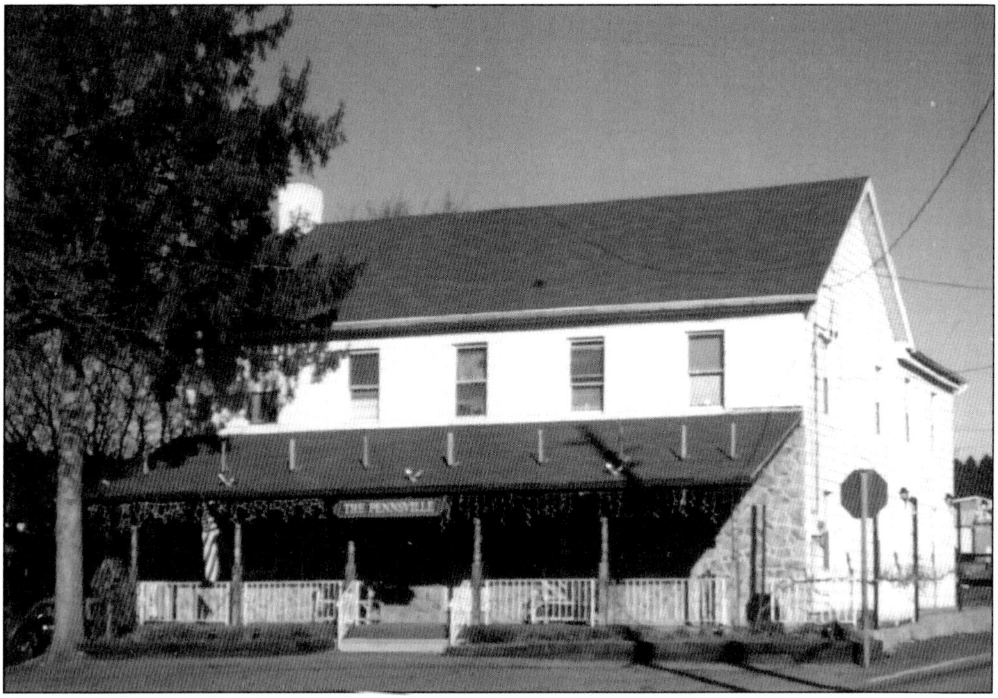

The Pennsville Hotel was a stagecoach stop on the King's Highway, part of which is now Route 248. (Courtesy Robert Mentzell.)

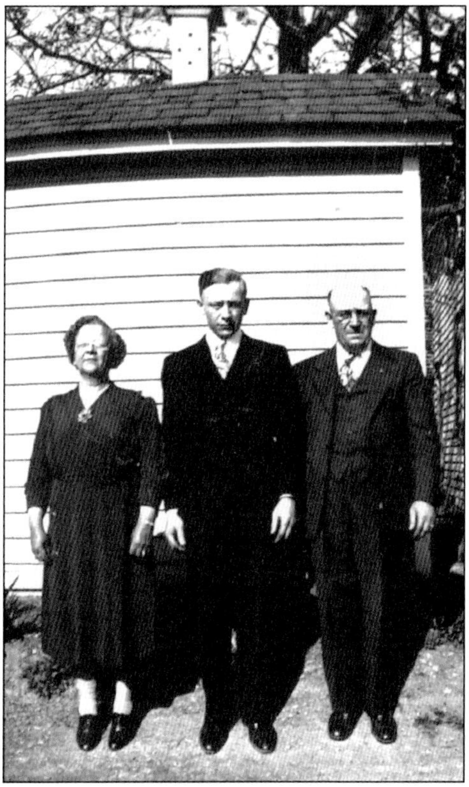

Bertha Reimer (left), son Lester (center), and husband Floyd stand near their summer house at the Petersville General Store in 1935. (Courtesy Lester A. Reimer.)

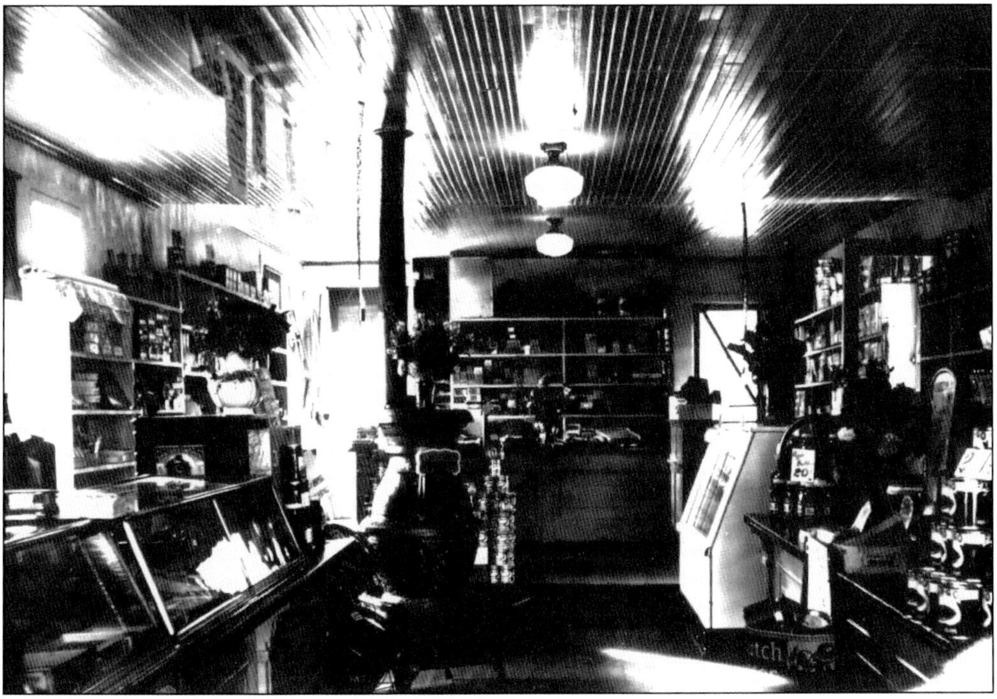

These interior views show the Petersville General Store in 1930, when it was owned by Floyd and Bertha Reimer. (Courtesy Lester A. Reimer.)

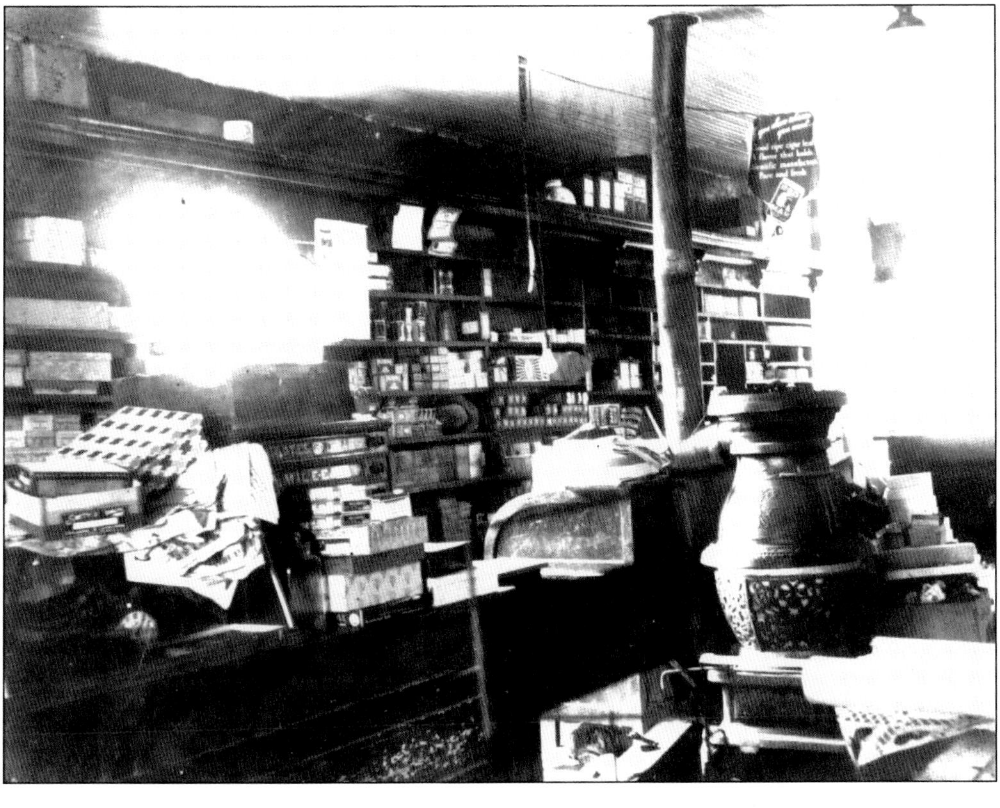

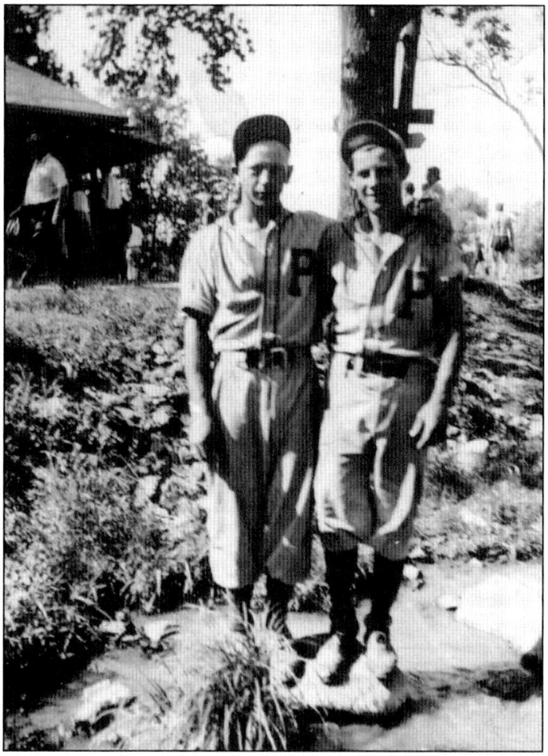

Petersville baseball team members Lester Reimer (left) and Charles "Shorty" Yost stand in the Petersville baseball field in this 1934 photograph. The field was located where the Whispering Hollow Mobile Home Park is today. (Courtesy Lester A. Reimer.)

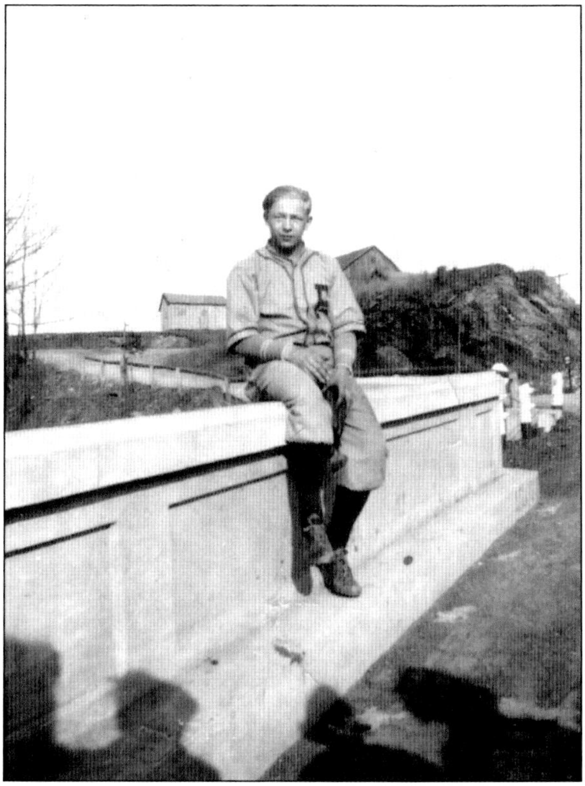

Lester Reimer, wearing his Petersville baseball uniform, sits on the bridge in Petersville. (Courtesy Lester A. Reimer.)

Five

THE TREICHLERS AREA

The village of Treichlers was originally known as Kuntzford. David Kuntz established a mill there in 1794 and, because it was said that the Lehigh River could be forded there by man or beast, the area became known as Kuntzford. Sometime before 1829, the Lehigh Coal and Navigation Company built the Slate Dam lower on the Lehigh to create a deeper river so the boats could use slackwater navigation to move downstream. This caused the Lehigh to be too deep to ford, so a flat-bottom scow was used to cross the river from Kuntzford to the opposite side, called Cherryford.

The opening of the Lehigh Canal through Kuntzford brought much traffic and trade to the settlement. A siding area for docking the boats overnight was constructed near the outlet lock, and a hotel and store were built to cater to the canal trade. For a time, Samuel Kuntz ran the store, a brick building that serves as a residence today. The village came to be known as Treichlers in the 1840s, when Henry Treichler became owner of the Kuntz mill.

George W. Bogh of Catasauqua purchased the mill and greatly expanded it but died soon afterward. Jacob Mauser took over in 1885–1886. In 1892, Mauser established a mill in Laury's Station near the Slate Dam. Other mills followed in Allentown, Palmerton, Danielsville, Hazleton, and Northampton. With the death of Mauser in 1908, control passed to his son J. Mark Mauser and George Lerch. In 1924, George Lerch's son Harry J. Lerch took over. The last of the family to run the mill was J. Mauser Lerch, who ran it from 1927 to 1967.

By this time, Mauser Mill was one of the largest independent mills in the northeast. It generated all its own electric power by directing the flow through the millrace onto a horizontal waterwheel. A work force of 30 to 40 people processed 2,000 bushels per day. Animal feed was shipped on the adjacent rail line. Flour was packed in 5- to 140-pound cloth and paper bags. Until 1927, two coopers were employed to make barrels that held 196 pounds of flour. Soft wheat brands produced at the mill included Fairy Kist, Full Bloom, and Rising Star. Hard wheat was made into Mauser's Best, Gibralter, Oven Buster, and Bread Maker.

In 1942, floodwaters covered the entire first floor of the mill. A June 1953 fire swept through part of the plant and, although most of the grain was saved, a section of the mill was destroyed and production was halted for several months. In 1967, Nebraska Consolidated Mills purchased the business. Today, it is part of the Conagra Corporation. A staff of only 11 employees working three shifts over seven days ship out some 40 truckloads of hard wheat and feed each week.

When the Lehigh and Susquehanna Railroad opened in 1867 with a combination freight-passenger station, Thomas Kuntz became the first stationmaster. A water tower was erected to feed the thirsty locomotives, and it was filled by a pipe leading to the "Dikey Dam." Much later, the A & P supermarket chain constructed a large building by the tracks to store potatoes for its grocery stores.

By the late 1800s, it became obvious that the slow and cumbersome ferry system had to give way to a bridge. On February 13, 1884, a meeting of Treichlers residents resulted in 44 citizens subscribing $12,000 in stock to fund a toll bridge to be constructed across the Lehigh by the

Franklin Bridge Company. The bridge was opened for traffic at the end of October 1884. In 1890, the bridge was purchased by Lehigh and Northampton Counties for $10,000, at which time the tolls were abolished.

Although it solved one problem, the bridge presented a new and growing concern. After exiting the bridge, traffic crossed another short bridge over the canal and then had to cross Central Railroad of New Jersey tracks. With alarming frequency, people, horses, wagons, and cars were victims of this unsafe condition. As cars became heavier, the safety of the old wooden-plank bridge was itself questioned.

The need for an overhead span to carry traffic above the tracks became clear. Two residents of Treichlers, William H. Anthony and Laura Steckel Kuntz, undertook what proved to be a three-year campaign to get such a bridge built. At one point, Kuntz personally invited Cornelia Pinchot and her husband, Gov. Gifford Pinchot, to Treichlers to see the hazardous situation for themselves. Exactly what was discussed when the Pinchots met with Kuntz and Anthony is unknown, but shortly thereafter, things started to happen. The second Treichlers bridge was opened to traffic on November 27, 1934, and lasted until it was replaced with the current bridge on November 24, 1997.

To the northwest of Treichlers is the area known as Lockport, which derives its name from the presence of locks on the Lehigh Canal near the mouth of the Bertsch Creek. Lockport was a boatbuilding and boat-repair center during the heyday of the Lehigh Canal in the late 1800s. In 1850, Beck's tavern and store was located here. Lockport was also a station on the railroad running through the town. The hotel in Lockport is said to have been built in the late 1700s and to have been used by travelers going to the Lehigh Gap.

Lockport was the center of a river-dredging operation for the recovery of anthracite fines. Wilson D. Putt began the dredging operation in this area in 1942. He owned two trucks, two pump boats, a steam-powered tugboat, and four scows. The trucks hauled different sizes of coal to the Zinc Company in Palmerton. This operation continued until 1959.

The Drifted Anthracite Coal Company dredged the river closer to Treichlers. This business had four partners: Jonathan Reber, David Wolfe, William Fry, and Grant Alleman. In the early 1920s, the company had two dredge boats. The company folded in 1947 when Jonathan Reber died.

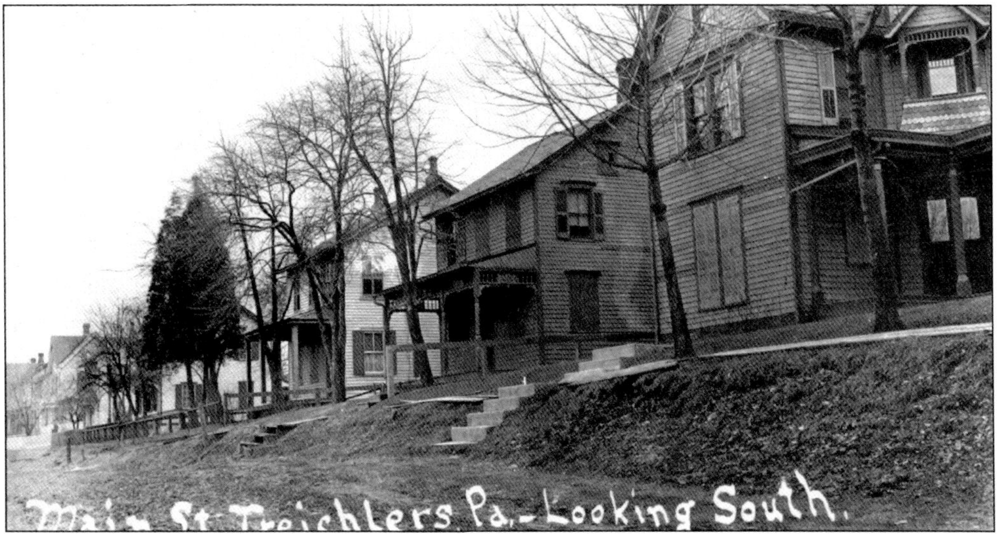

This view of Main Street in Treichlers looks south *c.* 1908. Notice that Treichlers had sidewalks at the time. (Courtesy Larry Hillborn.)

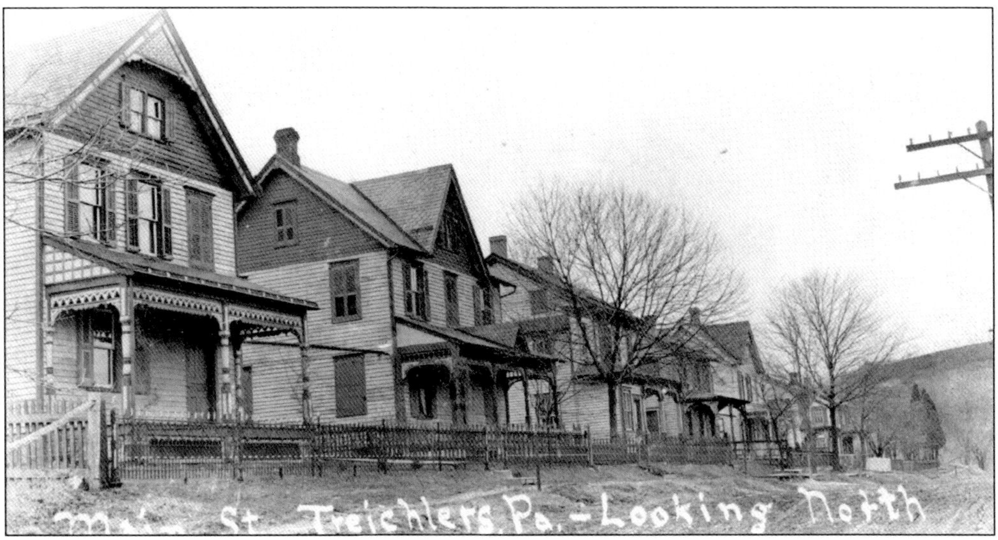

Main Street in Treichlers is shown in a view looking north *c.* 1908. (Courtesy Larry Hillborn.)

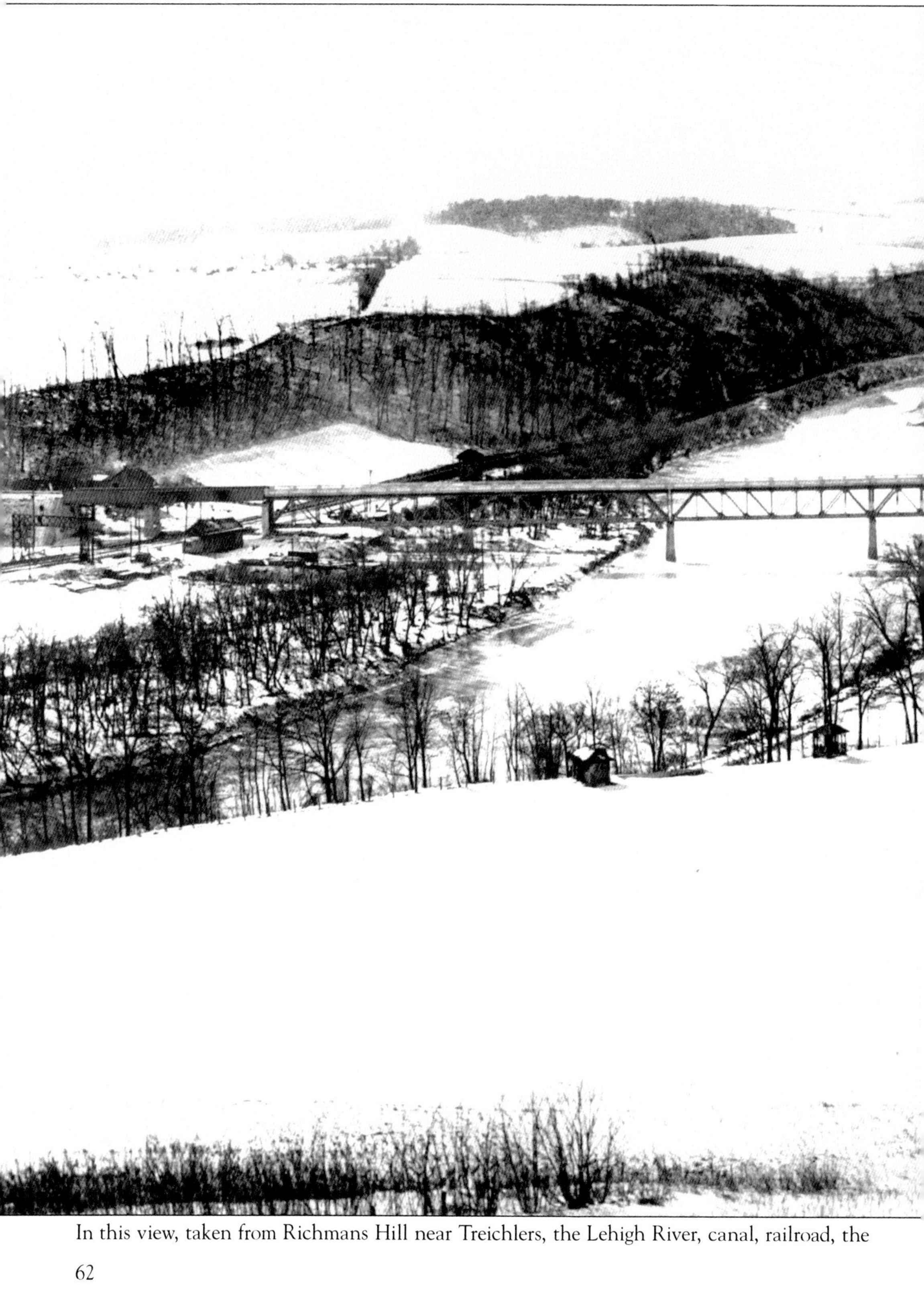

In this view, taken from Richmans Hill near Treichlers, the Lehigh River, canal, railroad, the

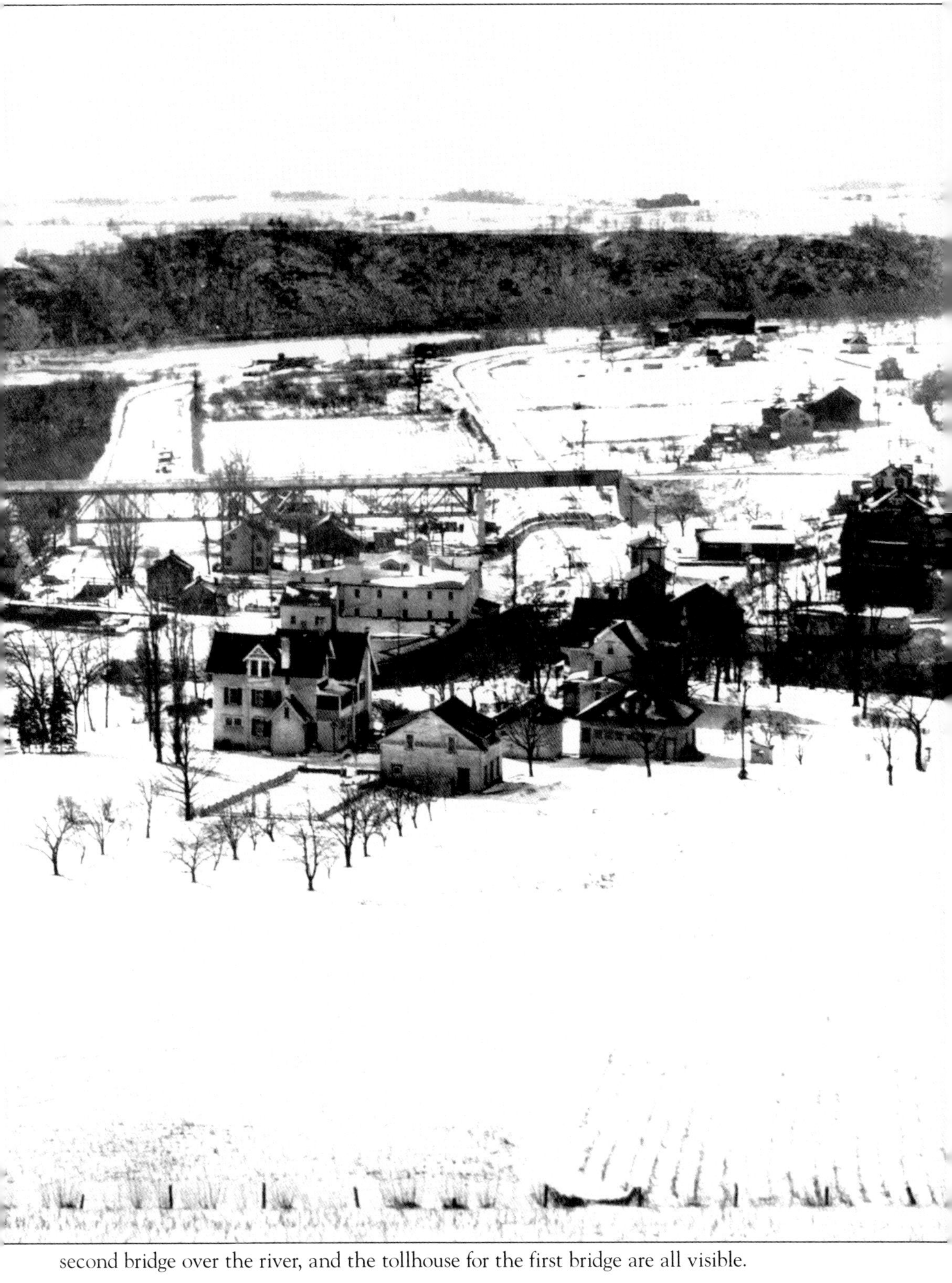

second bridge over the river, and the tollhouse for the first bridge are all visible.

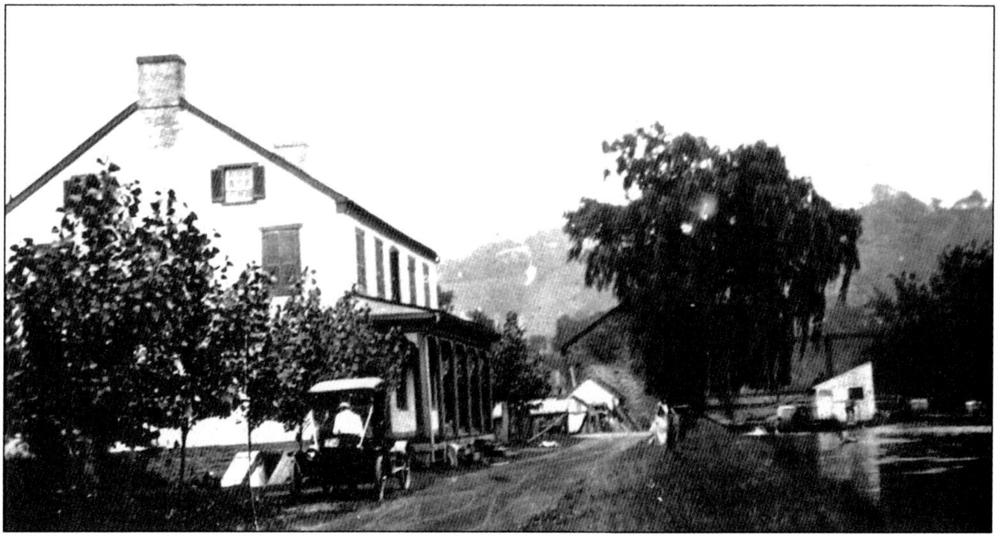

The hotel next to canal lock No. 28 in Treichlers is pictured here.

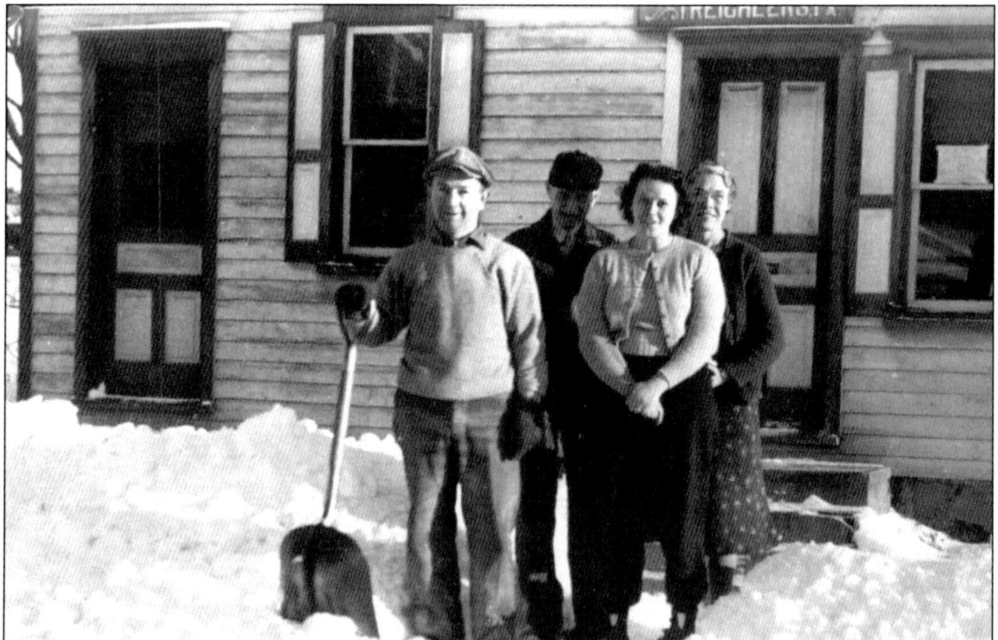

The old Treichlers post office, shown here on January 26, 1943, had to be removed for the building of Blue Mountain Drive. From left to right are L. Clarence "Shorty" Kuntz, Henry Bossard, Janet Lentz Snyder, and Hattie Lentz Shoemaker.

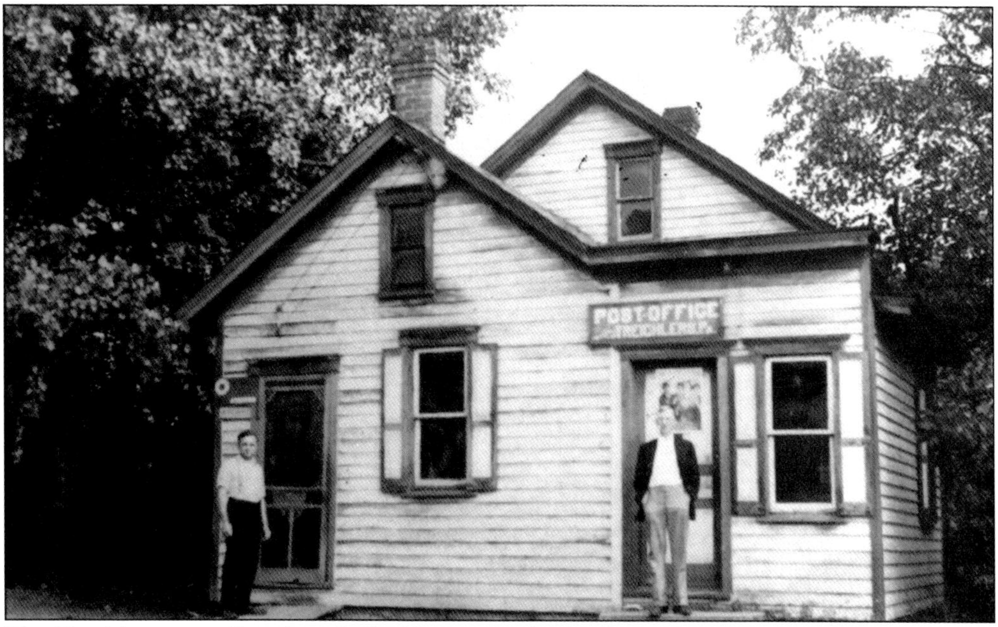

The Treichlers post office shared a building with a barbershop when this photograph was taken. Charles Stever (left) stands in front of his barbershop, and postmaster Benjamin Hall stands in front of the post office.

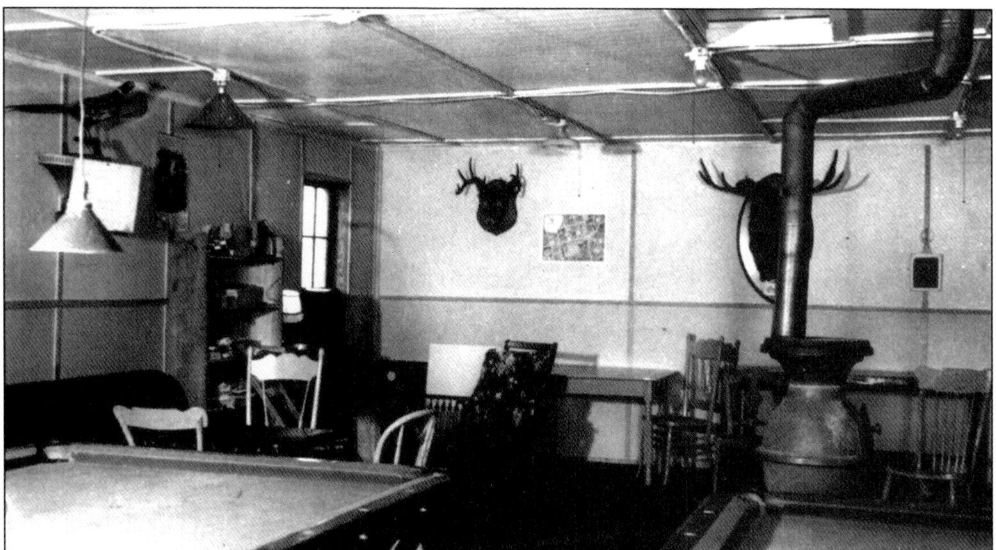

The Treichlers "clubhouse," located in the rear of the current post office, was a meeting place that was owned by a Mr. Peters but was open to the public. It was used for card games and parties.

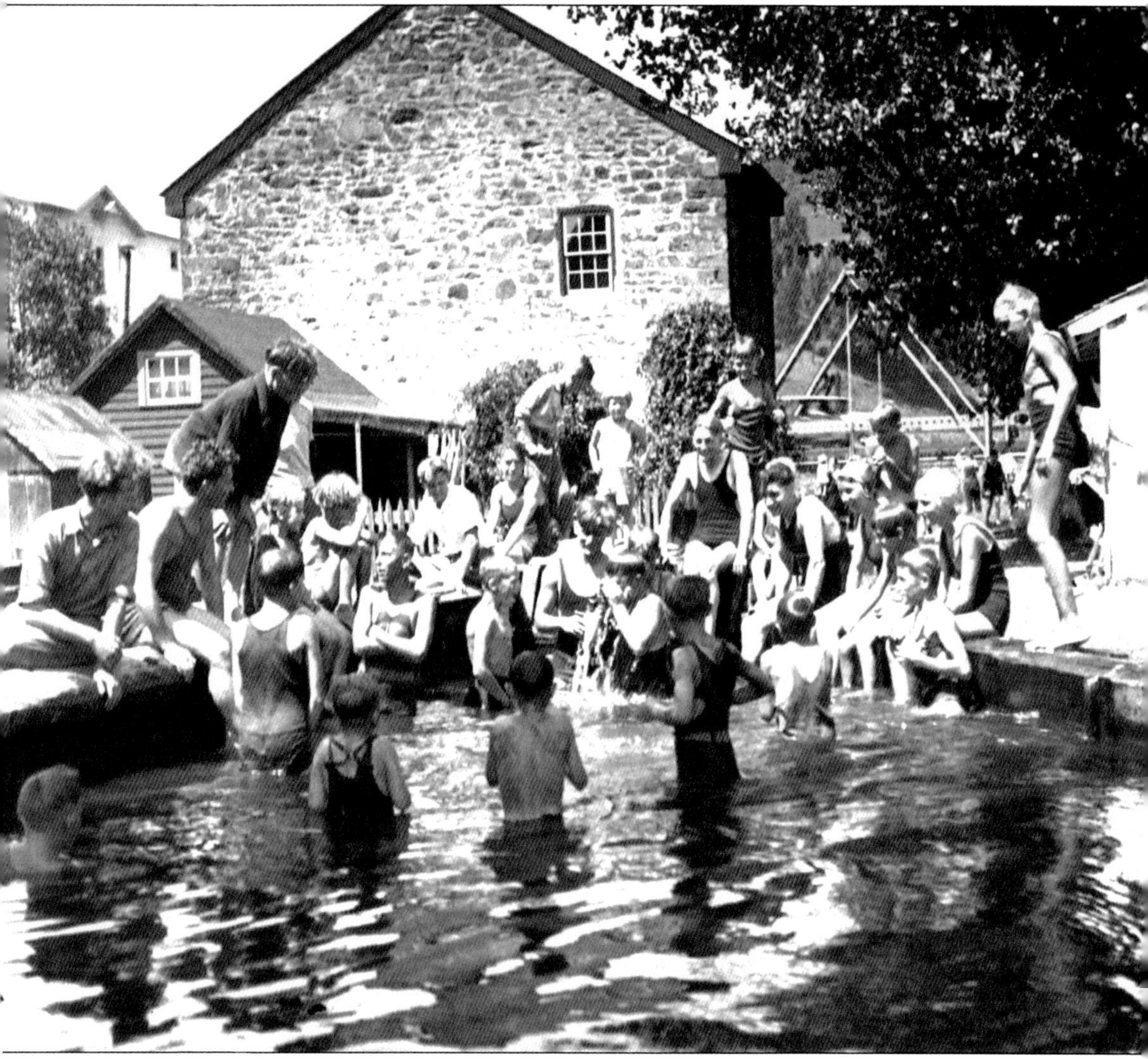

Many children in the area learned to swim in the canal. Shown here are children swimming near the locktender's house in Treichlers.

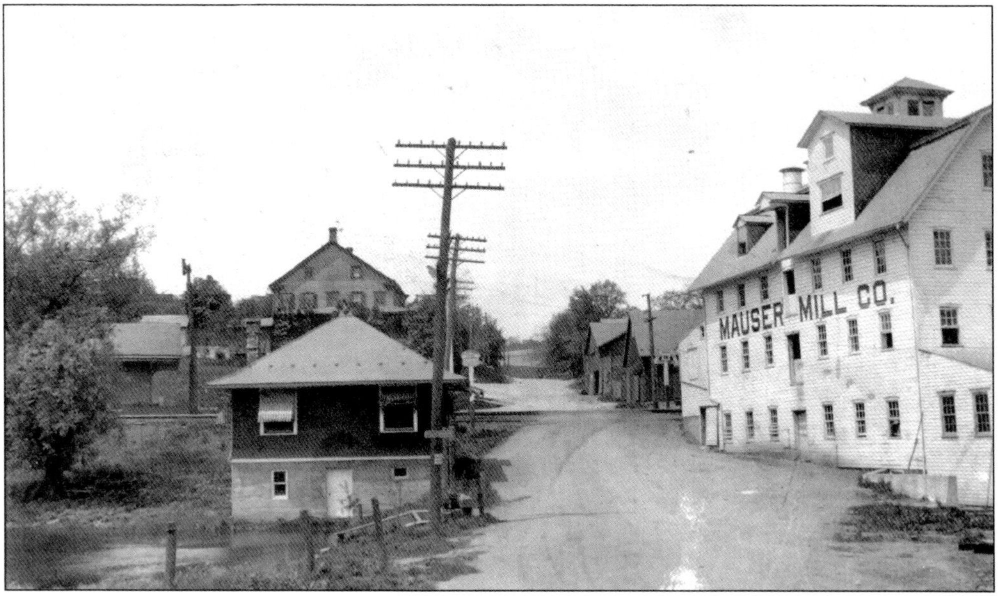

This *c.* 1913 view shows the old road to the first bridge past Mauser Mill. The Treichlers Hotel can be seen in the distance. (Courtesy Larry Hillborn.)

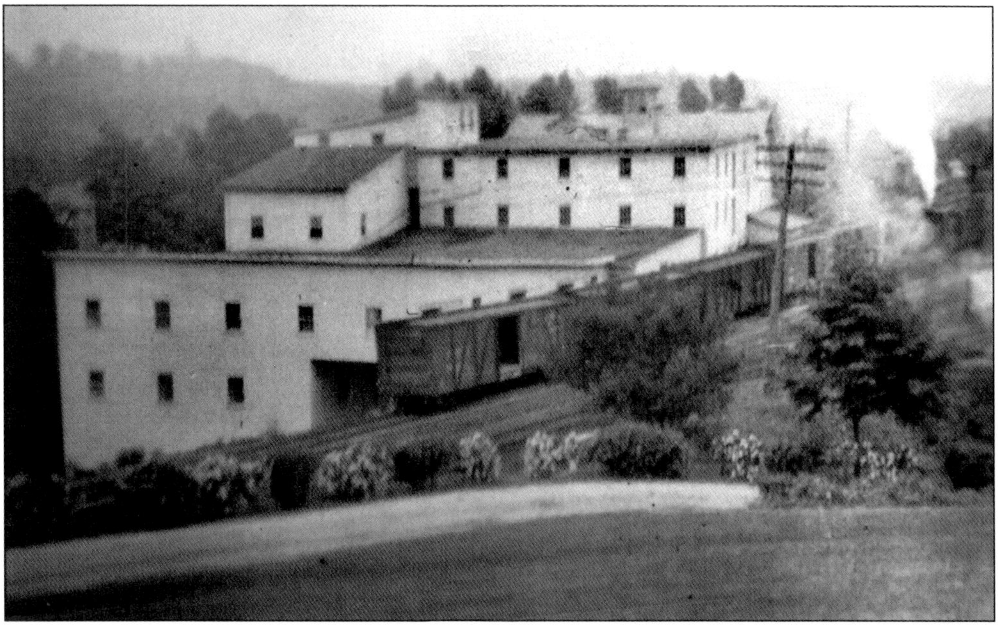

Rail cars at Mauser Mill are waiting to be loaded or unloaded in this photograph.

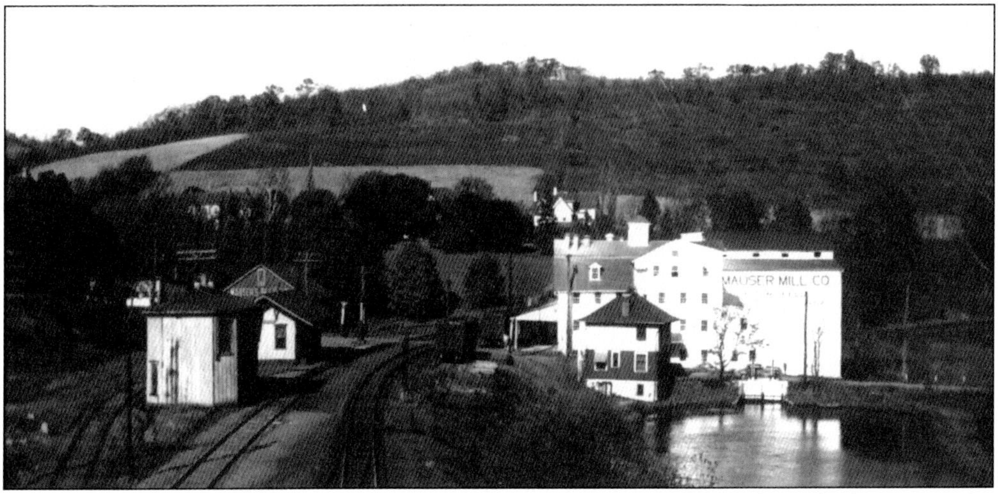

In this photograph, Treichlers is seen from the second bridge over the Lehigh River. The Central Railroad of New Jersey station at Treichlers is on the left, and the millpond at Mauser Mill is on the right.

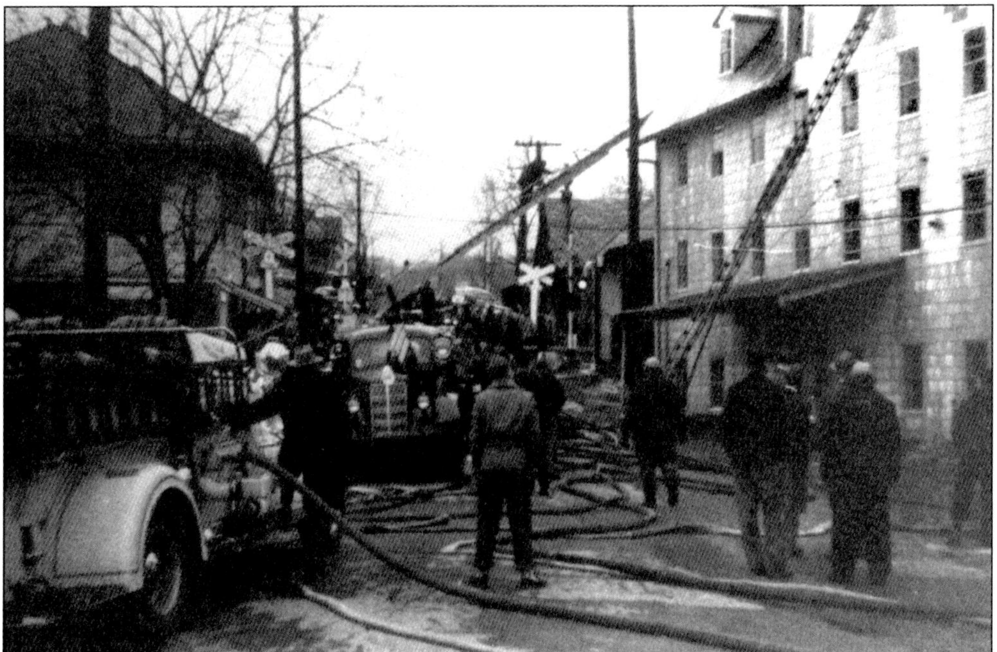

The Lehigh Township Fire Company fights a fire at Mauser Mill in January 1953. The fire caused $175,000 damage and destroyed the flour-manufacturing section of the mill. An additional $75,000 worth of flour was lost.

Oscar Lentz looks at the camera while working at Mauser Mill.

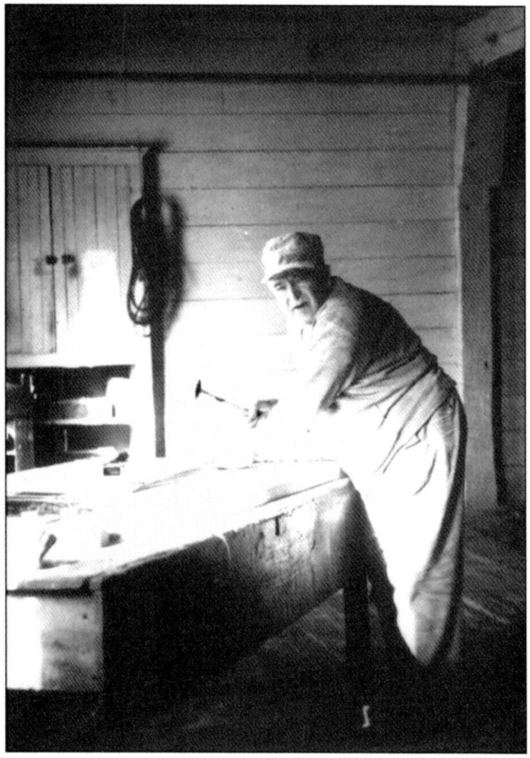

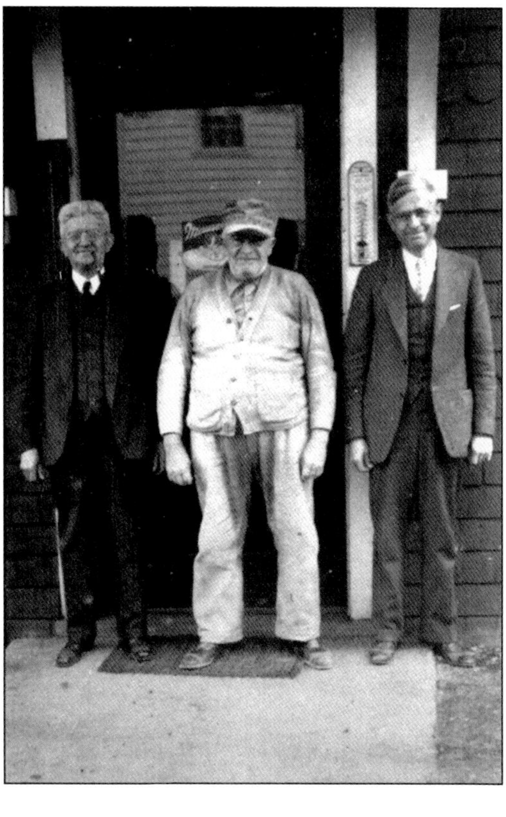

John Brader (left), Oscar Lentz (center), and Norman Hall stand in front of the Mauser Mill office.

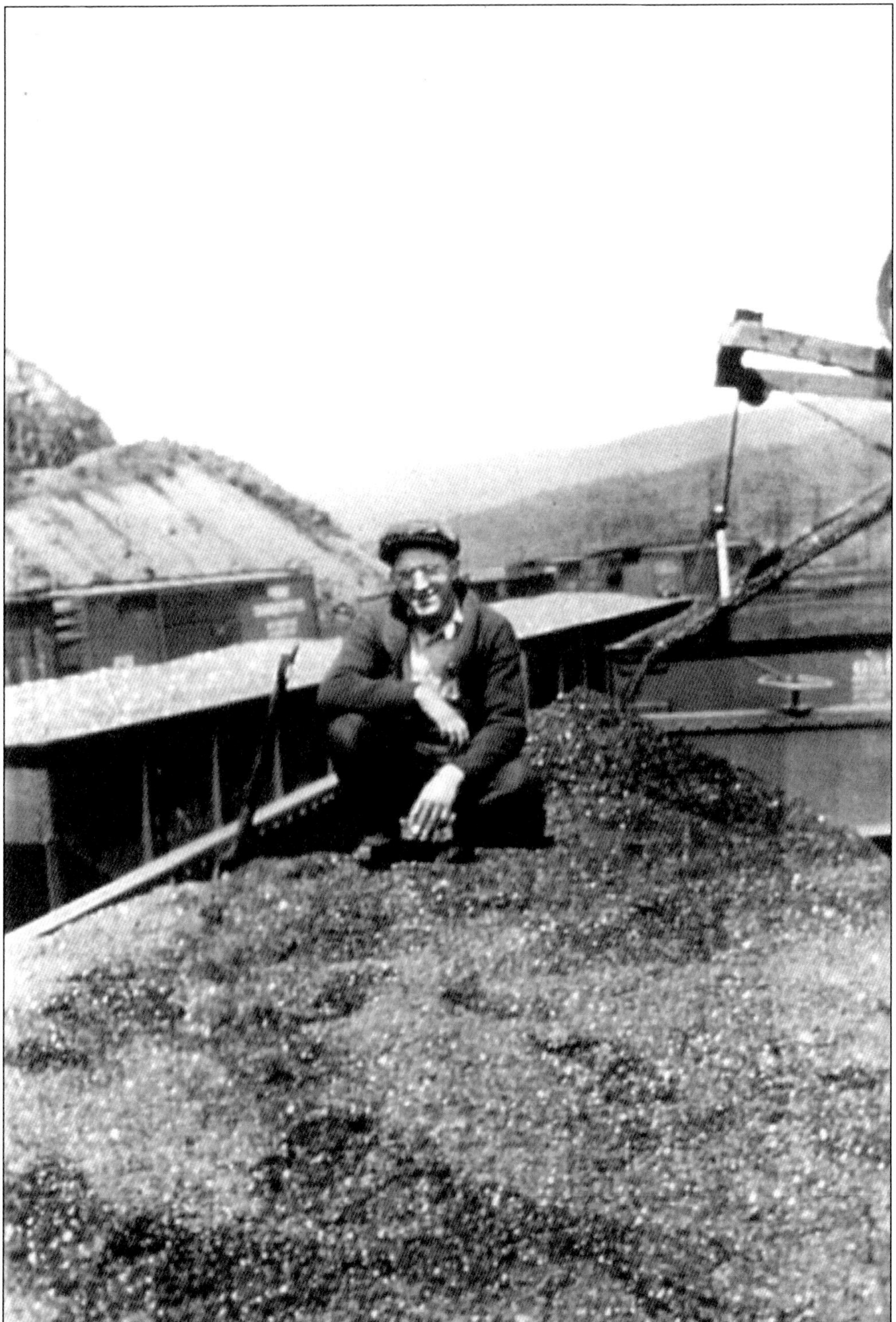

Coal dredged from the Lehigh River by Wilson D. Putt's dredging operation filled this coal car. This photograph was taken in 1930. (Courtesy Beverly and Wilson Putt.)

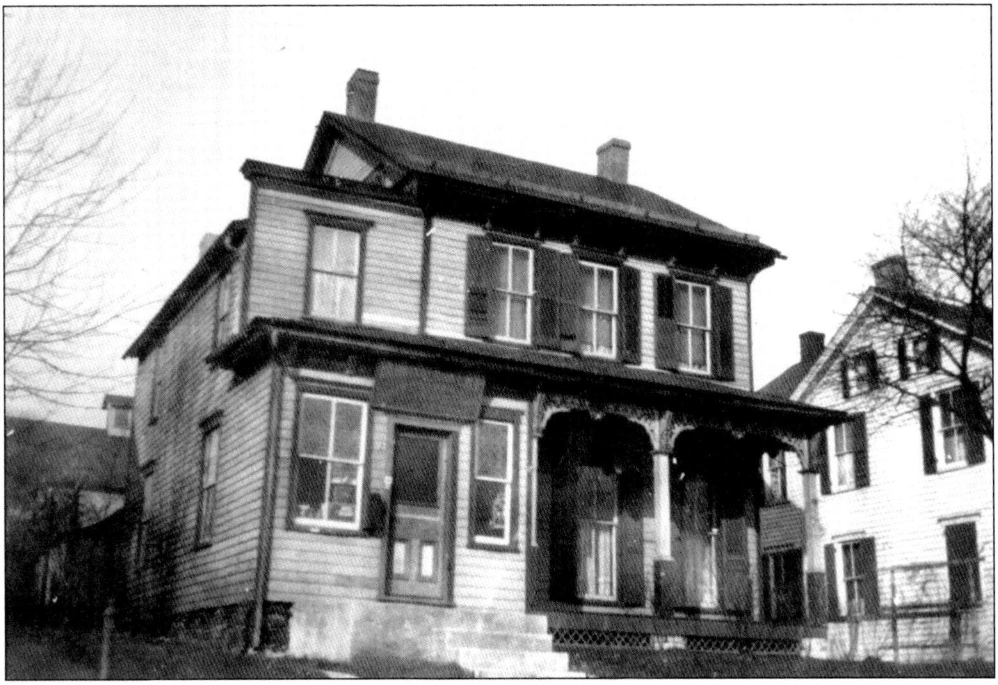

What looks in this photograph like an ordinary residence actually housed John Sheirer's store (later known as Newhart's, a store and bakery).

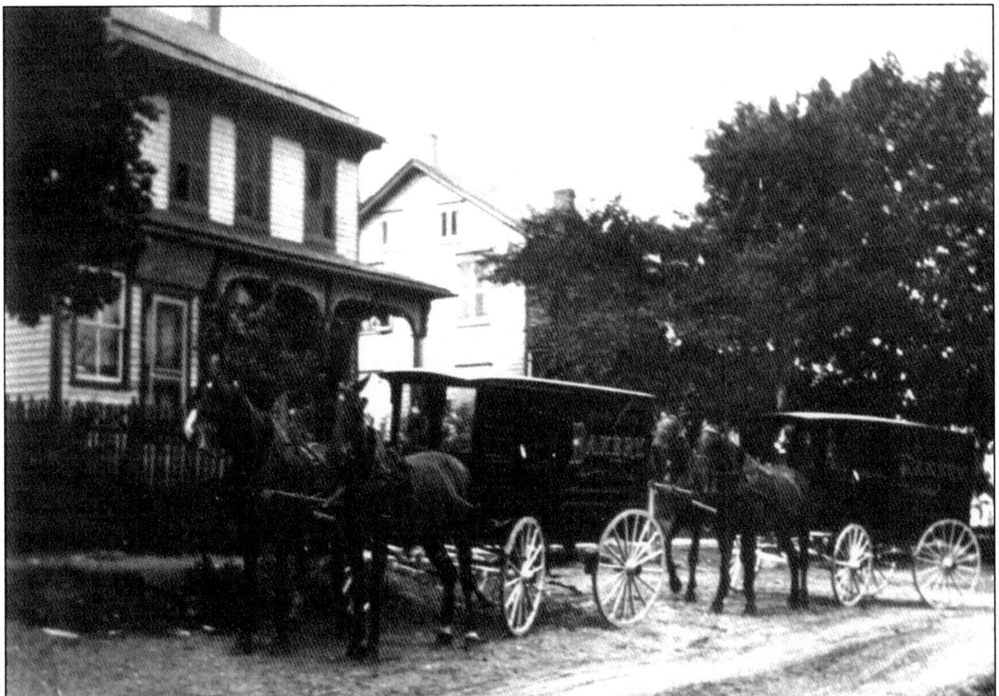

Sheirer's store with delivery wagons are shown here in front of the store. Sheirer started the Bon Ton Bakery, and the name was continued when the store was purchased by Elvin and Stella Newhart c. 1918–1920.

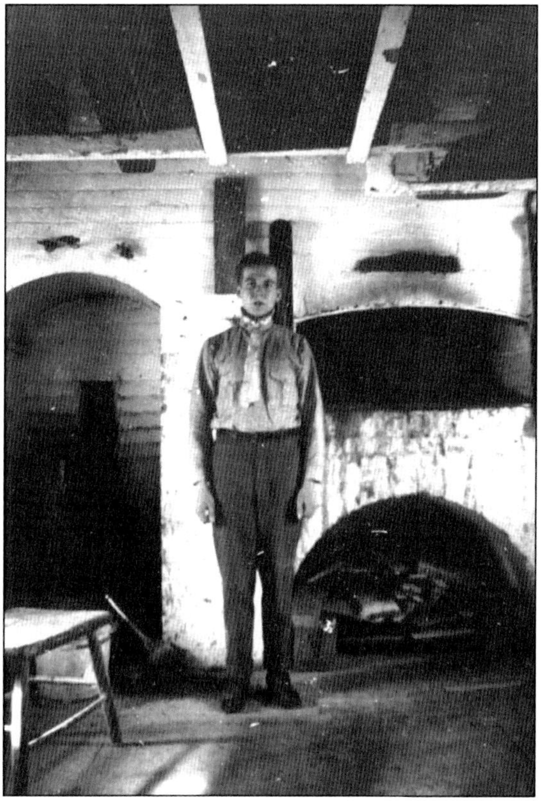

This 1917 photograph shows Stanley Shiffert standing in front of the oven in Scheirer's bakery before it became known as Newhart's bakery.

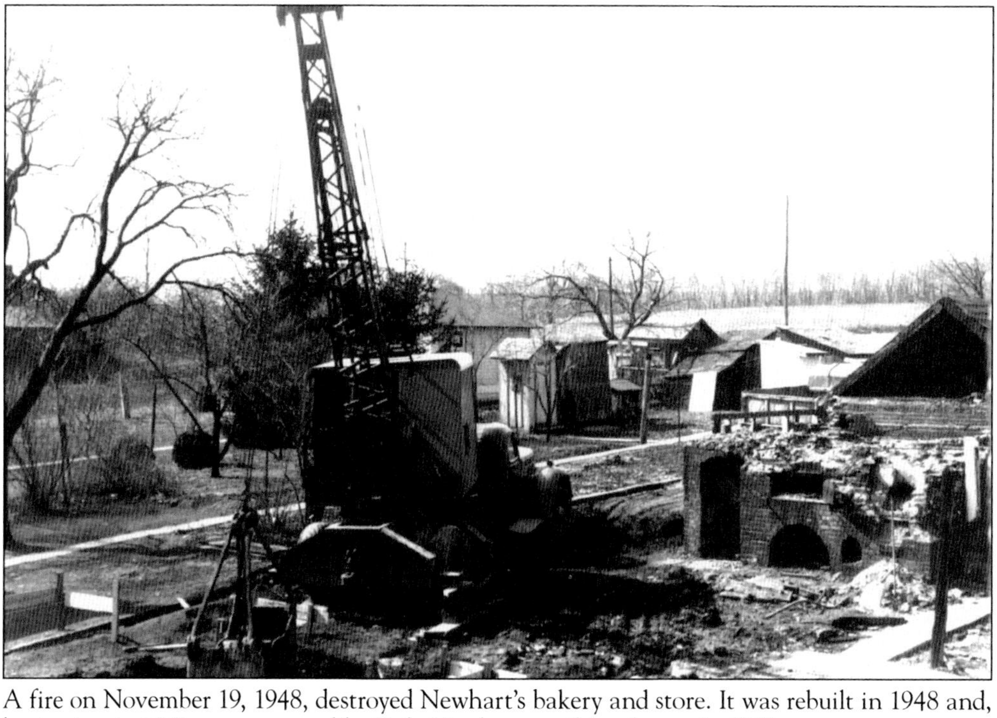

A fire on November 19, 1948, destroyed Newhart's bakery and store. It was rebuilt in 1948 and, beginning in 1961, was operated by Dale Newhart until its closure in 1973.

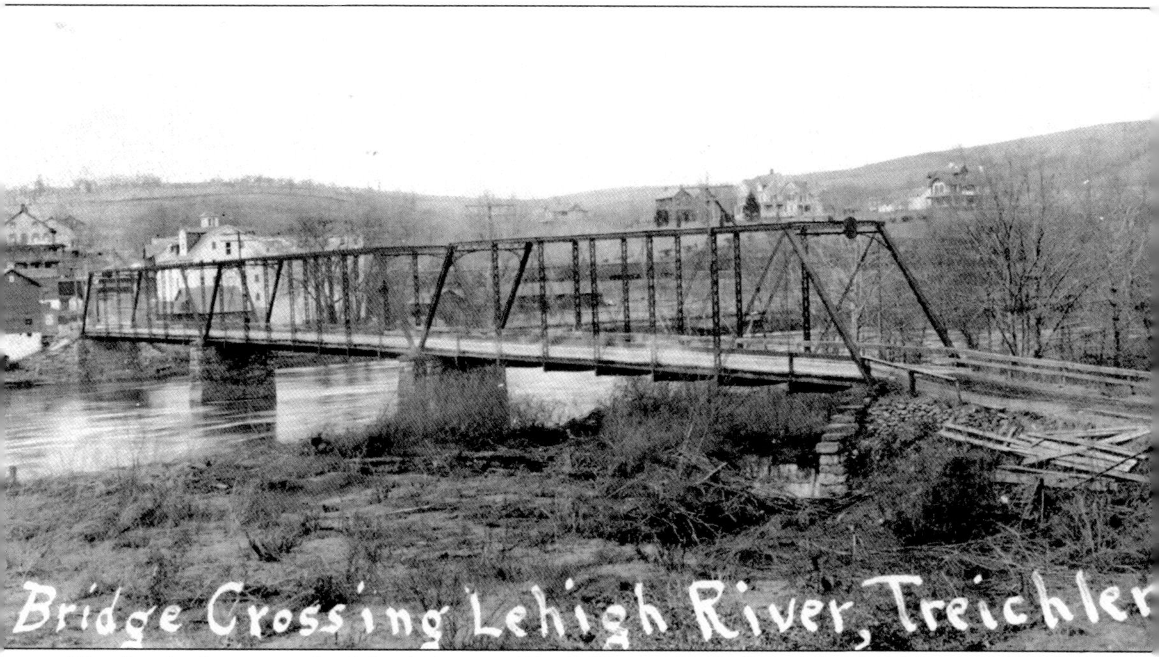

The first bridge across the Lehigh River in Treichlers was located past the Treichlers Hotel and Mauser Mill. Constructed by the Franklin Bridge Company, it opened for traffic at the end of October 1884. (Courtesy Larry Hillborn.)

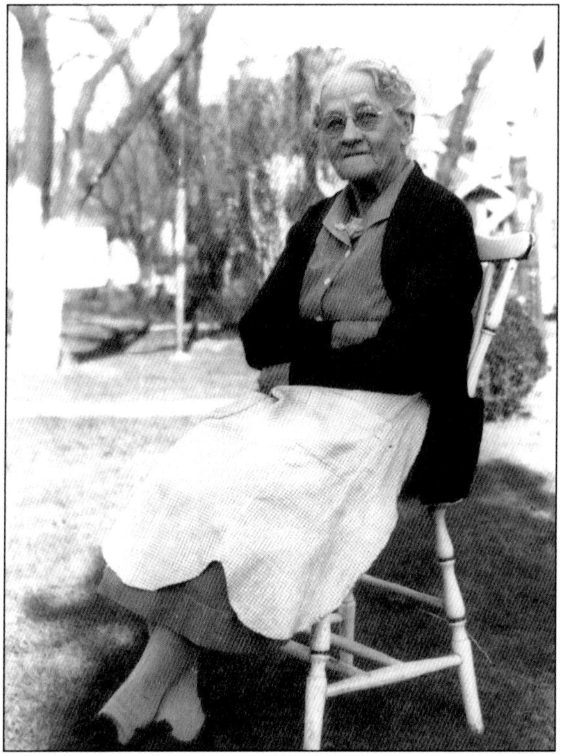

Laura Steckel Kuntz, shown here sometime in the 1930s, undertook what proved to be a three-year campaign to get the second Treichlers bridge built. (Courtesy Phaon Kuntz.)

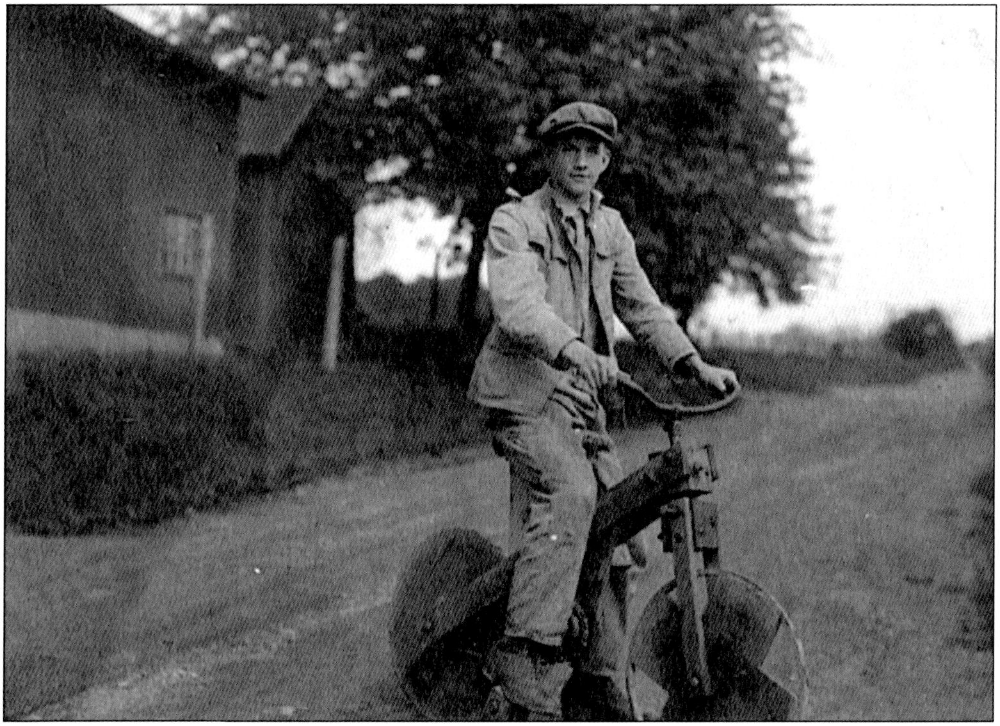

Phaeon Kuntz is shown in 1924 on his homemade bike. His family did not have enough money to buy him a bike, so he made one himself. (Courtesy Phaeon Kuntz.)

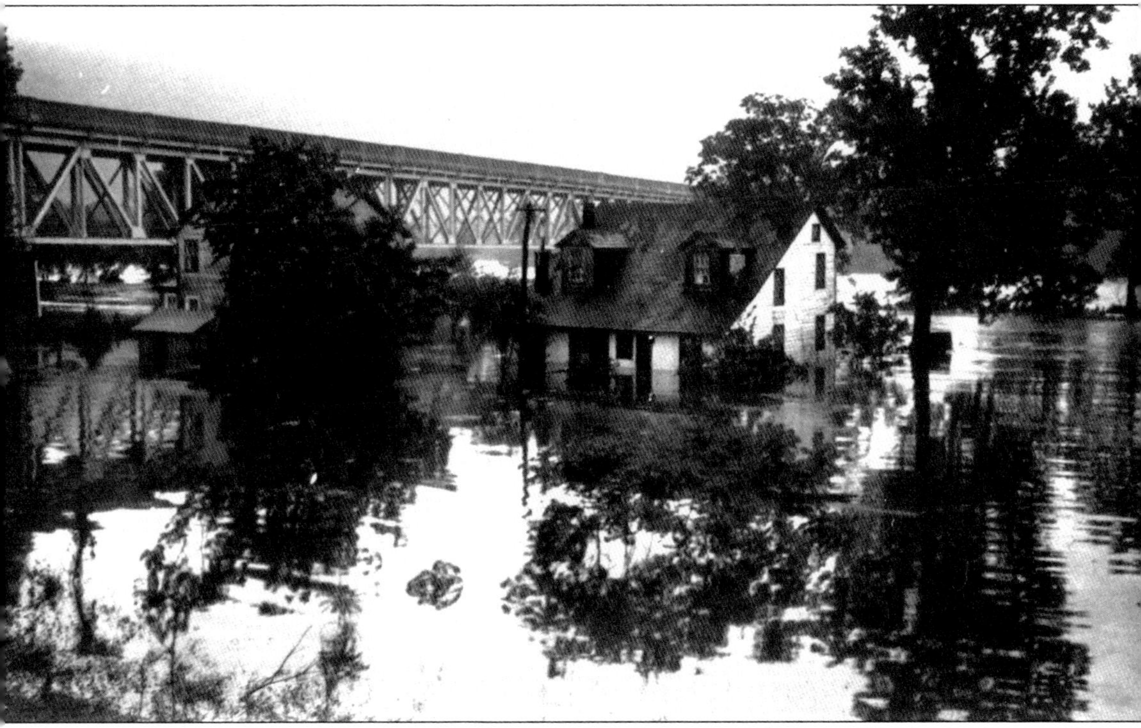

This photograph, taken during the flood of 1942, offers a view of the second bridge built over the Lehigh River at Treichlers.

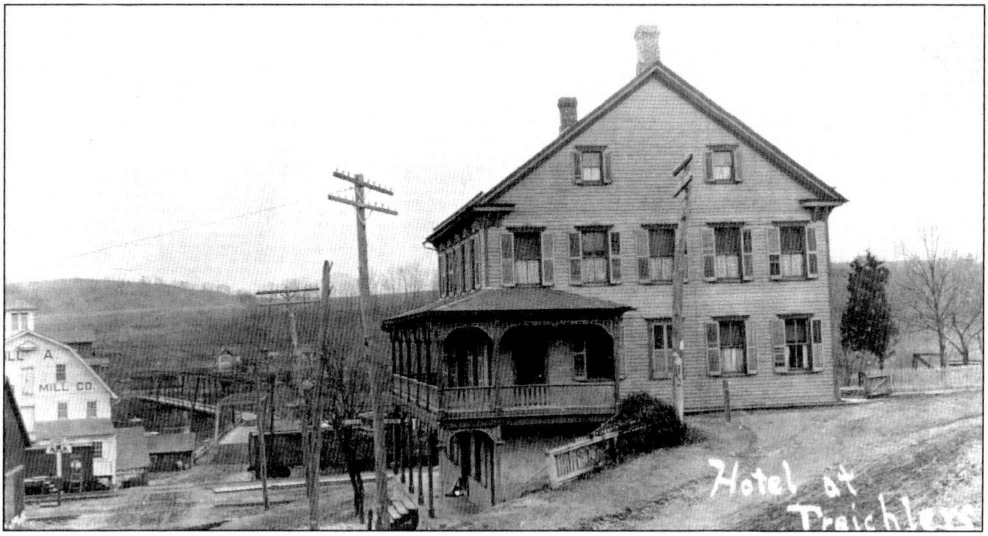

Mauser Mill and the first Treichlers bridge can be seen in the background of this *c.* 1910 photograph of the Treichlers Hotel. Notice the hotel's large porch, now gone, and the window on the right front where the door is now. (Courtesy Larry Hillborn.)

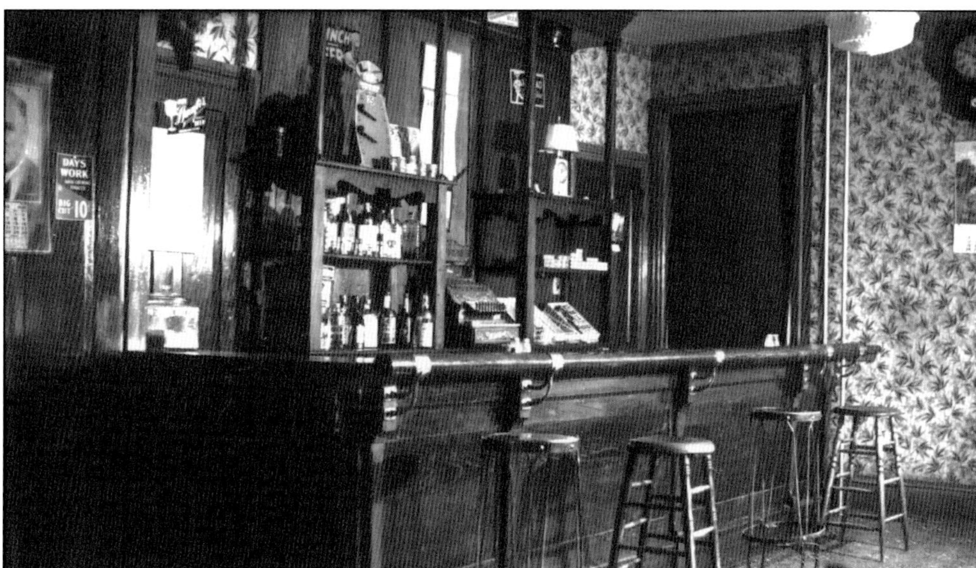

The interior of the Treichlers Hotel is pictured *c.* 1933.

This political advertising card was used by Clement S. Frederick, former owner of the Treichlers Hotel.

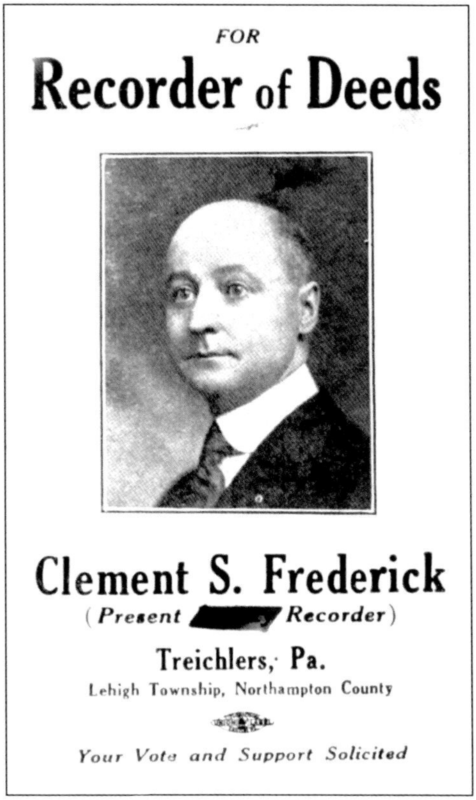

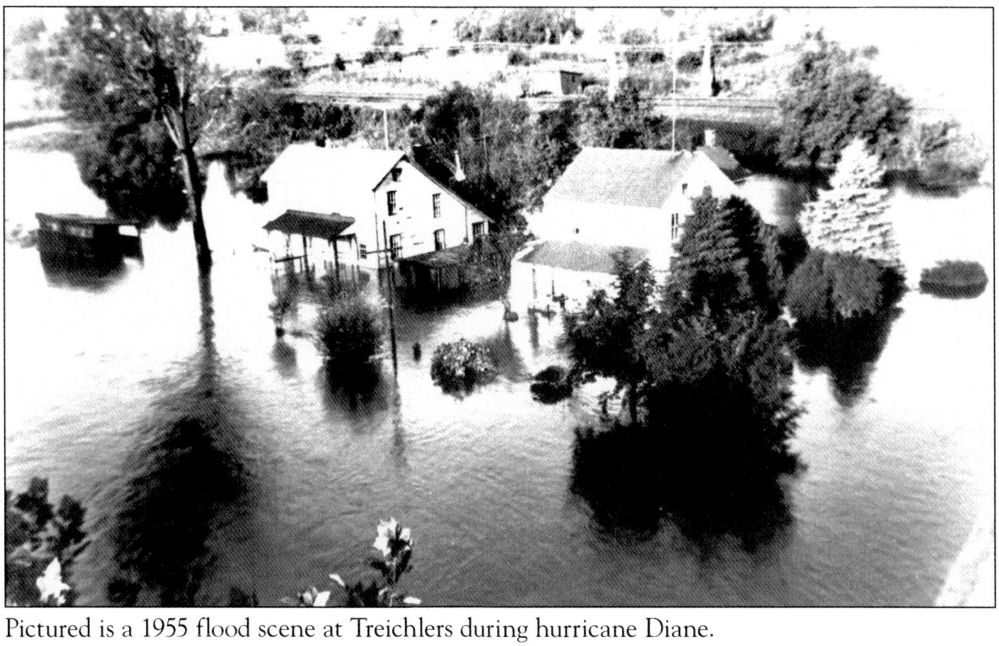

Pictured is a 1955 flood scene at Treichlers during hurricane Diane.

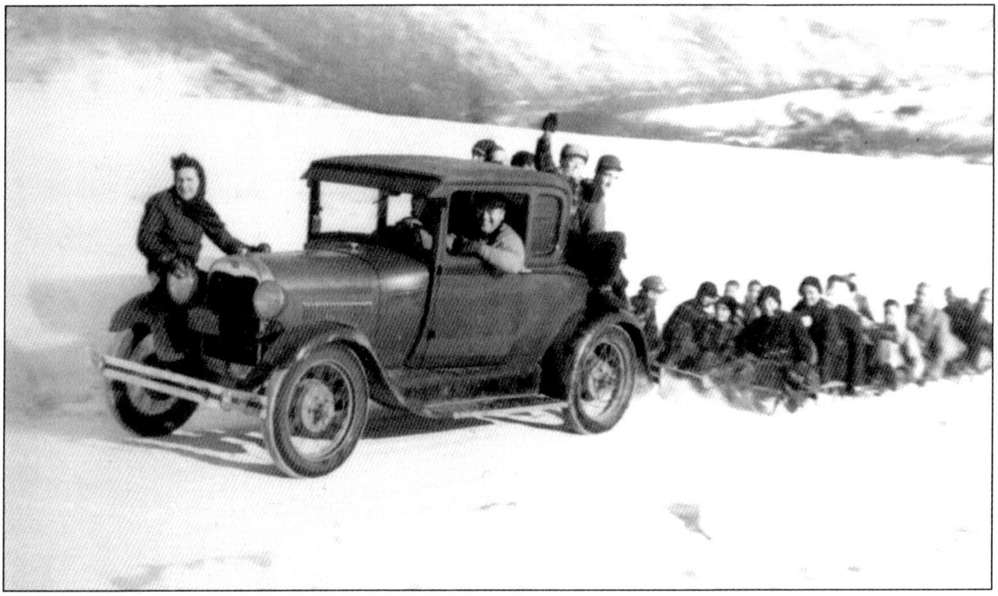

A motor car driven by Asher Snyder pulls sleighs up Long Lane in Treichlers. Catherine Hall is on the front fender of the car in this February 1948 picture.

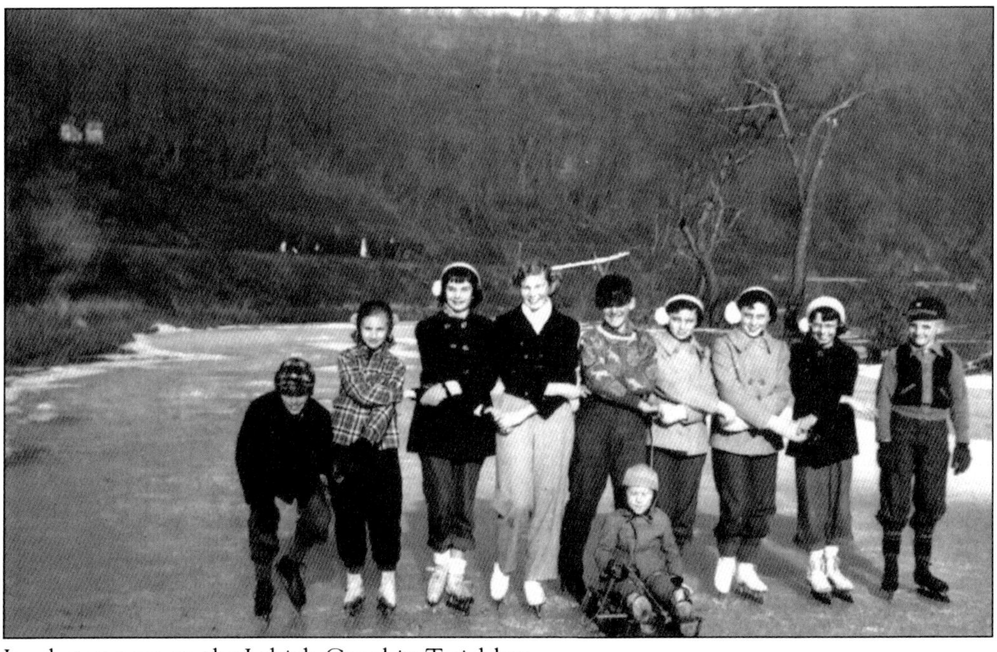

Ice-skaters pose on the Lehigh Canal in Treichlers.

Six

Amusement Parks

Indian Trail Park is located on 20 acres on the banks of Indian Creek in Pennsville. Allentown building contractor Samuel E. Solliday and his brother William J. Solliday purchased the property on May 15, 1929, from James O. and Mary J. Hower. William Solliday wanted his own park, and he convinced his brother that it was a good investment.

The brothers sold the land to the Indian Trail Park Company (which they formed for the project) and began promoting it as a picnic grounds. The location was perfect. It was easily accessible to all from the tri-county area—Lehigh, Northampton, and Carbon. In 1932, the Sollidays promoted the park in brochures as a "Cool Retreat from the Summer's Heat."

More than 20 summer bungalows, each with a 50- to 60-foot frontage and a depth to ensure proper privacy, were built along the hillside, overlooking the park. According to brochures from the early 1930s, lots in this "paradise" were priced from $275 to $400. The bungalows, which even then had access to electricity and telephone hook-ups, still stand today, remodeled into permanent homes.

Indian Trail Park offered a lifeguarded concrete swimming pool, graded from two to nine feet in depth and shaded by hemlock and beech trees. Guests had access to modern dressing rooms and steel lockers, and the perimeter of the pool was lined with benches and umbrellas for guests to relax and enjoy the beautifully landscaped gardens. Just steps away, the Trading Post served cool drinks.

A modern restaurant was located on the second floor of the 18th-century gristmill that continued to generate electricity for the park each day until 10 p.m., when the park tapped into commercial power.

About five acres along the creek were made into picnic grounds that offered shade, shelter, tables, benches, fountains, and more. Campsites were also available. The resort also provided the finest of free playground activities—sandboxes, slides, swings, and seesaws.

The Trading Post offered a large porch for sitting outside to enjoy the surroundings. Inside, there was an open fireplace, comfortable and spacious rooms, and a modern soda fountain with a restaurant that served good food at reasonable prices. One of the specialties was chicken and waffles. Water from the creek provided cool temperatures to store the watermelons, along with water and electricity for the park and swimming pool. Another concession stand, located near the merry-go-round, sold popcorn, soda, candy, hot dogs, and novelties.

Located in front of the Trading Post was a goldfish pond, which was later replaced with two gasoline pumps. Across Route 45, free parking was available in a meadow, but the park was so popular that many were forced to park along the road.

The penny arcade was set up in an old house on Cinchona Road. For both young and old, it offered hours of fun and revelry, with strength testers and a multitude of other penny-in-the-slot machines. Over the years, the arcade prices increased until they reached a quarter. Ed Conrad, a vendor, kept a live monkey in the building.

Other forms of entertainment included a dance pavilion, billed as one of the finest in the Lehigh Valley. Back in the 1930s, the park featured local dance bands such as the

Broadway Buck-A-Roos, who played on Wednesdays and weekends and for roller-skating during the week.

Amusement rides in the early days of the park were the merry-go-round, the Mohawk miniature train, and the roller coaster. A wooden octagonal building with open sides protected the three-abreast carousel from the elements. The carousel had hand-carved horses, goats, and deer. The outside row was stationary, and the two inner rows were jumpers (horses that went up and down). Six burros from Texas were brought to the park to provide rides for a nickel, the same price as the amusement rides.

Indian Trail Park was like other amusement parks, opening Memorial Day weekend and closing around Labor Day. Each evening, the park would close while playing "The Star-Spangled Banner" at the merry-go-round.

On November 30, 1949, the Indian Trail Park Company sold the park to Thomas Long and Leroy Kahle, and Kahle bought out Long on April 8, 1957. On November 9, 1972, Kahle and his wife, Alyce, sold the park to Leslie and Judith Tuttle. According to newspaper reports, antiques the Tuttles had stored in one of the buildings of the park were stolen, causing financial difficulties that led to the property being sold at a sheriff's sale on September 9, 1977, to the First National Bank of Allentown. Then, on April 21, 1978, the bank sold it to the Lehigh Township recreation system for $72,000.

Saullo Amusements was the last of the park operators. Leasing it from Lehigh Township in 1981, the company brought in rides such as the looper, the octopus, a little train, the cuddle-up, a Ferris wheel, a little merry-go-round, and children's bumper cars. By this time, the carousel was gone and the building had been converted into a picnic pavilion. Saullo changed the old swimming pool into a miniature golf course and renovated the Trading Post into an arcade with pinball machines and the office. In 1984, however, the firm ended the amusement park's days by terminating the lease.

Edgemont Park was located in Harpers on Route 946, west of Danielsville. The Blue Ridge Traction Company trolley lines ran through the area, so trolley company owner Franklin M. Hower started the park. Popular for picnics and reunions, the park contained a merry-go-round, a dance hall, and other amusements.

After Hower's death, his daughter Amanda and her husband, Silas Marsh, took over. The couple's financial troubles eventually brought park ownership to Pat Gallager, who added a swimming pool and roller-skating rink. Rollin Minnich owned the ice-cream stand in the park.

In 1945, George Wanisko purchased the park and added an arcade. He brought in silent movies and featured famous personalities, such as Sally Star of television fame.

The park faded out of existence over time, but the skating rink has managed to stay open.

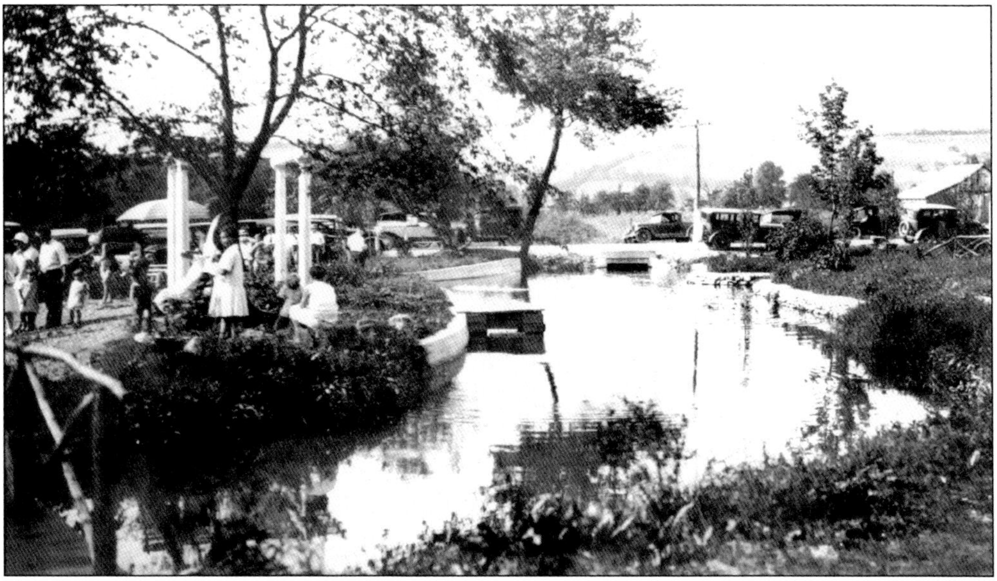

This view of Indian Trail Park along Indian Creek dates from c. 1931. (Courtesy Larry Hillborn.)

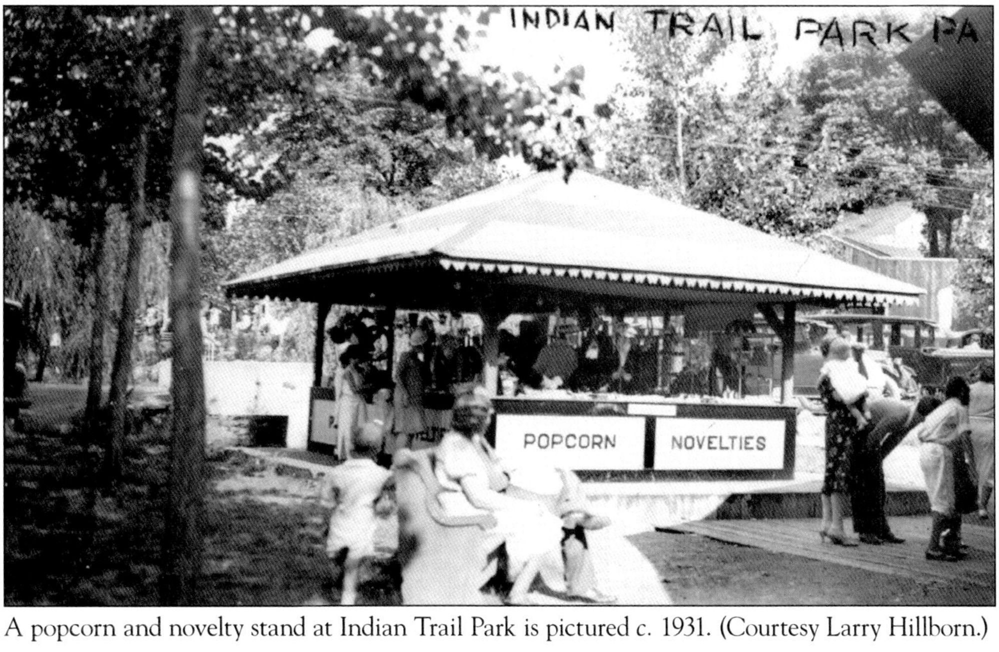

A popcorn and novelty stand at Indian Trail Park is pictured c. 1931. (Courtesy Larry Hillborn.)

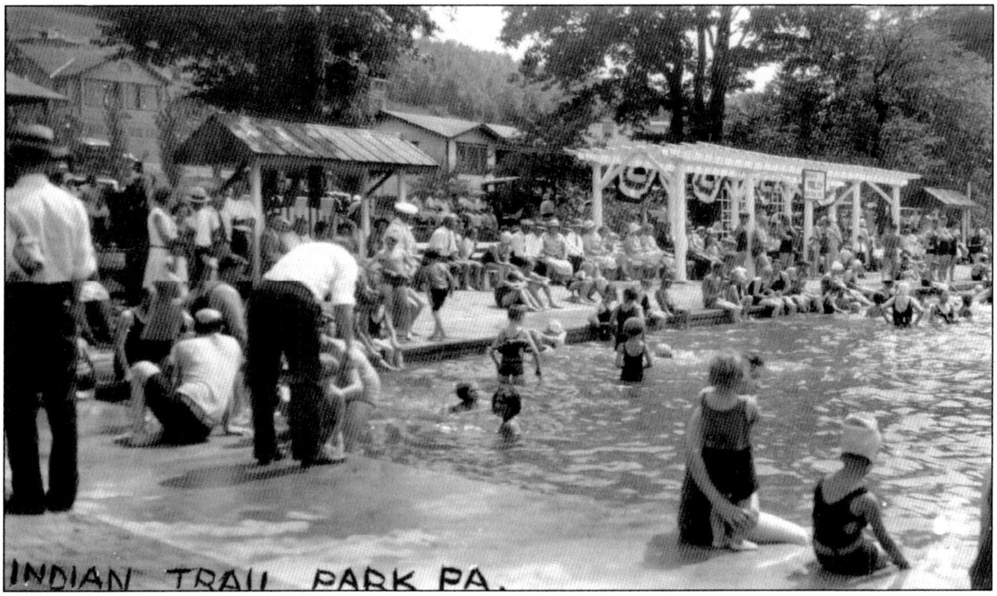

The pool at Indian Trail Park, shown here in 1931, was fed by water from the creek. (Courtesy Larry Hillborn.)

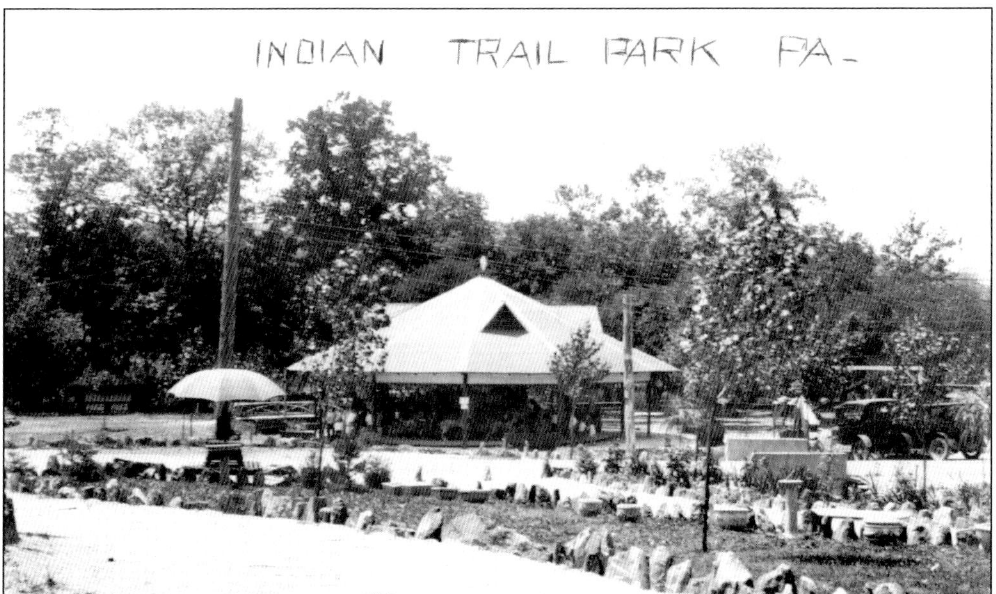

The merry-go-round at Indian Trail Park is shown c. 1931. (Courtesy Larry Hillborn.)

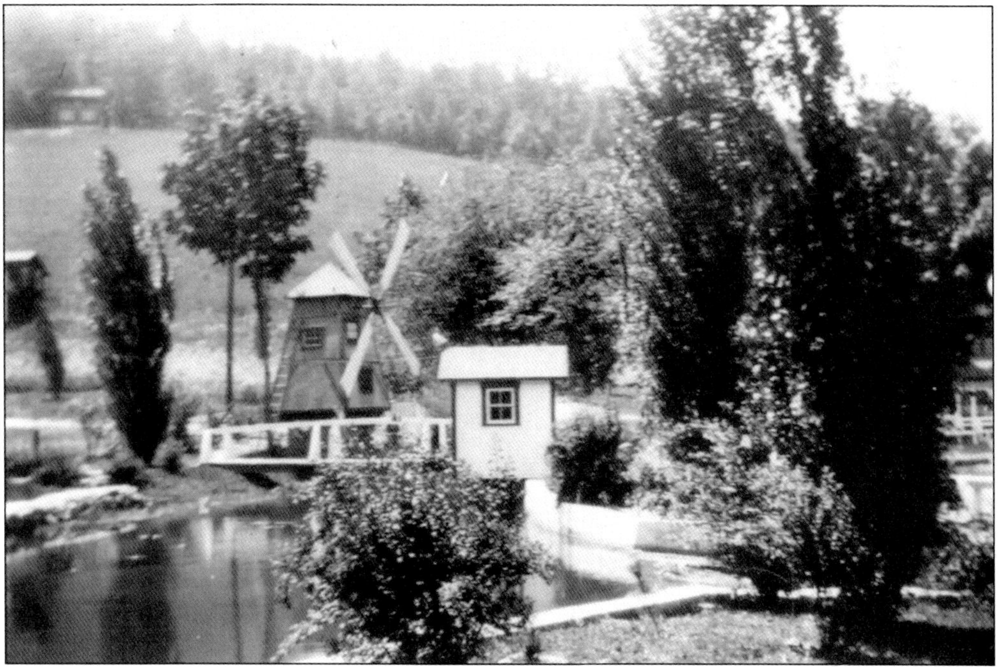

This 1932 photograph of Indian Trail Park shows how the park was landscaped to emphasize nature and to offer a relaxing place to cool off. (Collection of the Lehigh Township Historical Society.)

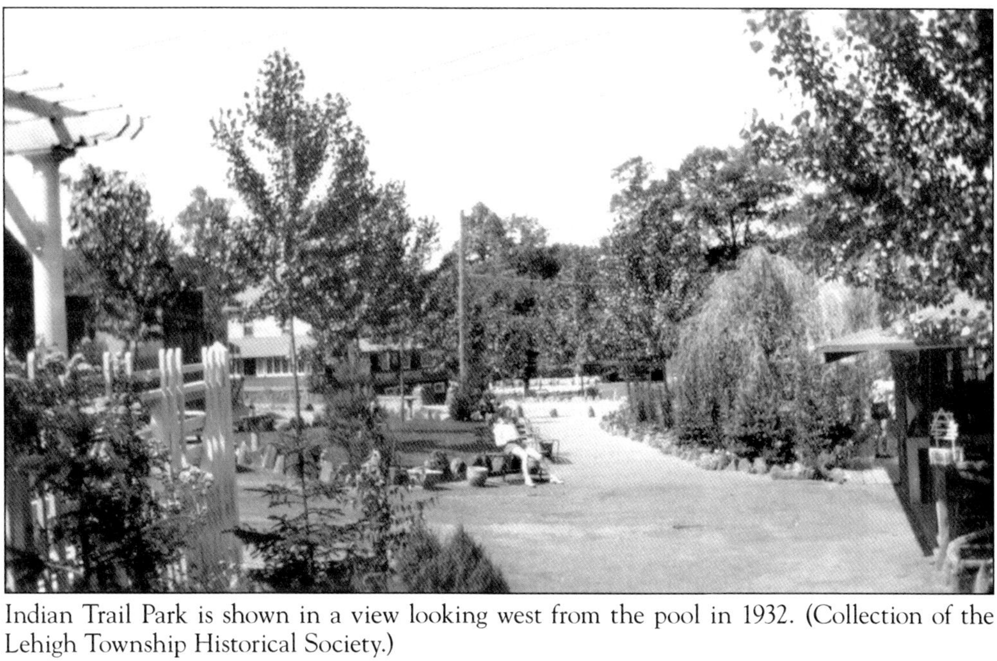

Indian Trail Park is shown in a view looking west from the pool in 1932. (Collection of the Lehigh Township Historical Society.)

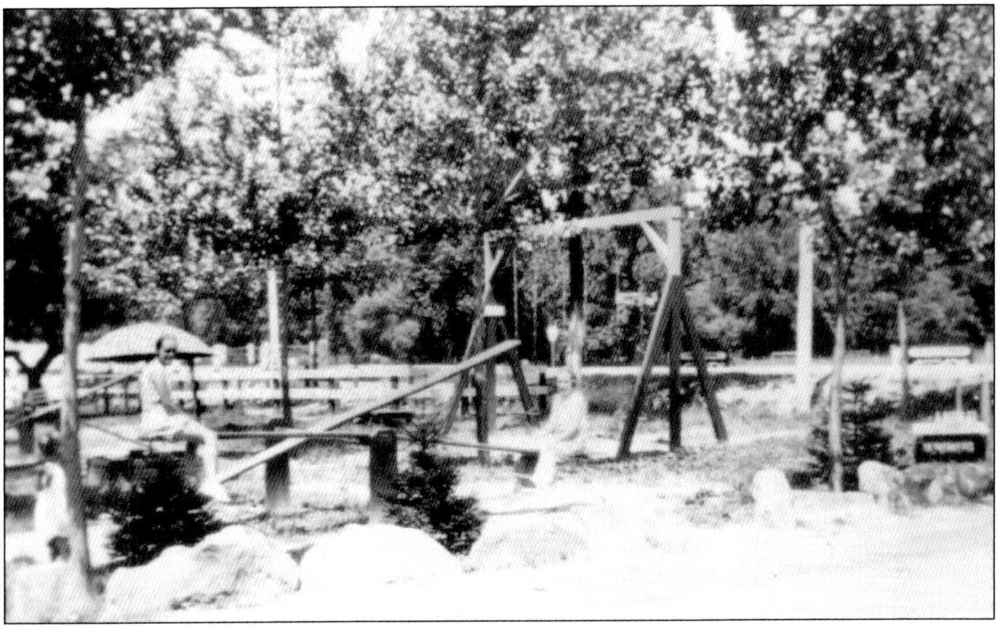

The Indian Trail Park playground is pictured c. 1940. (Collection of the Lehigh Township Historical Society.)

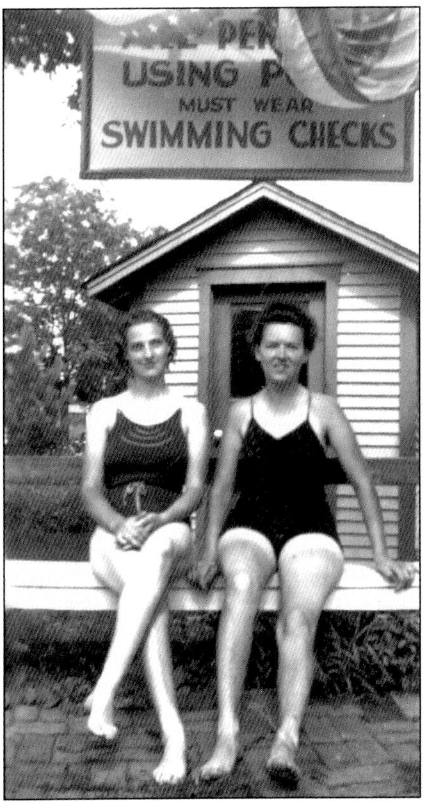

Emily Jones (left) and Sis Uhnak are shown at the Indian Trail Park swimming pool in 1941. (Courtesy Alverta and Emily Jones.)

Jean Rau stands on the diving board at the Indian Trail Park swimming pool in July 1940.

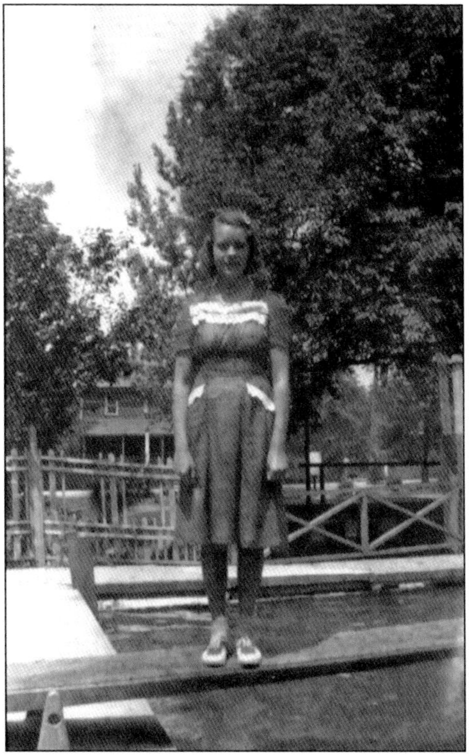

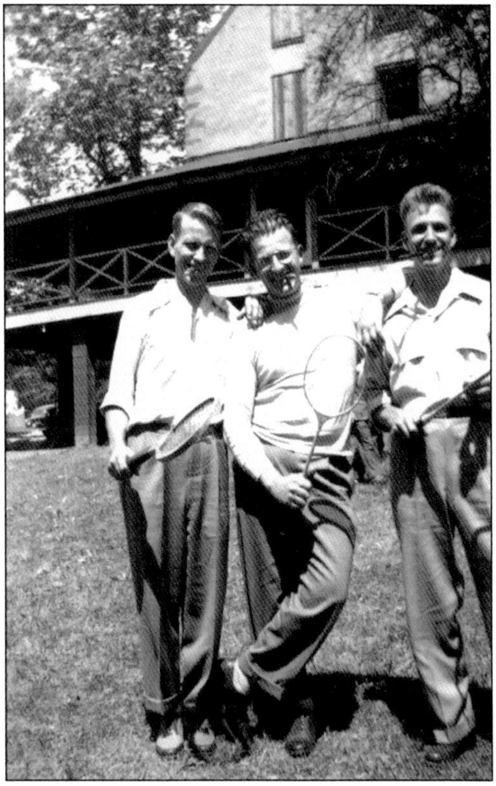

A group stands in front of the gristmill at Indian Trail Park *c.* 1940.

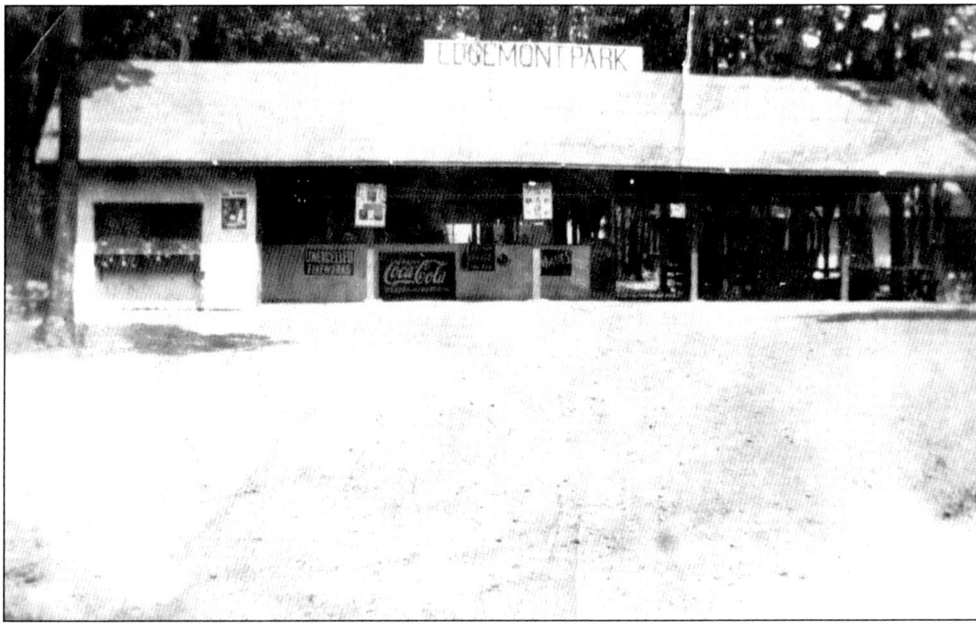

This 1940 image offers a view of Edgemont Park. (Courtesy Alverta and Emily Jones.)

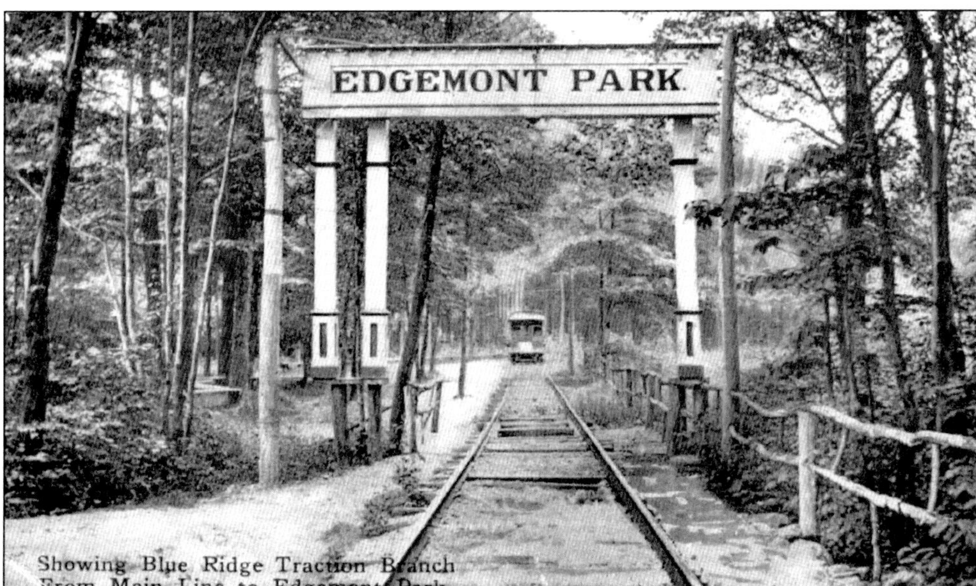

The Blue Ridge Traction Company trolley is pictured at Edgemont Park. (Courtesy Sean and Johanna Billings.)

Nature was an important part of Edgemont Park, as this 1907 photograph of the promenade shows. (Courtesy Larry Hillborn.)

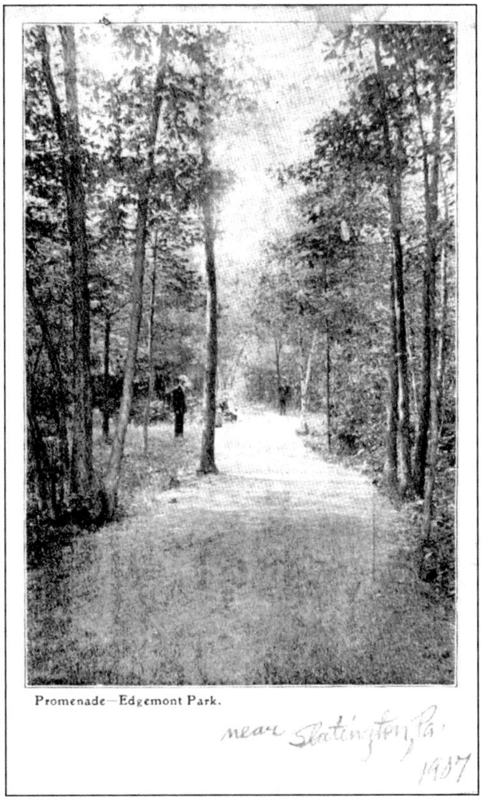

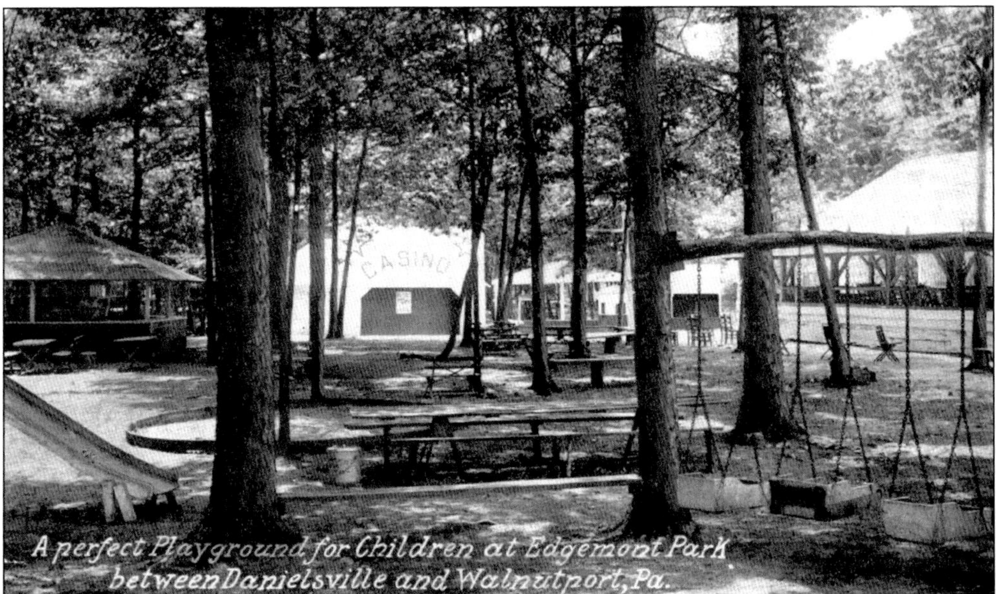

The casino can be seen in the background of this 1914 photograph of the Edgemont Park playground. (Courtesy Sean and Johanna Billings.)

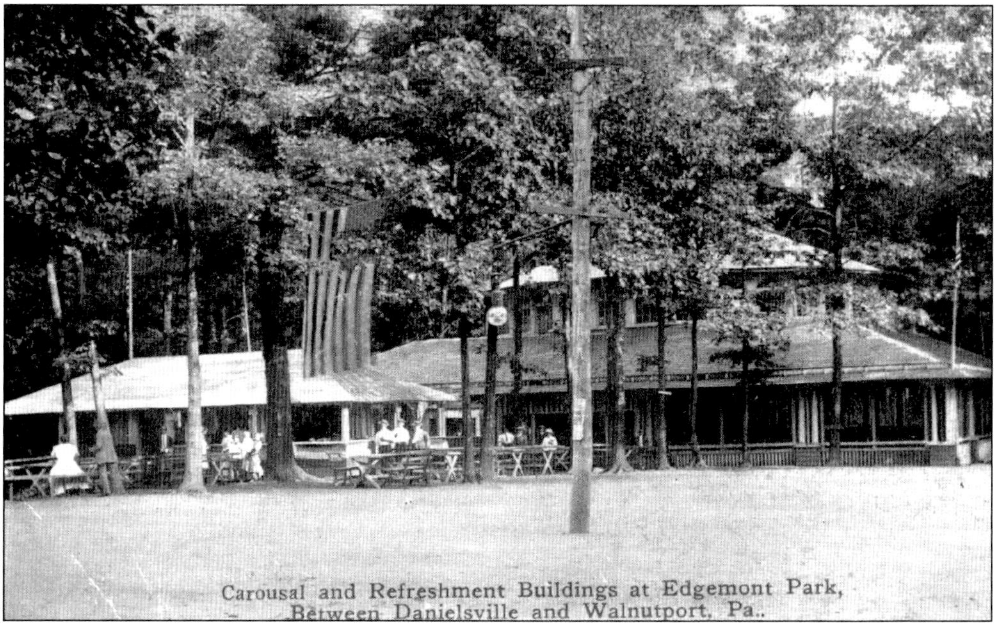

Edgemont Park featured both a carousel and refreshment buildings, as seen in this *c.* 1914 photograph. (Courtesy Larry Hillborn.)

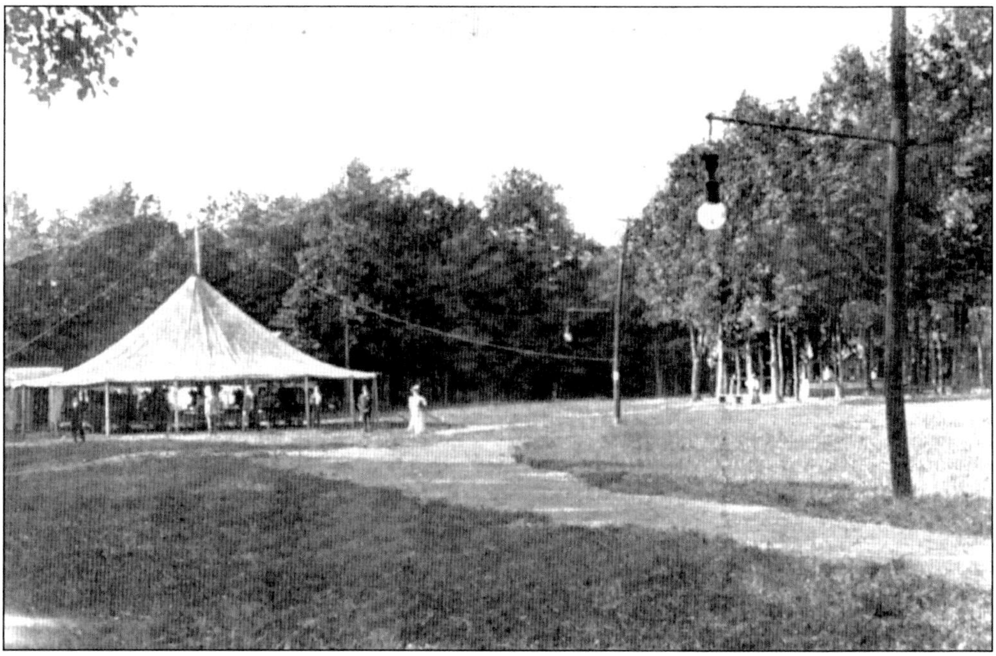

Open space and nature can be seen in this *c.* 1914 view of Edgemont Park. (Courtesy Larry Hillborn.)

Seven

Lehigh Township Schools

The first schools in the township were probably set up in connection with one of the churches and supported by payment made directly to the teacher. Compulsory education was not required by the state until 1895, and it was not consistently enforced until 1931. Before 1976, when the state mandated a minimum school year, schools stayed open only as long as they had money.

Most township schools served eight grades in one- or two-room brick buildings with slate roofs. Four grades shared each room in the two-room schools.

In 1837, the township had six schools with six male teachers earning an average of $8 per month. School was open for two months, with 175 students attending. By 1859, the number of schools and teachers doubled, as did the length of the school year. Teachers earned an average of $21.14 per month and taught 474 boys and 367 girls. Twelve of these students spoke English, 497 spoke German, and 332 were bilingual. By 1863, the number of students increased to 876.

By 1880, the number of schools jumped to 17. The 15 male teachers earned an average of $23.67 per month, and 2 female teachers earned $19.50. School was open for five months, with 466 boys and 379 girls attending.

At the turn of the century, the township had 20 schools, with 18 male teachers earning an average of $39.47 per month and 2 females earning $40. The 435 boys and 412 girls attended school that year for seven months.

Pennsville's one-room schoolhouse, constructed of stone, has no date stone. The stone house that shares its driveway is said to have a cornerstone from the 1840s. The school was probably used until 1908, when Pennsville's two-room school was built. The larger school was open until the Lehigh Township Elementary School was built in 1956.

Another Pennsville school, known as the "upper school," was located on the hill south of Pennsville toward Stone Church. The school was eventually purchased by the Harmony Grange for $300.

The Lehigh Gap schoolhouse was built in 1856 and closed in 1951. The school is currently a residence.

The Indianland schoolhouse was built in 1865 and closed in 1951. The cornerstone reads, "St. Paul's 1865," and St. Paul's Church in Indianland still owns the building. It is one of the few remaining schoolhouses not converted into a home or a business.

The Kuntzford schoolhouse was built in 1868 in what was later known as Treichlers. It was used until 1906, when the two-room school was built. Like many schoolhouses in the township, the two-room one closed in 1956.

No cornerstone has been found on the Lockport one-room schoolhouse, but it is believed to date from the 1870s. It closed in 1947.

A one-room schoolhouse was built in Harpers in 1871. In use as a school until 1948, it now serves as the American Legion post. Its date stone, located toward the peak, is still visible.

An 1874 map of Lehigh Township shows a schoolhouse in Howersville at the intersection of what is now Dogwood and Cedar Drives. No sign of the school remains.

The Berlinsville schoolhouse shows up on an 1874 map as being located about where the Lehigh Township High School was built in 1906. It is possible that the school was taken down when the road was built from Berlinsville to Walnutport or that it was torn down when the high school was built.

Cherryville had a two-room schoolhouse, built in 1877 and used until the Lehigh Township Elementary School was completed in 1956.

Danielsville's one-room schoolhouse was built in 1879 and was also in use until 1956. The cornerstone identifies it as "Danielsville School 1879."

Danielsville also had a two-room schoolhouse, built in 1894. Delbert Benninger and his wife bought the building for $1,600 when it closed in 1956.

The Farbers one-room schoolhouse was used until 1948. The cornerstone, which states, "Farbers 1884," was removed by a previous owner and is currently owned privately. The school was probably named after D. Farber, who owned land in the area, according to an 1874 map.

The Rockville one-room schoolhouse was built in 1886 and was used until 1948. A brick on the front of the school has "Built 1886" scratched into it, but no other cornerstone has been found.

The Petersville schoolhouse was built on land donated by Edwin Zader, whose farm sits behind it. The school closed in 1947 and now serves as a residence.

The Benningers one-room schoolhouse was built in 1902 and closed in 1947. Carl Benninger and his wife paid $1,500 for the school in 1957.

The Slate Valley one-room schoolhouse is located along Route 946, about a mile east of Danielsville. It is not known when it was built or when it closed.

In 1906, the Lehigh Township High School was built in Berlinsville. However, not all students living in the township attended the high school. Some still went to Northampton, Palmerton, and Slatington. Two students, Hilda Sabina Caskie and Stanley Nelson Coffin, were the first to graduate at commencement exercises, held on May 15, 1908, at the Union Chapel in Walnutport. In 1948, the last 15 students graduated, and then the school closed. The building was used for school functions until the 1975–1976 school year. Today, students attend classes at Northampton Area High School.

The Lehigh Township Elementary School was the last school to be built in the township. The groundbreaking for the building, located in the geographical center of the township, was on February 12, 1955. The school opened on February 13, 1956, followed by an open house on March 3 and 4, 1956. The school, now a part of the Northampton Area School District, is still in use today.

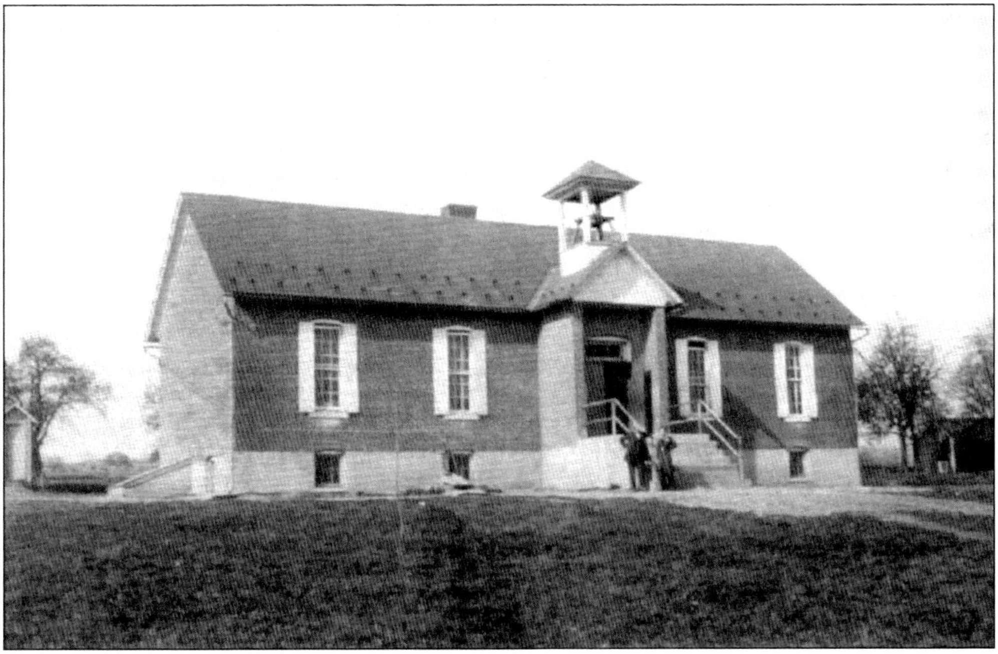

The Treichlers schoolhouse, located on Second Street in Treichlers, has been converted into a business. (Courtesy Josephine Miller.)

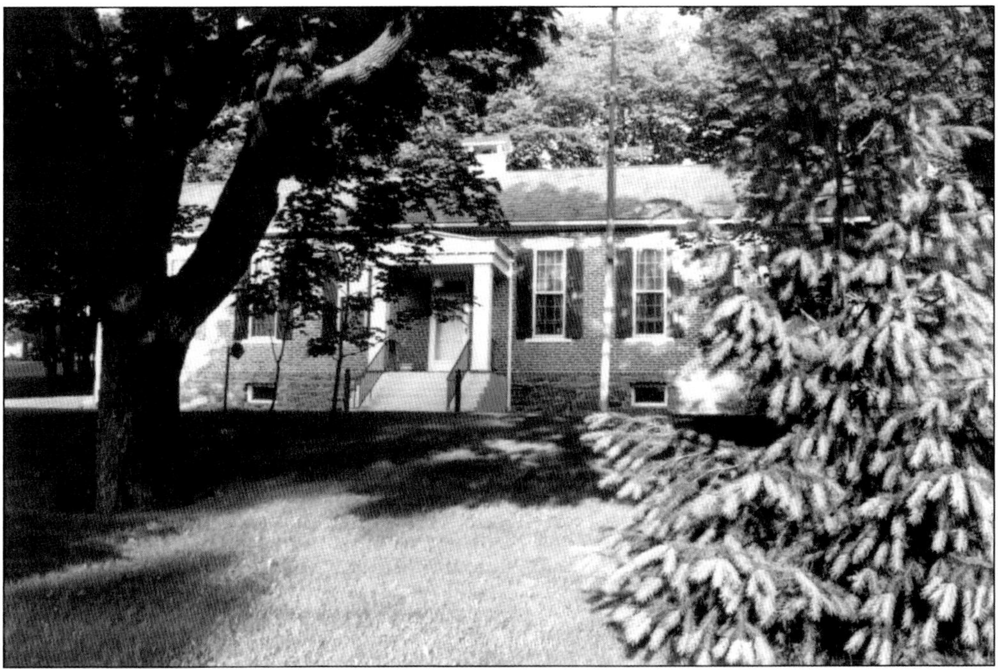

The Cherryville schoolhouse was built in 1877, south of the village on Blue Mountain Drive. It is currently a residence.

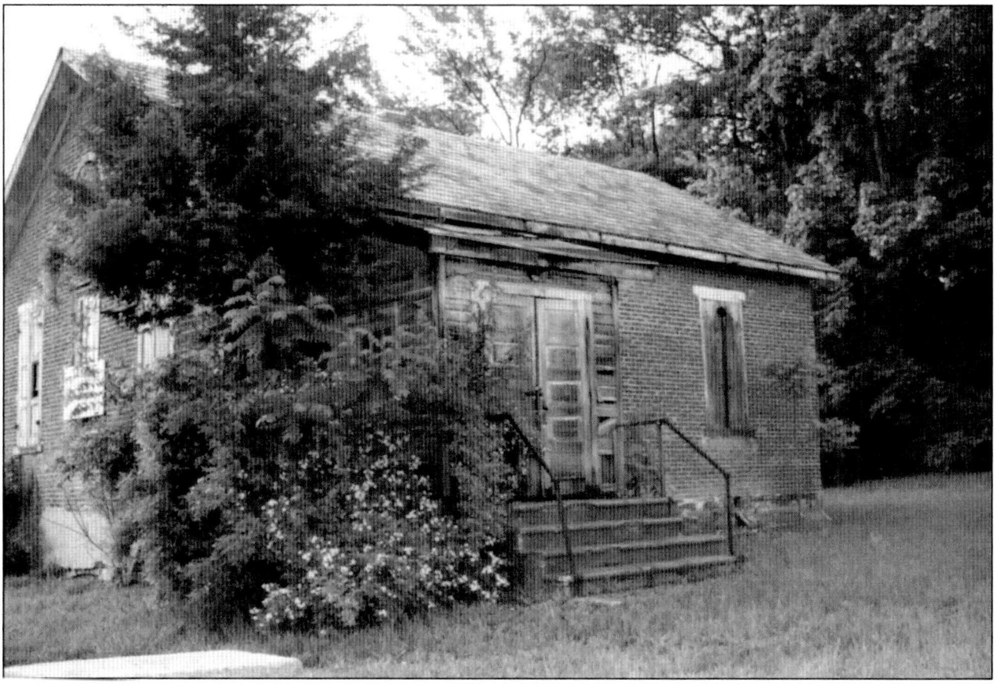

This is a modern view of the Slate Valley School. The school has been vacant for many years.

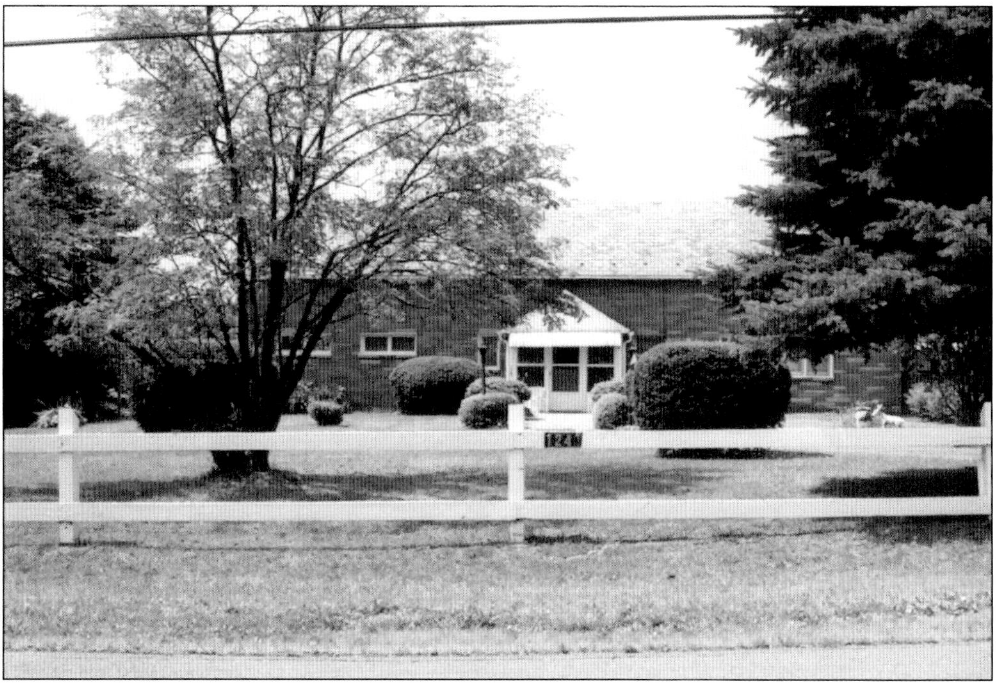

The Danielsville two-room schoolhouse, located on Walnut Drive in Danielsville, was built in 1894 and has since been converted into a house.

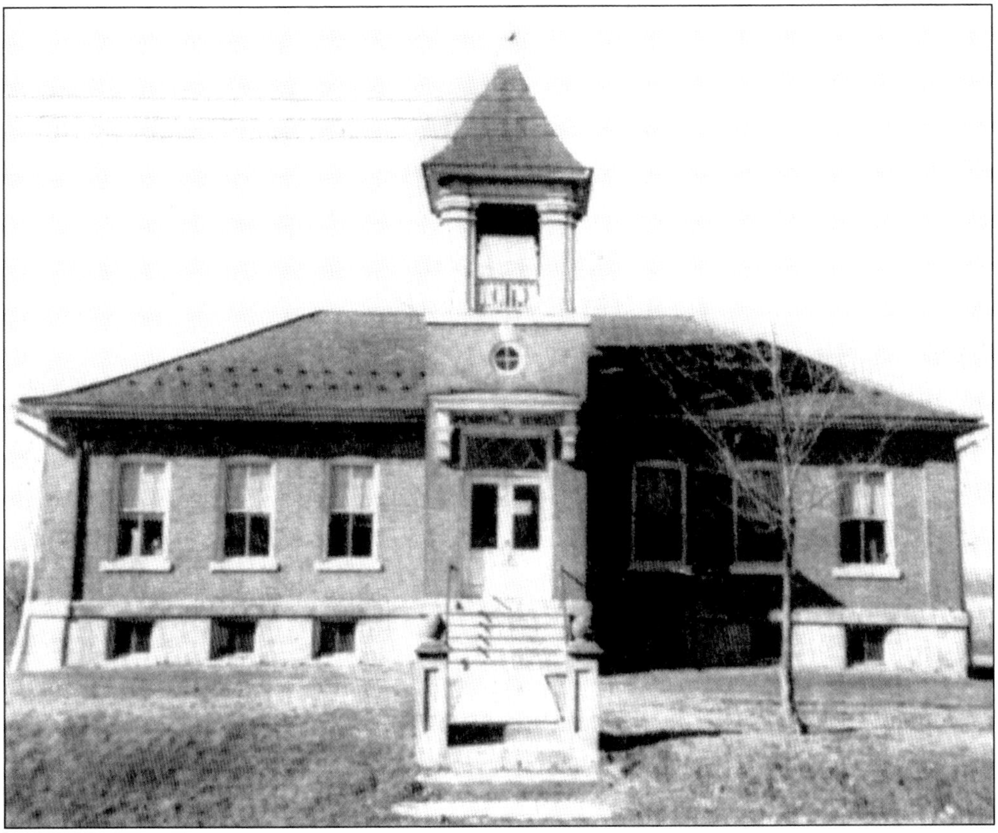

The Pennsville schoolhouse, on Walnut Drive in Pennsville, was used until 1956 and now serves as a home.

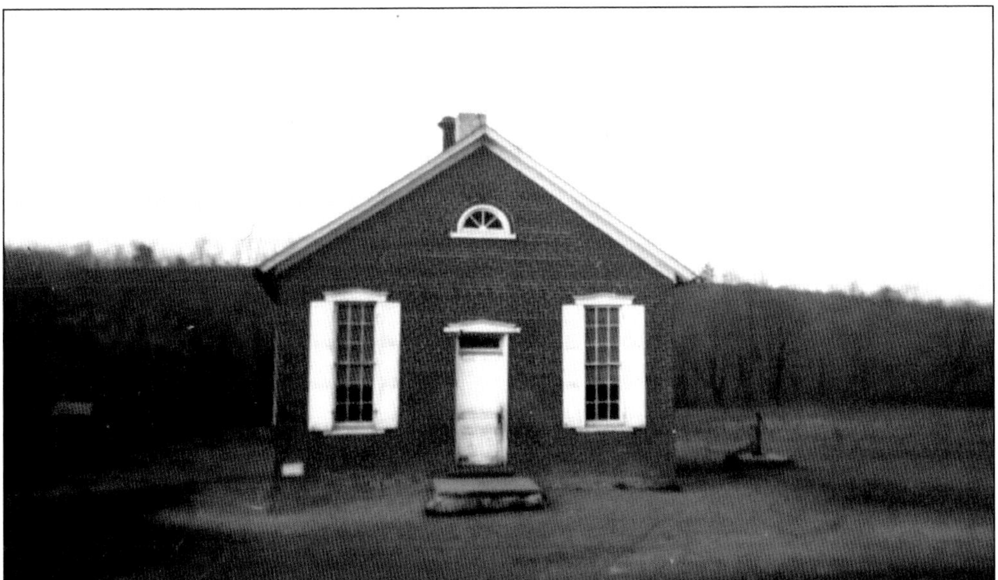

The Benningers schoolhouse, located on Maple Drive in Benningers, was converted into a home in 1957.

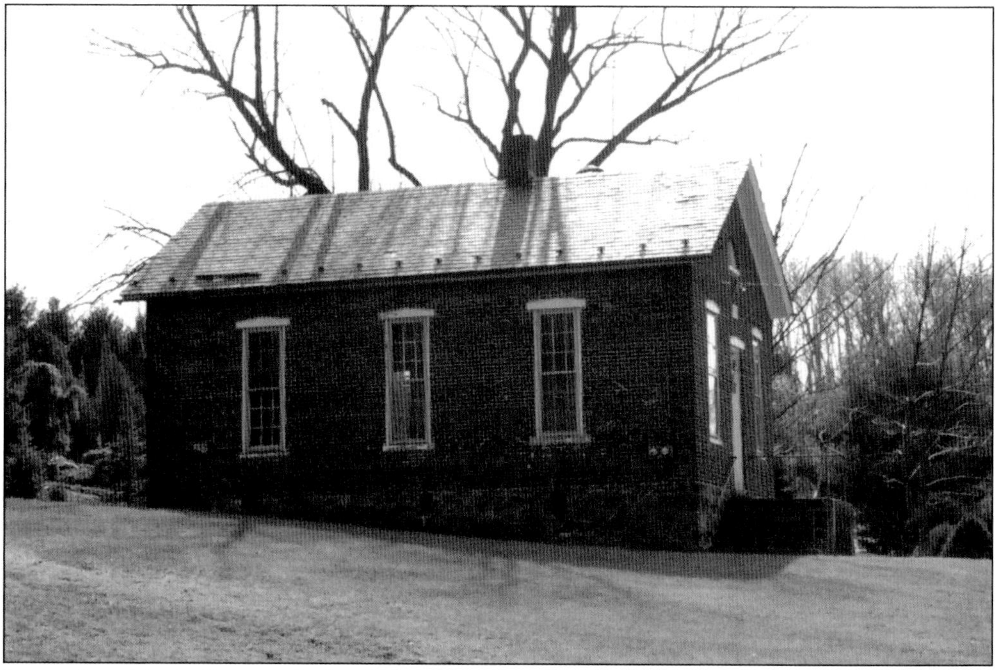

Located on Maple Drive in Indianland, the St. Paul's one-room schoolhouse has not changed much since it was last used in 1951. The school is owned by St. Paul's Church. (Courtesy Sean and Johanna Billings.)

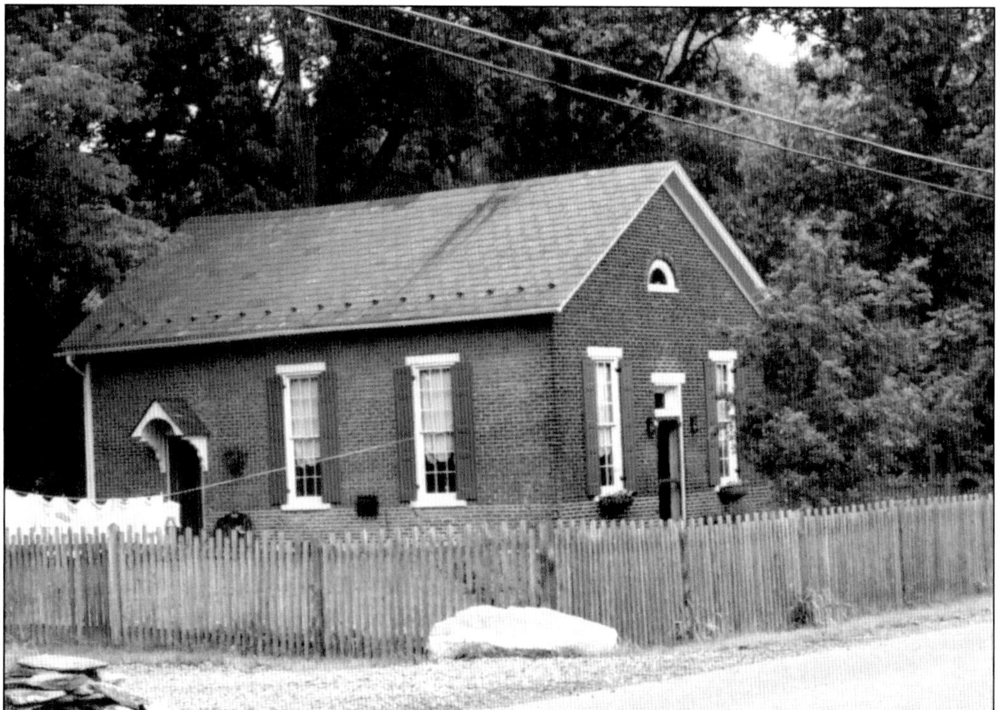

After the Rockville one-room schoolhouse closed in 1948, it was used as a chicken coop and was later remodeled into a home. (Courtesy Sean and Johanna Billings.)

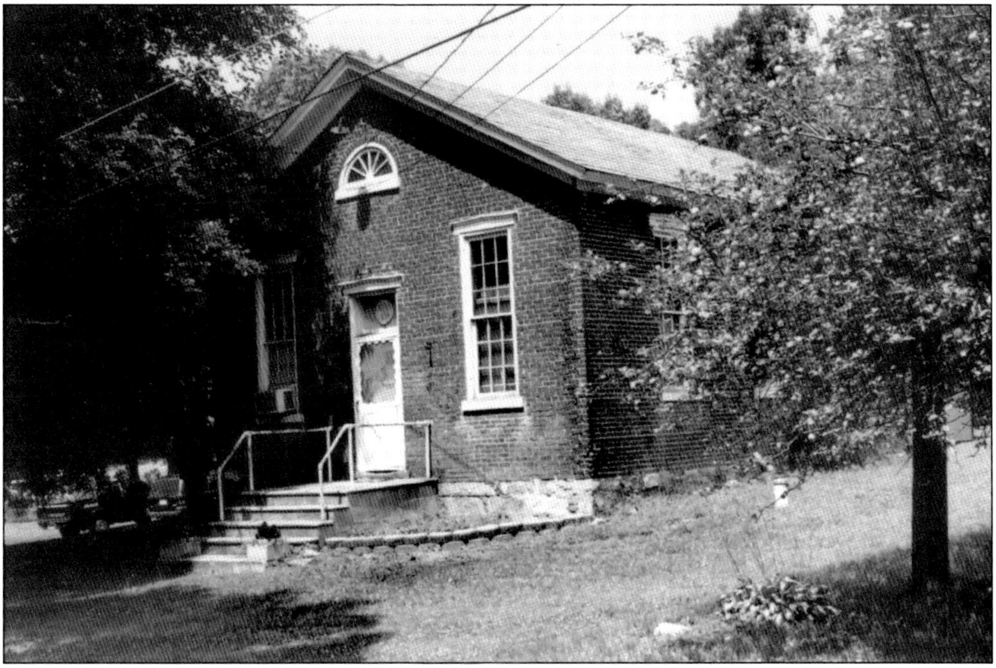

The Lehigh Gap one-room schoolhouse, located on Timberline Road, was built in 1856. The building is now a residence. (Courtesy Sean and Johanna Billings.)

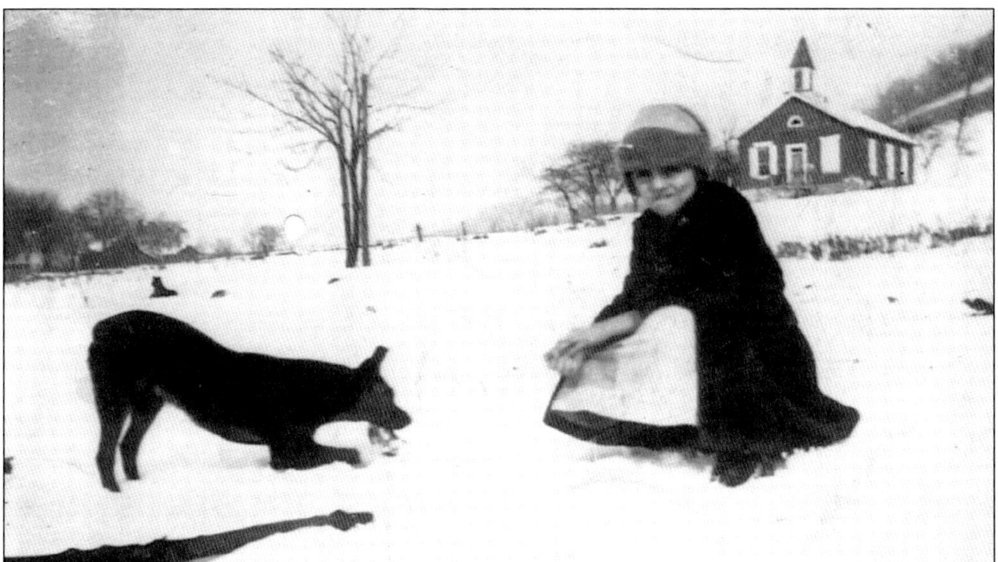

The Lockport one-room schoolhouse can be seen in the distance behind Grace Rehrig in this 1918 photograph. Notice the school's bell tower, which was removed sometime before 1943. Like other schoolhouses, this one has since been converted into a home. (Courtesy Florence Kline.)

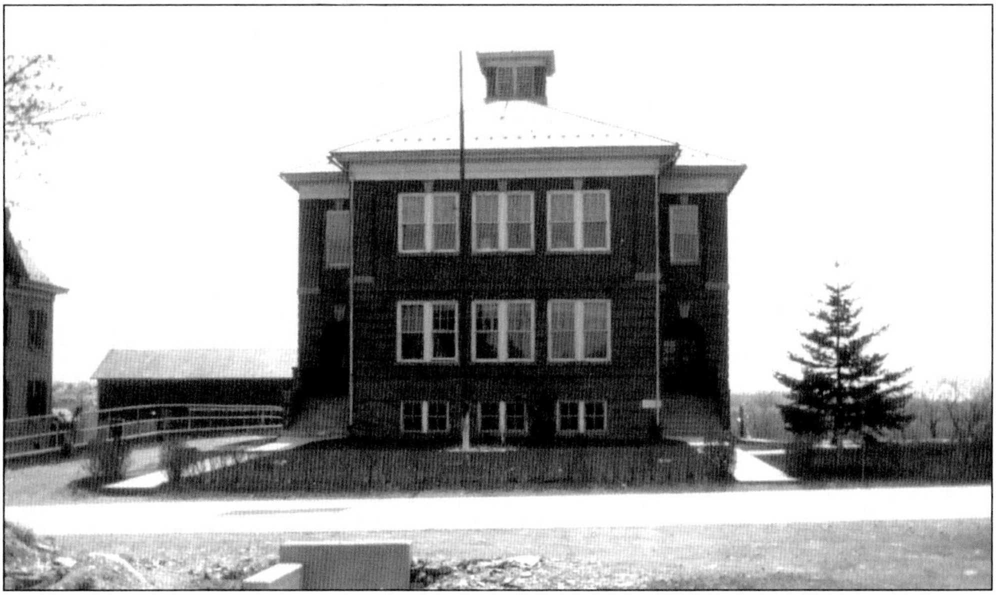

This is what the Lehigh Township High School in Berlinsville looked like when students still attended classes there. It has since been converted into a day-care center. (Courtesy Larry Hillborn.)

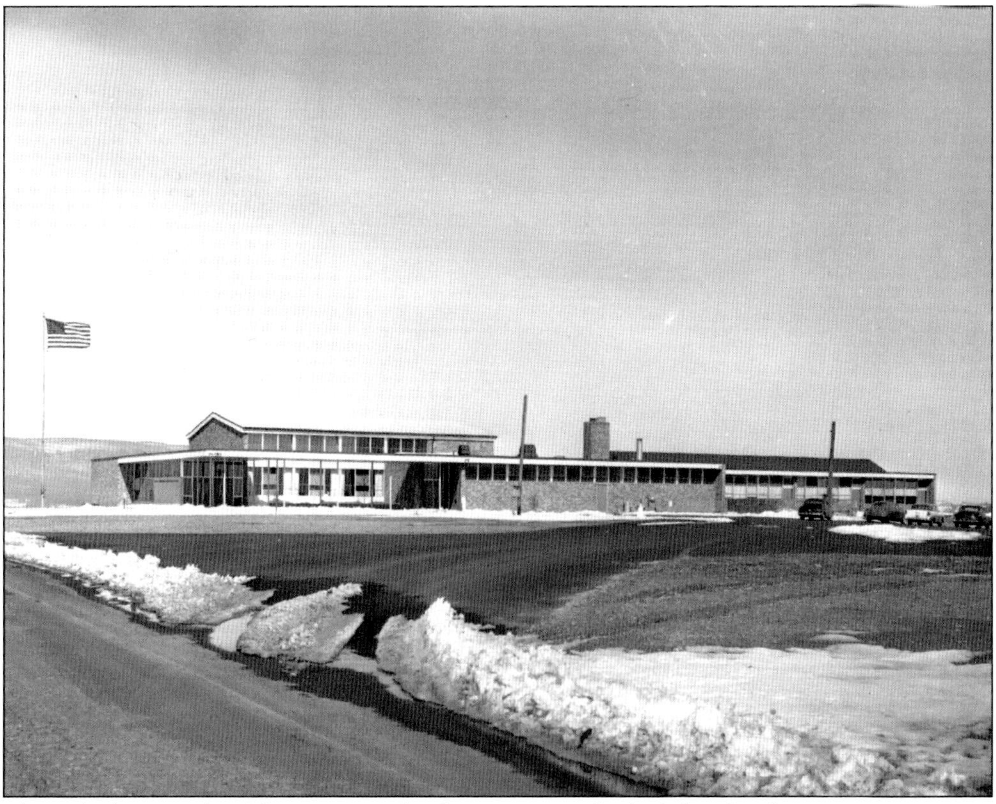

The Lehigh Township Elementary School is seen as it looked shortly after construction was completed in 1956.

As seen in this announcement for the first graduating class from the Lehigh Township High School, only two students graduated in 1906—Hilda Sabina and Stanley Nelson Coffin. (Courtesy Larry Hillborn.)

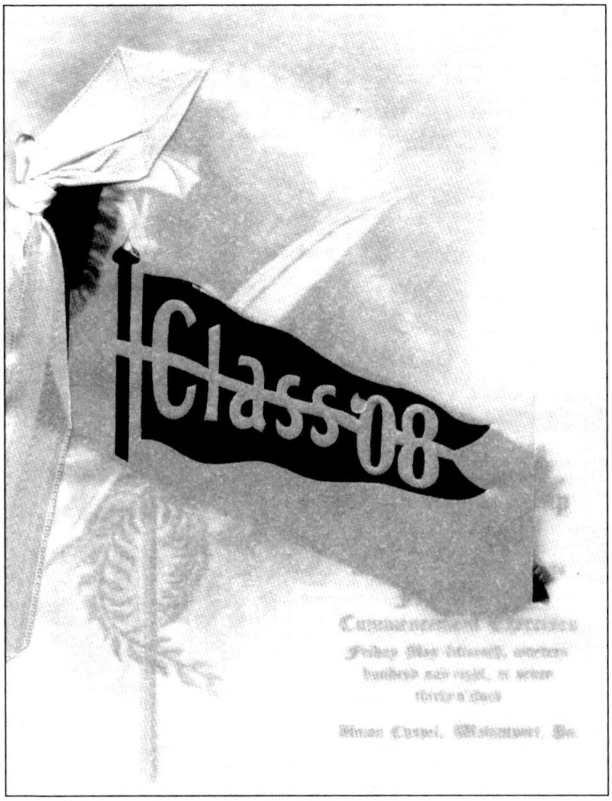

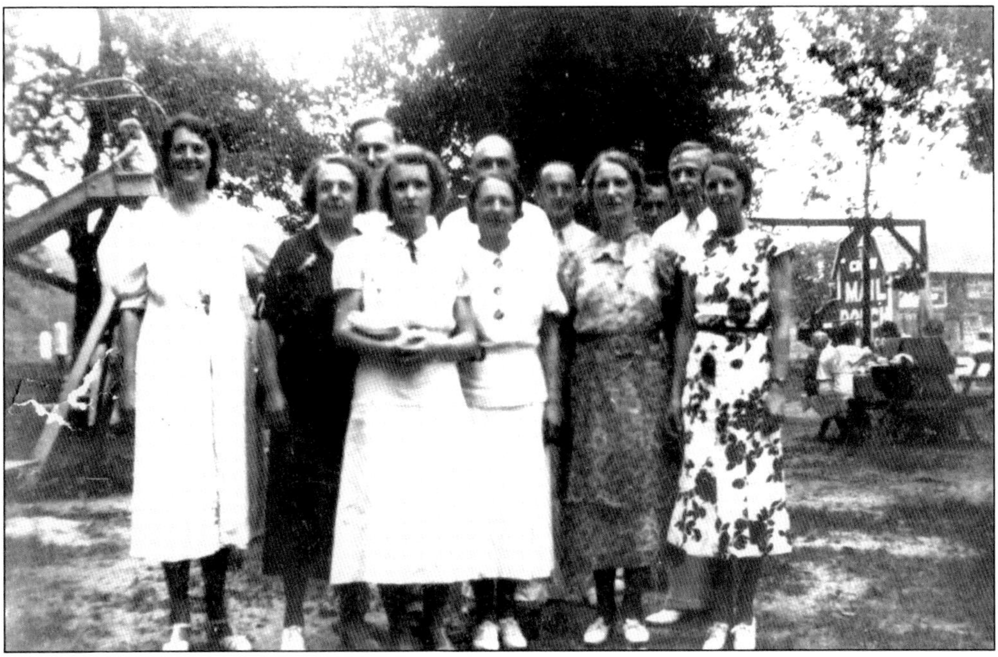

The Lehigh Township High School Class of 1917 held its 20th reunion at Indian Trail Park on July 10, 1937. (Courtesy Griffith Roberts.)

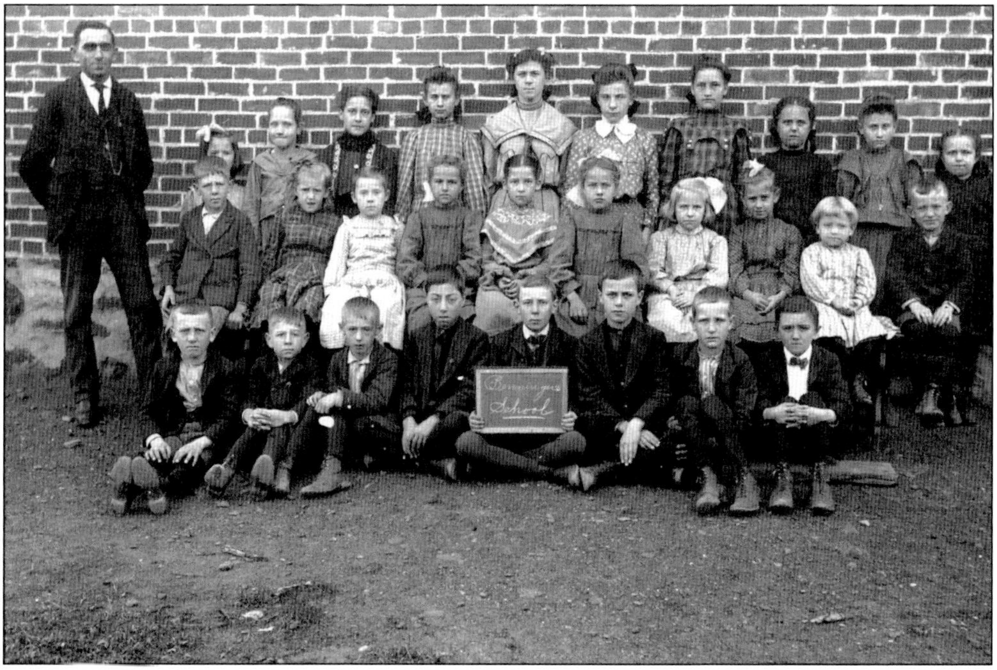

Teacher and students pose outside of Benningers School c. 1900. (Courtesy Griffith Roberts.)

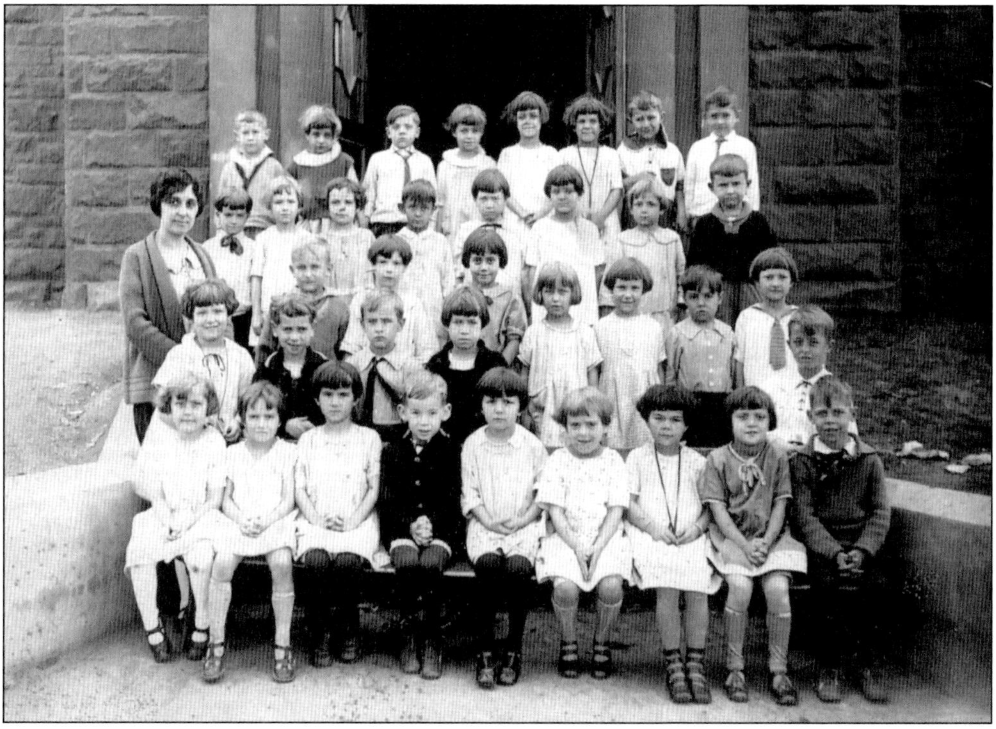

Teacher and students pose outside the Berlinsville school in 1924. (Courtesy Larry Hillborn.)

Teacher Vaughen Davis is pictured with unidentified students at the Treichlers two-room schoolhouse. Notice the 48-star flag.

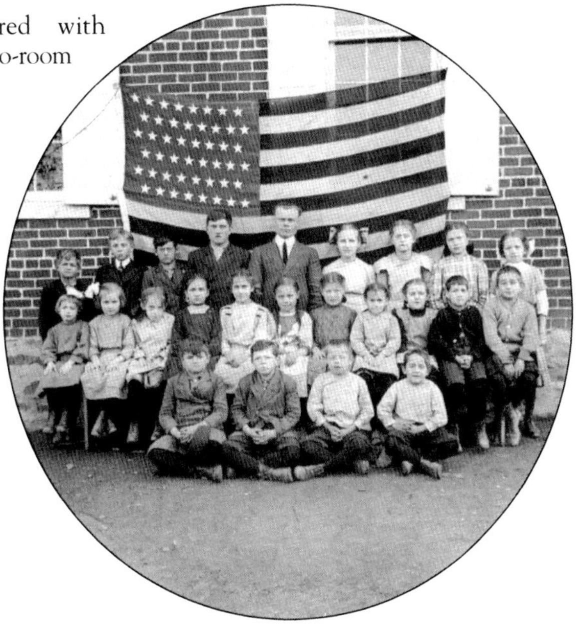

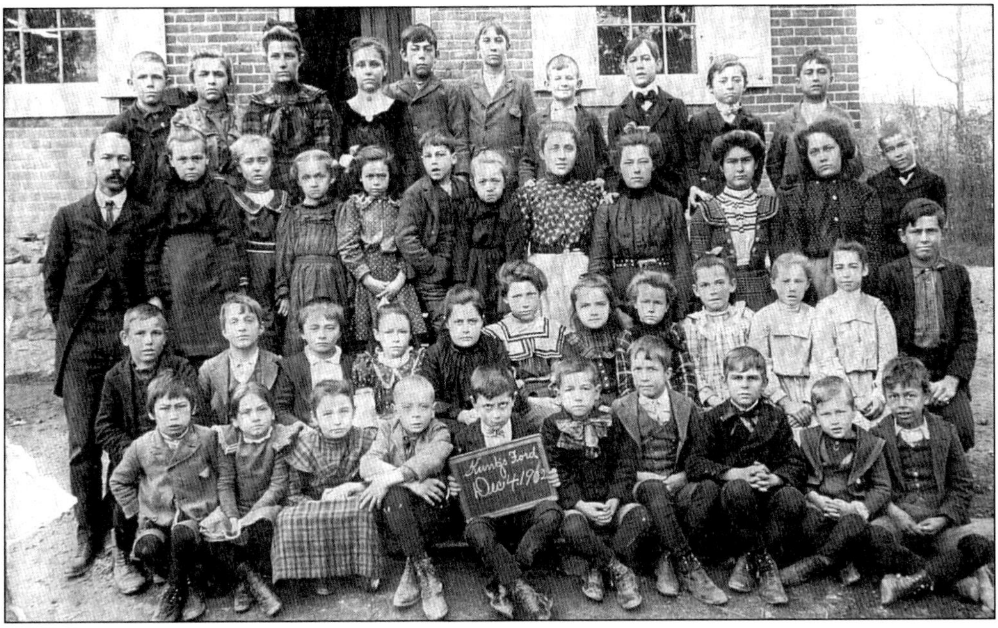

This class photograph was taken at Kuntz's Ford in 1902. From left to right are the following: (first row) James Kresge, Nellie Anthony, Kate Ackerson, Earl Anthony, Harvey Rinker, Clarence Kuntz, Ralph Rabert, Ray Benninger, Charles Hauseman, and Oliver Shoemaker; (second row) George Stever, Francis Robert, Jerry Snyder, Hattie Lutz, Ida Hauseman, Minnie Rinker, Grace Brader, Lillian Kuntz, Maude Shoemaker, Clara Kuntz, Nellie Nicholas, and Norman Hall; (third row) teacher Charles Kunkle, Ella Rehrig, Gertrude Benninger, Maude Handwerk, Lillian Lentz, Horace Anthony, Barbara Nicholas, Esther Newhardt, Bertha Kuntz, Irma Kuntz, Chloe Guldner, and Leon Kuntz; (fourth row) Horace Stever, Mabel Stever, Eva Kuntz, Mabel Benninger, Ed Shoemaker, Fred Snyder, Granville Redline, Henry Kester, William Nicholas, and Sam Snyder.

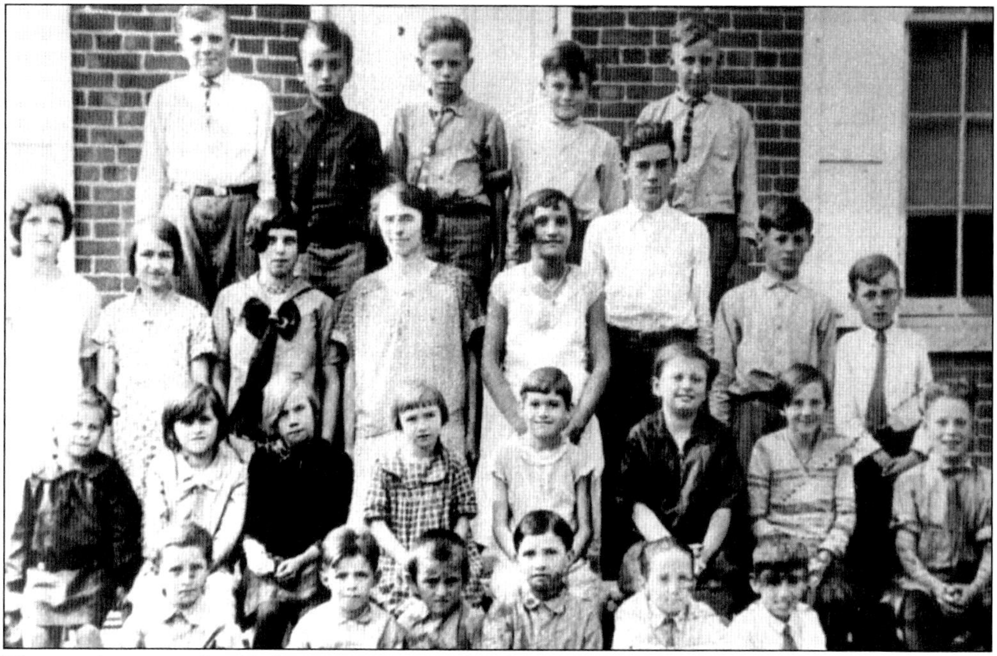

The students at the Farbers one-room school pose in 1929. From left to right are the following: (first row) Maurice Litchauer, Ray Heiny, John Skrapits, Frank Litchauer, Merritt Althouse, and Forrest Buskirk; (second row) Dressie Kepp, Anna Skrapits, Mabel Billig, Minerva Billig, Doris Weiland, Laure Kepp, Myrtle Althouse, and Harold Heiny; (third row) Ethel Buskirk, Aquilla Billig, Arlene Heiny, teacher Katie Bachman, Mary Litchauer, Alben Mascoy, John Borbacs, and Martin Csencsits; (fourth row) Ralph Kepp, Joe Skrapits, Homer Heiny, Eric Weiland, and Howard Atherhold. (Courtesy Caroline Cook.)

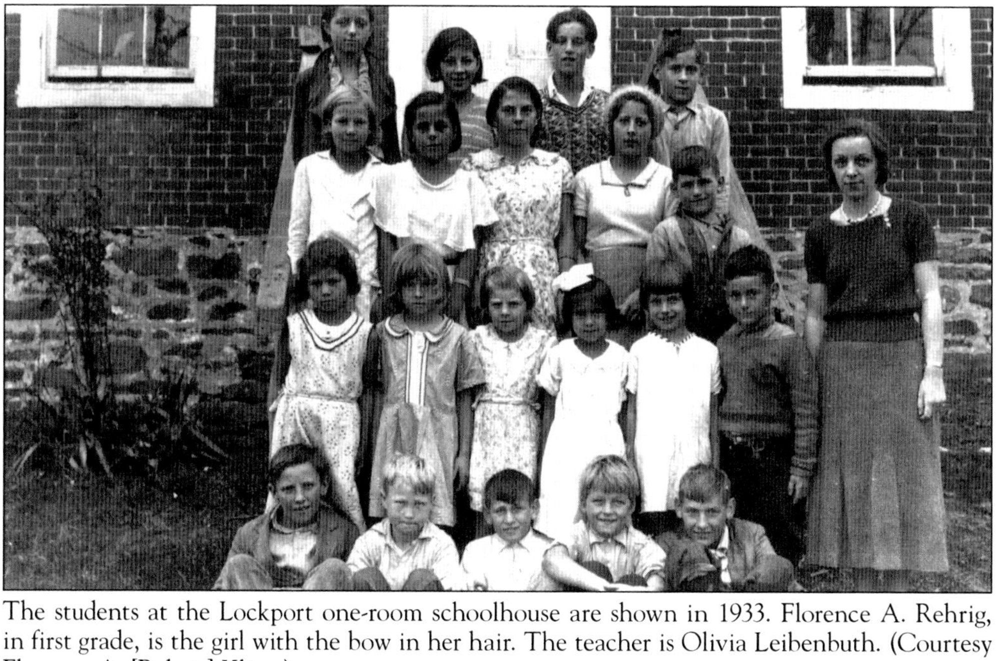

The students at the Lockport one-room schoolhouse are shown in 1933. Florence A. Rehrig, in first grade, is the girl with the bow in her hair. The teacher is Olivia Leibenbuth. (Courtesy Florence A. [Rehrig] Kline.)

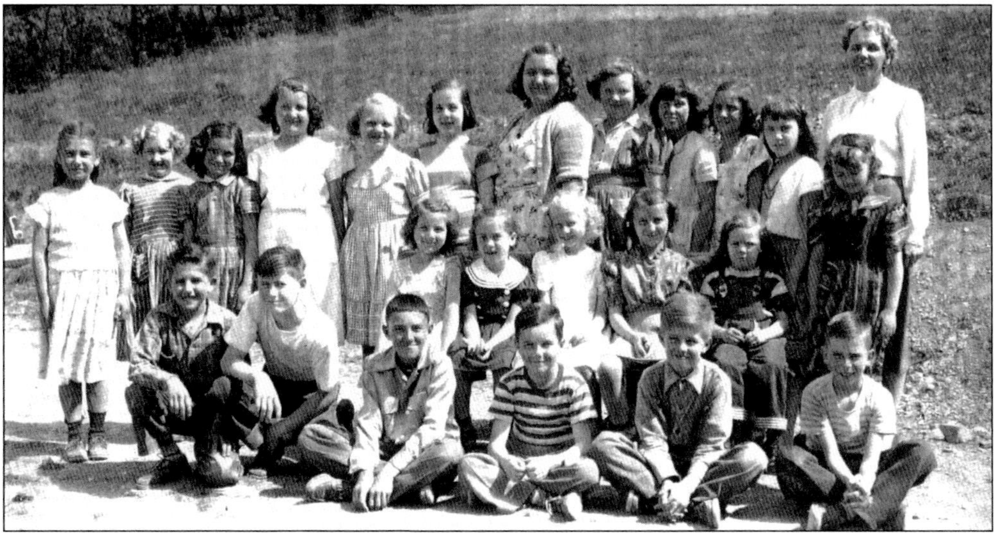

A Mrs. Day poses with her classes from the one-room schoolhouse at St. Paul's in Indianland. From left to right are the following: (front row) Donald Schaffer, Dale Eastman, Vincent Uhnak, Donald Dieter, Dale Schaffer, and Charles Fink; (middle row) Judy Andrews, Mary Ellen Leibenguth, Carol Kuntz, Betty Andrews, and Nancy Blose; (back row) Iris Solt, Sandra Hummel, Judy Wieand, Shirley Andrews, Barbara Klutzaritz, Marie Blose, Lorraine Andrews, Shirley Fatzinger, Maryann Schneck, Joan Wieand, Suzan Blose, and Barbara Beigi.

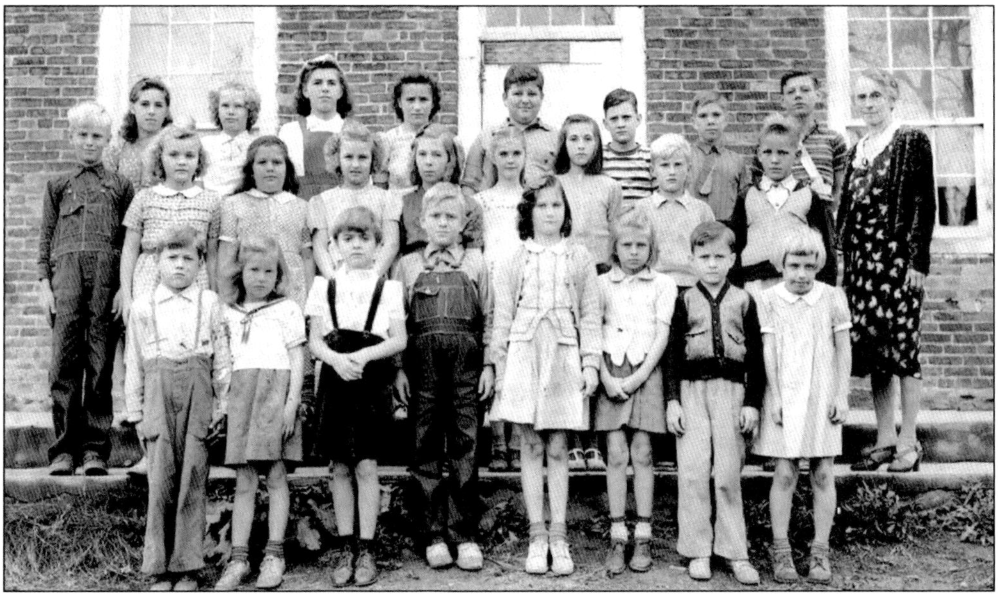

Katie Bachman taught at the Petersville one-room schoolhouse from 1916 to 1946 (when the school closed) and then went to Pennsville to teach. In this 1942 photograph, she is shown with, from left to right, the following: (front row) Rolland Kratzer, Betty Kratzer, Dorothy Hanzel, Richard Kulp, Christen Koch, Dolores Portarious, Jay Koch, and Mildred Kulp; (middle row) Robert Kulp, Dorothy Gilbert, June Schneburger, Pearl Kulp, Helen Dorhner, Joyce Borger, Maryann Koiber, Edward Kratzer, and Junior (Frances) Silfies; (back row) Margaret Dorner, Marian Kulp, Margaret Branigan, Regina Schneburger, Kenneth Becker, Grant Koch, Edward Borger, and Eldin Altrich. (Courtesy Betty Wattson.)

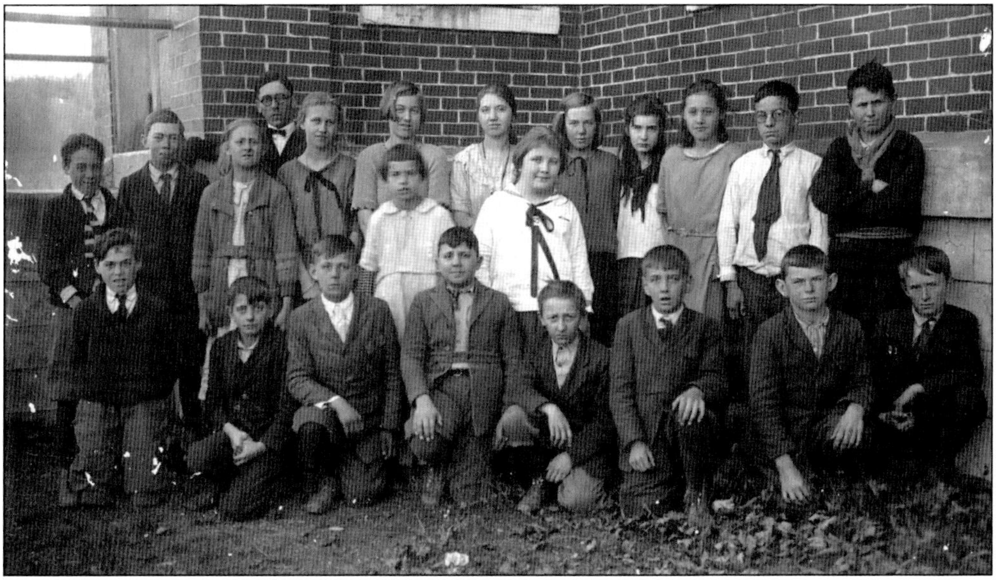

This school photograph at the Pennsville two-room school was taken *c.* 1920. The teacher and students are unidentified.

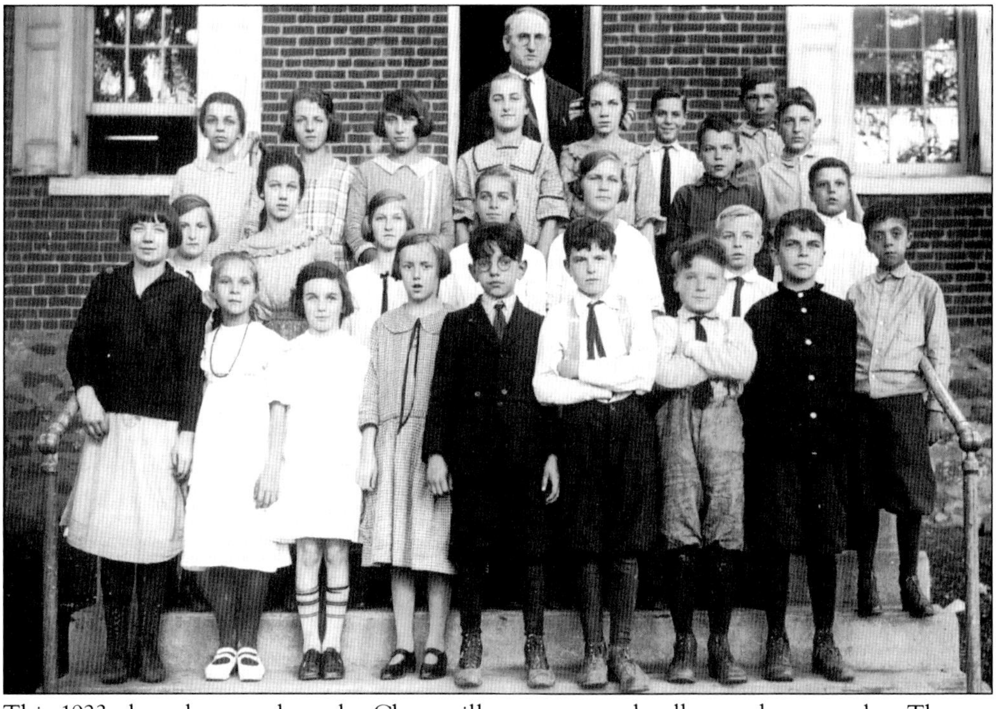

This 1923 class photograph at the Cherryville two-room schoolhouse shows teacher Thomas Arndt with students. From left to right are the following: (front row) Behlah Snyder, Melba Herbert, Catherine Ryan, Pauline Easterday, Robert Johnson, Herman Traub, Raymond Williams, Roland Dieter, and John Copenhaver; (middle row) Alice Royer, Evelyn Marsh, Isabel Royer, Helen Heckman, Alberta Gangaware, James Gable, and Harvey Gangaware; (back row) Florence Johnson, Mildred Tolan, Hertella Bleich, Naomi Dieter, Dorothy Marsh, Forrest Easterday, and Thomas Royer.

Eight

Railroads and the Canal

On March 20, 1818, the state gave virtual ownership of the Lehigh River to the Lehigh Navigation Company in exchange for making and keeping the river navigable. The bear trap lock, invented by Josiah White in 1819, released water on which boats could float to the next dam and lock, achieving downstream navigation.

The Lehigh Canal was built to achieve upstream navigation. The canal was the brainchild of Josiah White and his partner, Erskine Hazard of the Lehigh Coal and Navigation Company. Using both dug canals and a technique called slackwater navigation, the canal ran from Mauch Chunk (present-day Jim Thorpe) to Easton, following the path of the Lehigh River. The canal, completed in 1829, consisted of 44 lift locks, 5 guard locks, and 3 guard lift locks. It dropped 353 feet in 46 miles of length. In Lehigh Township, including Walnutport, there are eight locks, two guard locks, two dams, and one aqueduct.

Today, the 76-acre stretch of canal running from the Lehigh Gap down through Walnutport is a park owned by the Walnutport Borough and maintained by the Walnutport Canal Association. At lock No. 23, the original stone locktender's house, one of only two still in existence, was restored by the association in 1989. The association restored the lock in 1998.

One of the earliest railroads in Lehigh Township was the Lehigh and Susquehanna, founded on March 13, 1837, to run along the Lehigh River on its way from Wilkes-Barre to White Haven. In 1862, when floodwaters damaged the canal north of Mauch Chunk, the railroad was extended through the township to Easton. The first coal train arrived in Easton from Mauch Chunk on March 16, 1864. The Lehigh and Susquehanna was leased and then sold to the Central Railroad of New Jersey. On April 1, 1976, Conrail took over these rails, which are now owned by the Norfolk and Southern.

A second line, the Slate Valley Railroad, was organized on April 28, 1886, with $125,000 capital stock. From 1886 to 1887, Franklin Moyer Hower of Danielsville and a Dr. Hughes of Philadelphia constructed six miles of single track from the Hower slate quarries below Danielsville to Lockport, where the line connected to the Central Railroad of New Jersey. A small shed near Danielsville housed the company's only locomotive, numbered 21 and named the *F.M. Hower*. This small slate-hauling line was purchased by the Pennsylvania, Poughkeepsie and Boston Railroad on January 19, 1891, and changed hands numerous times afterward.

On September 15, 1887, the Pennsylvania, Poughkeepsie and Boston Railroad acquired the Pennsylvania, Slatington and New England Railroad. This line was born of a merger between the Delaware and Slatington Railroad and the Pennsylvania and New England. The merger, completed on June 20, 1882, included plans to build a line from Slatington across New Jersey to Pine Island, New York. The firm began grading the route between Slatington and Benders Junction through the township but did not finish before filing for receivership on June 9, 1885, and being sold two years later.

The buyer (the Pennsylvania, Poughkeepsie and Boston Railroad) did not fare much better. Although the company began service from Slatington to Campbell, New York, on January 1,

1890, it fell into receivership by February 17, 1891. In an attempt to recover, the line leased its tracks to the Philadelphia and Reading from May 1, 1892, to July 31, 1893, and then to the Lehigh Valley Railroad from August 1, 1893, to December 31, 1896. On December 14, 1894, the line was sold to the Lehigh and New England Railroad, which began service with its own equipment on January 1, 1897, and came under the control of the Lehigh Coal and Navigation Company on May 9, 1904. In 1909, Lehigh Coal and Navigation reinforced the railroad bridge across the Lehigh River from Walnutport to Slatington.

The September 29, 1910 *Engineering News* reports that the Lehigh and New England intended to build the "Tamaqua Extension," a 30-mile addition from the main line in Danielsville to Tamaqua, at a cost of $3 million. On July 1, 1911, the firm reached an agreement with the American Bridge Company to construct a 110-foot span across the Lehigh River at the Lehigh Gap, the first step toward completing the extension.

By 1918, the slate business virtually disappeared over the old line running from the Danielsville area to the Hower quarries, so it was abandoned. On October 6, 1934, the railroad abandoned the Slatington branch from Slate Junction near Danielsville to Slatington, a distance of six miles. On June 9, 1960, the Lehigh and New England petitioned the Interstate Commerce Commission to abandon operations and officially did so on October 31, 1961, at 12:01 a.m. The bridge across the Lehigh at the Lehigh Gap was removed from 1967 to 1968.

The Blue Ridge Traction Company, chartered by the Hower family on April 11, 1902, was a small trolley line that ran from Danielsville to Walnutport with four stops: Danielsville, Edgemont Park, Berlinsville, and Walnutport. Construction commenced in the summer of 1902, and service began on February 9, 1903. The company used two types of cars, closed and open. The closed cars were dark green and the open, or summer, cars were bright red. The 1910 time table lists a 5:15 a.m. start time in Danielsville, with trolleys running about every 40 minutes until 11:25 p.m.

Unfortunately, the trolley line did not directly tie in to other trolley systems. A rider at the Walnutport end had to get off and walk across the bridge to Slatington to catch another trolley there. To correct this problem, the company established a mule-drawn tally-ho service between Slatington and Walnutport.

At first, the electricity to operate the trolleys was generated in the powerhouse in Danielsville. On February 12, 1908, the company began to purchase electricity from the Lehigh Valley Transit Company in Slatington, whose wires hung above the Lehigh River to Walnutport. The trolley line was abandoned on May 30, 1924, making it the first electric railway company in the Lehigh Valley to disappear entirely.

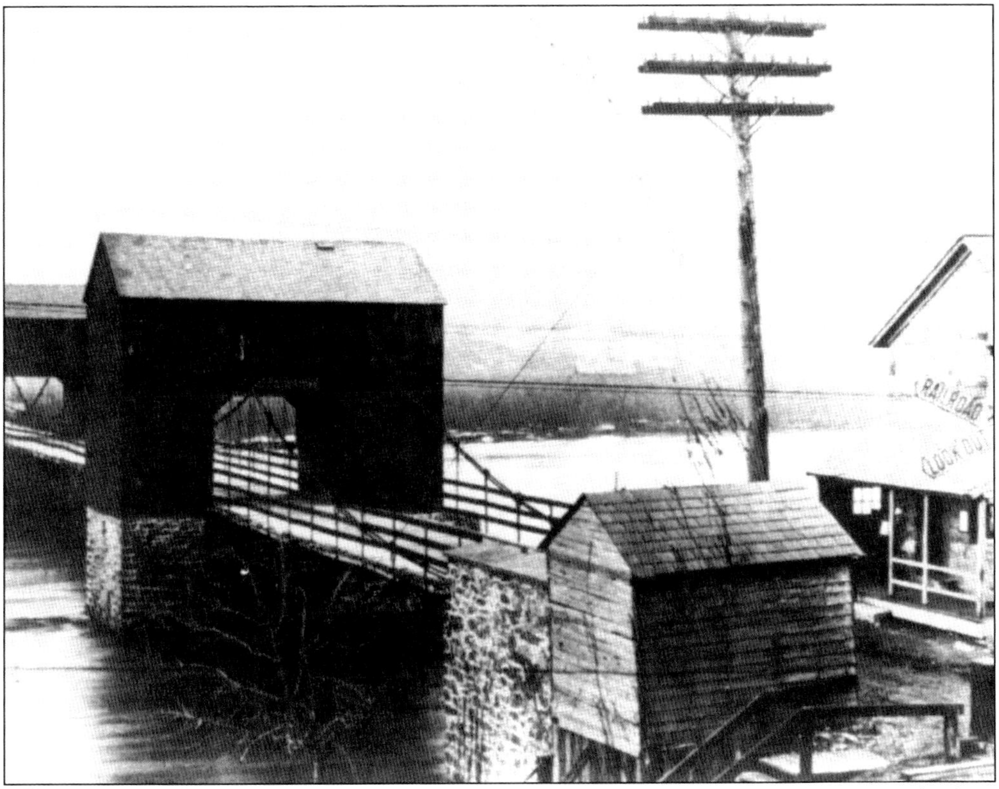

Pictured here *c.* 1900, the chain bridge across the Lehigh River at the Lehigh Gap was built in 1825 and dismantled in 1934.

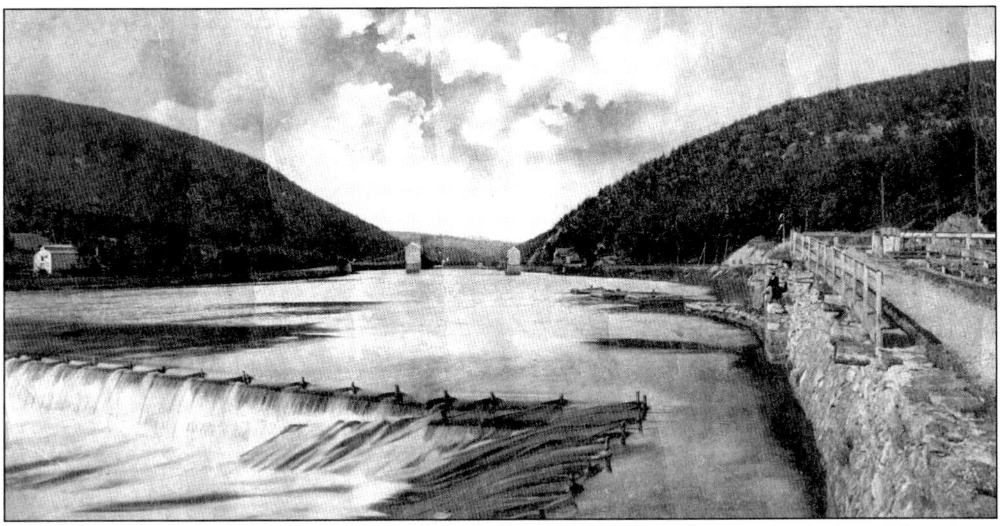

This view shows the Lehigh River and dam No. 3, just south of the Lehigh Gap. The chain bridge can be seen in the distance. On the right is the start of this section of the Lehigh Canal. (Courtesy Florence Kline.)

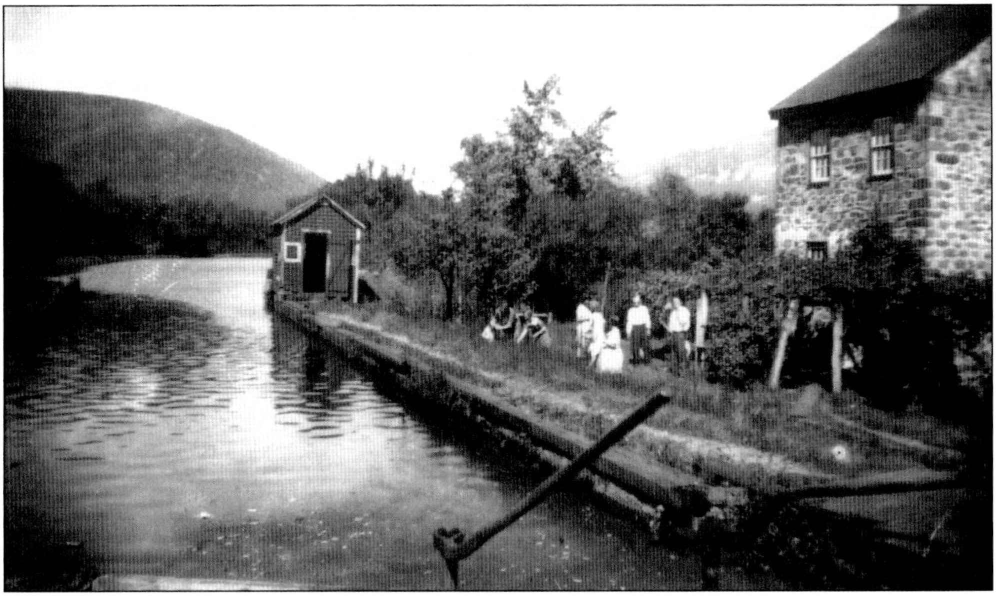

Lock No. 22, north of Walnutport, is known as "Frantz's lock" after the last locktender. The house was razed in 1954. (Courtesy Walnutport Canal Association.)

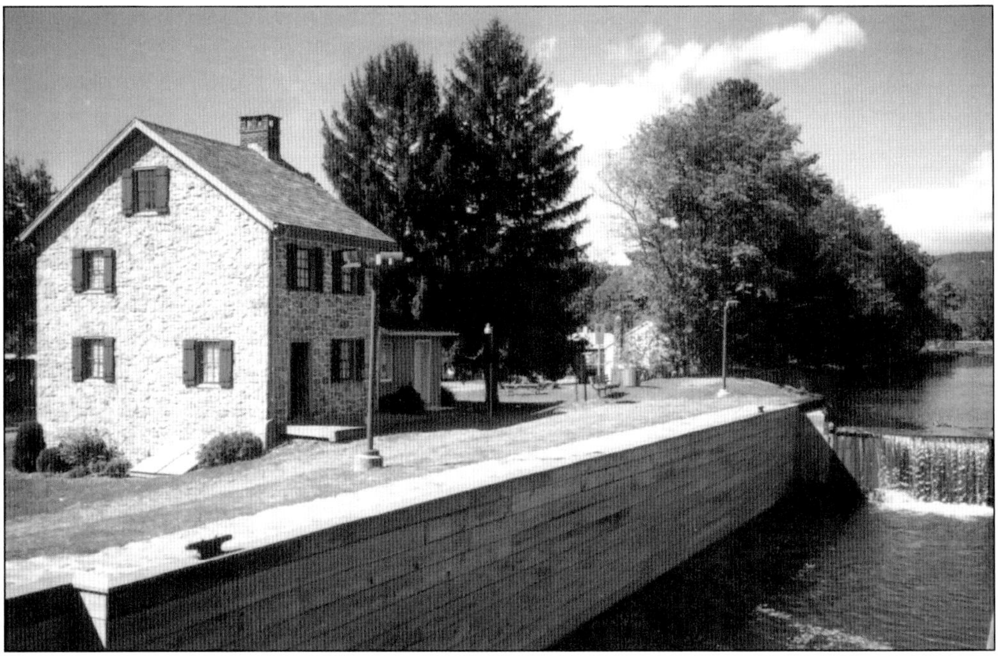

Lock No. 23, in Walnutport, is pictured here. The original stone locktender's house, one of only two still in existence, was restored by the Walnutport Canal Association in 1989. The lock was restored in 1998. Frank Kelchner was the last locktender here. (Courtesy Walnutport Canal Association.)

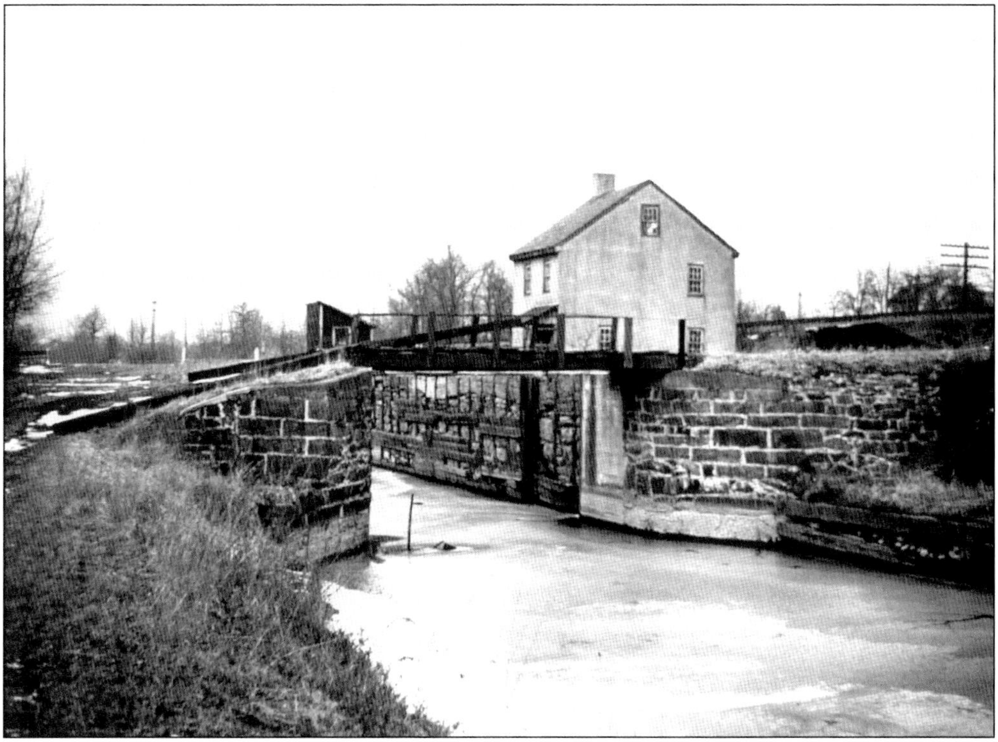

Lock No. 24, south of Walnutport, was known as "Shafer's lock" after the last locktender. The house was razed *c.* 1960. (Courtesy Walnutport Canal Association.)

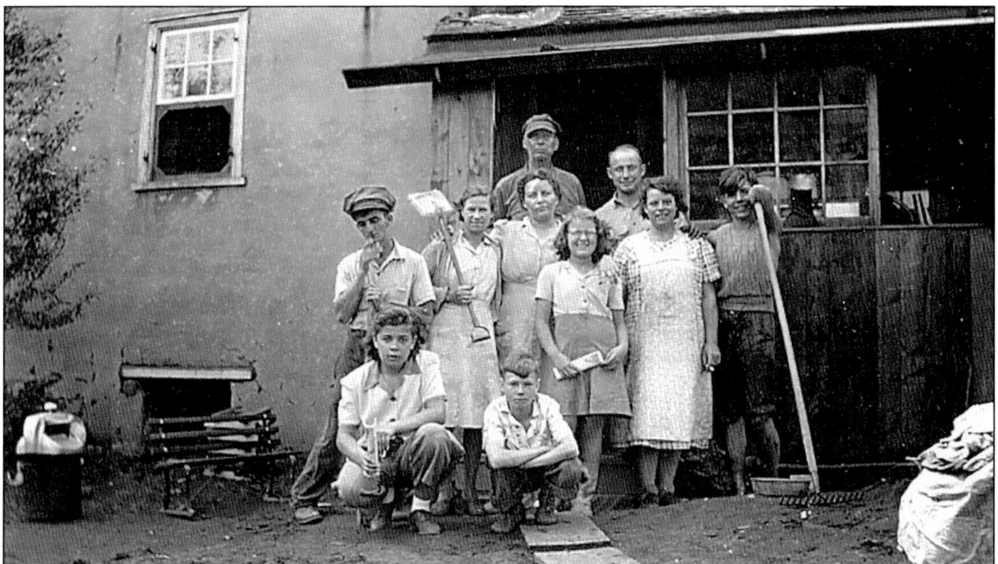

The Sheckler family poses while cleaning the house at lock No. 25 after the flood in 1942. Charles W. Sheckler (wearing a hat in the back, center) was the locktender. (Courtesy Walnutport Canal Association.)

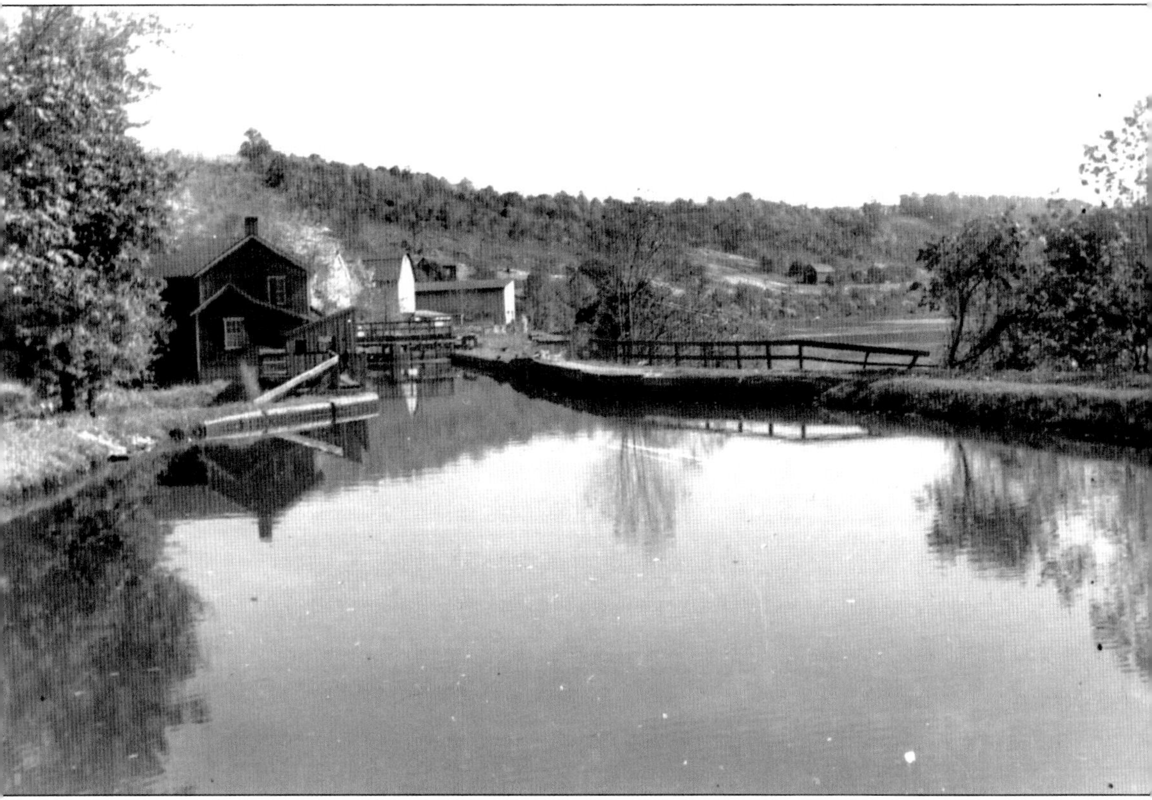

The Lehigh Canal at Lockport is pictured in 1941. Lockport had two locks, Nos. 26 and 27. An aqueduct also crossed the Bertsch Creek before reaching lock No. 26. From lock No. 27, a boat would enter the Lehigh River on slackwater behind dam No. 4 in Treichlers. (Courtesy Carson and Joanne Jones.)

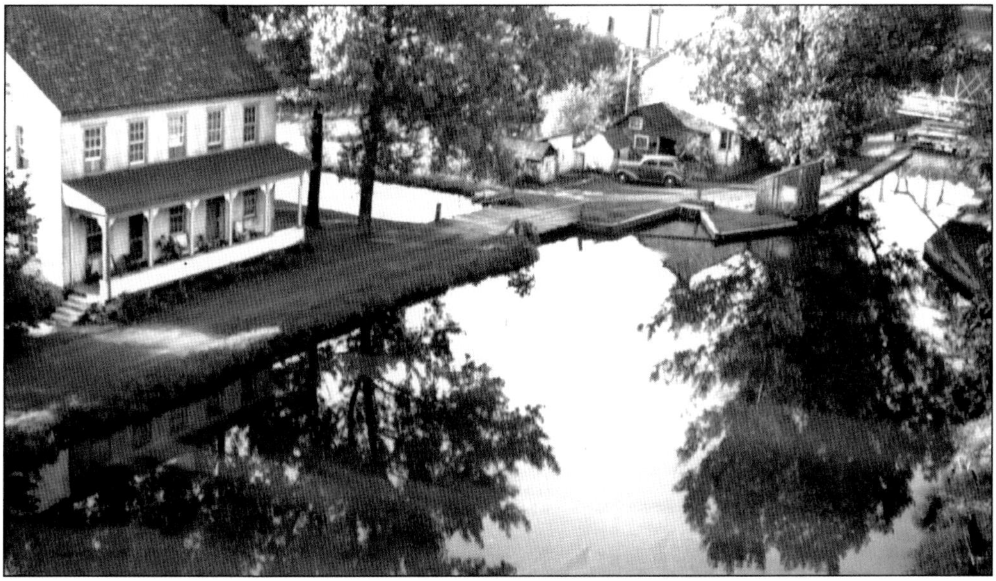

Shown is a view of the canal at lock No. 28 in Treichlers. Canal boats entered the canal at guard lock No. 4 at dam No. 4, west of Treichlers. Because there was no lock No. 29, boats would continue to lock No. 30.

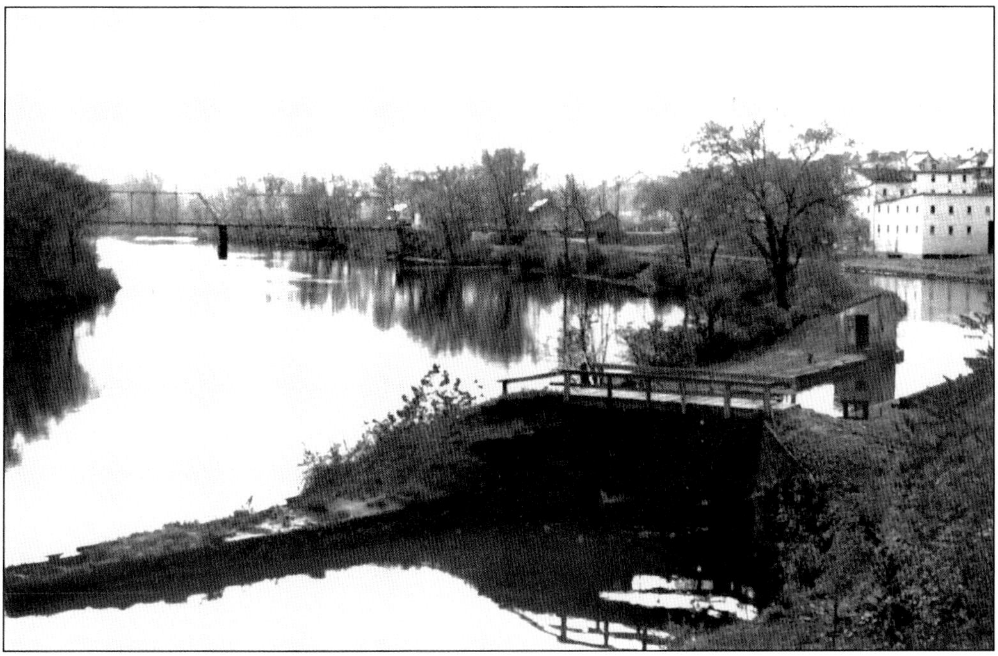

Boats would leave the canal at lock No. 30 (shown here), in Treichlers, and go back into the river on slackwater behind dam No. 5. The first bridge over the Lehigh in Treichlers can be seen in the distance to the left.

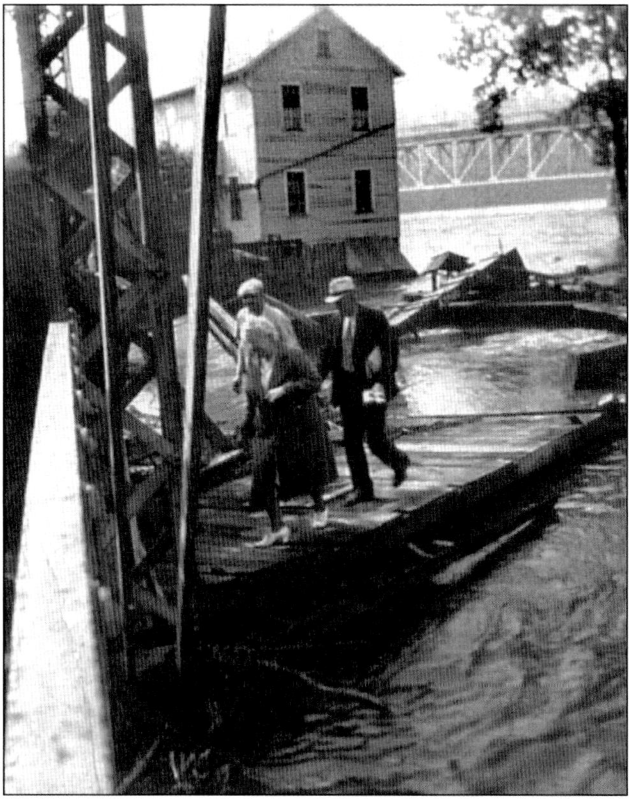

In this photograph of the 1942 flood, the toll taker's house for the first bridge at Treichlers can be seen in the background.

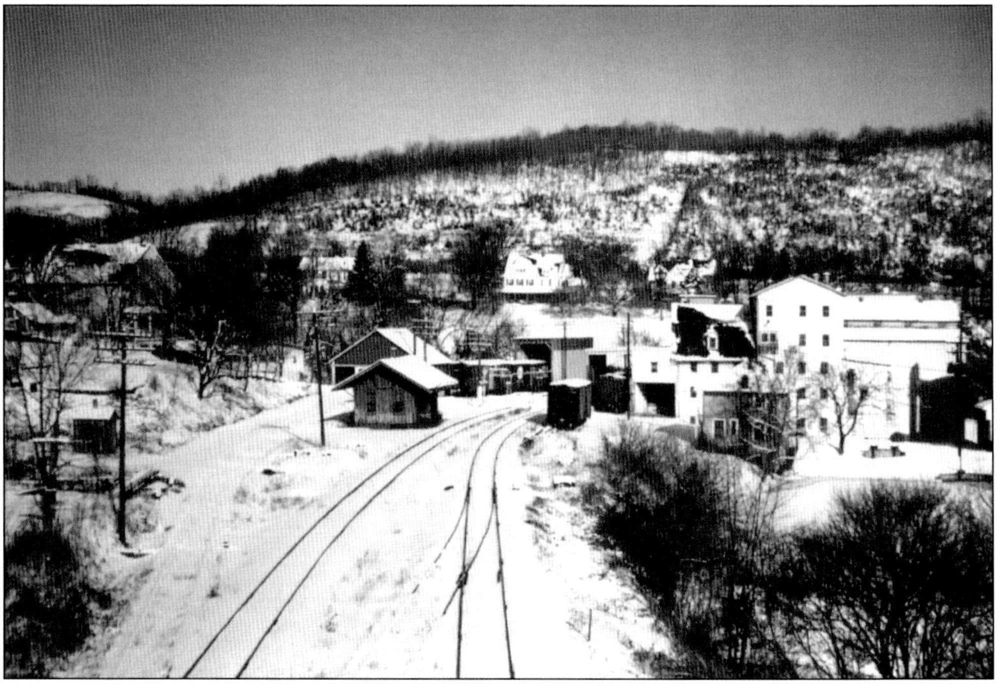

The Central Railroad of New Jersey station stands in the center of this view of Treichlers, and Mauser Mill is on the right.

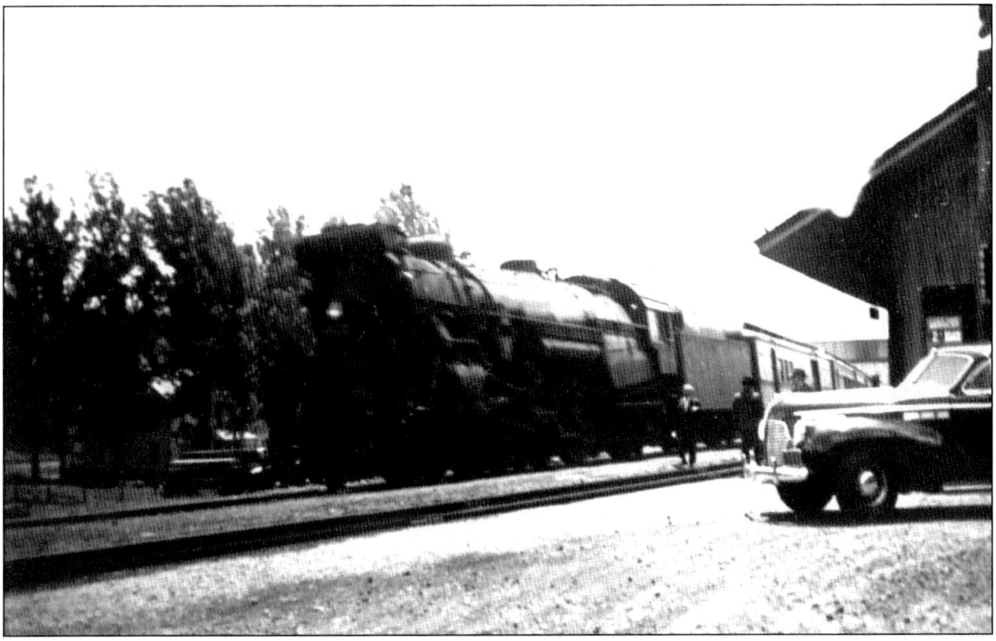

A steam locomotive is stopped at the station at Treichlers.

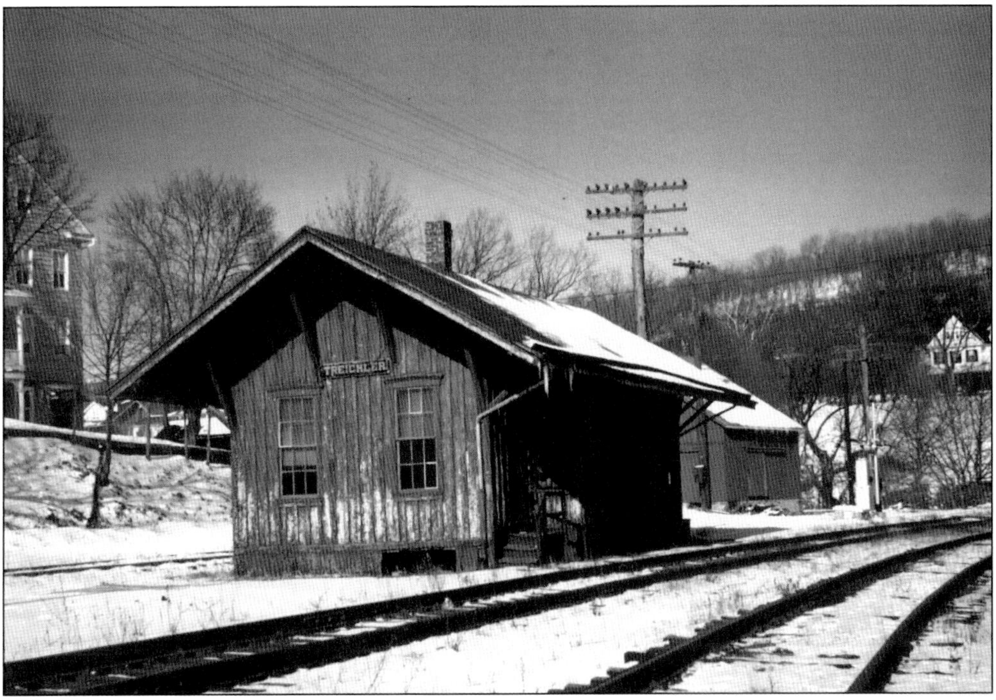

The Central Railroad of New Jersey station at Treichlers is shown in 1966, shortly before it was razed. (Courtesy Charles Houser Jr.)

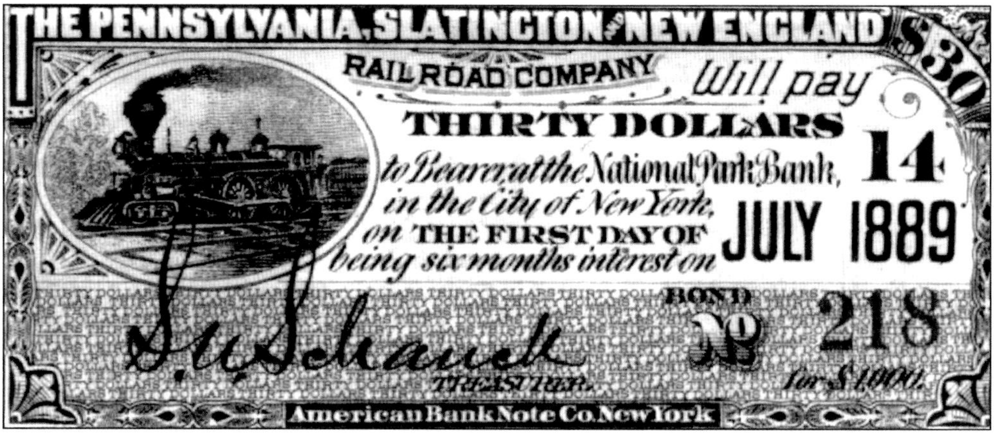

This stock coupon was for the Pennsylvania, Slatington and New England Railroad. (Courtesy Sean Billings.)

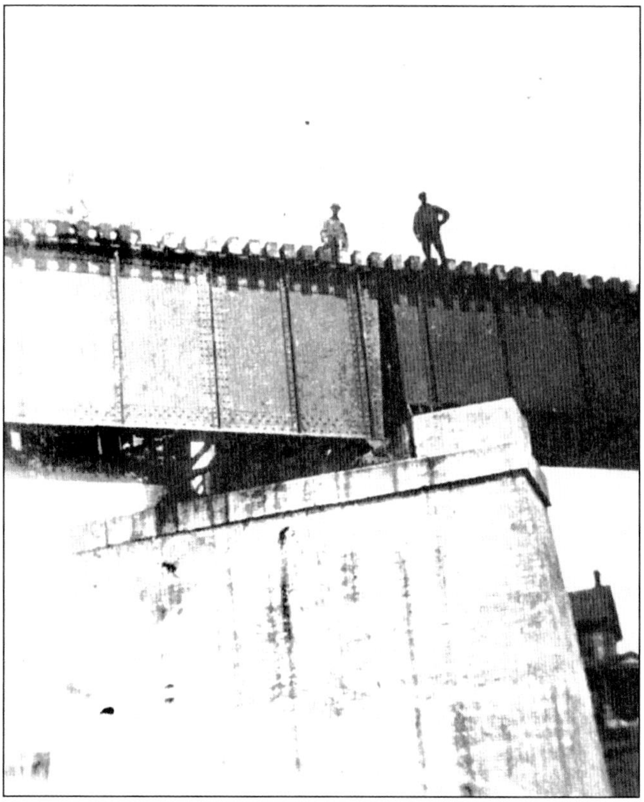
This Pennsylvania, Poughkeepsie and Boston bridge crossed the Lehigh River below Walnutport. The bridge is gone, but the piers still stand today. (Courtesy Griffith Roberts.)

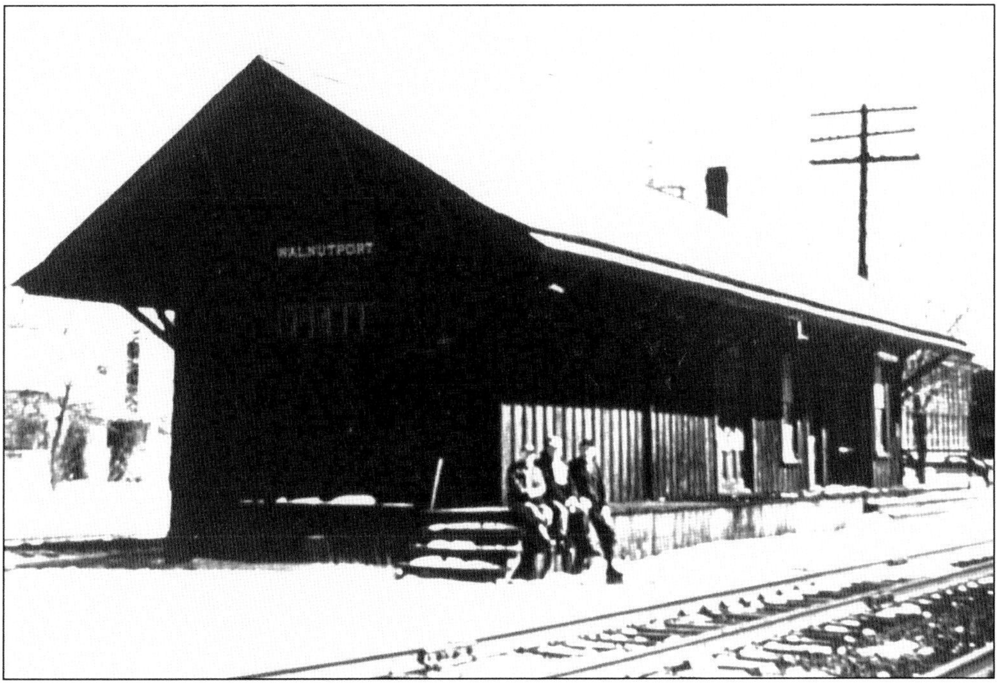

The Central Railroad of New Jersey station in Walnutport is pictured here. (Courtesy Walnutport Canal Association.)

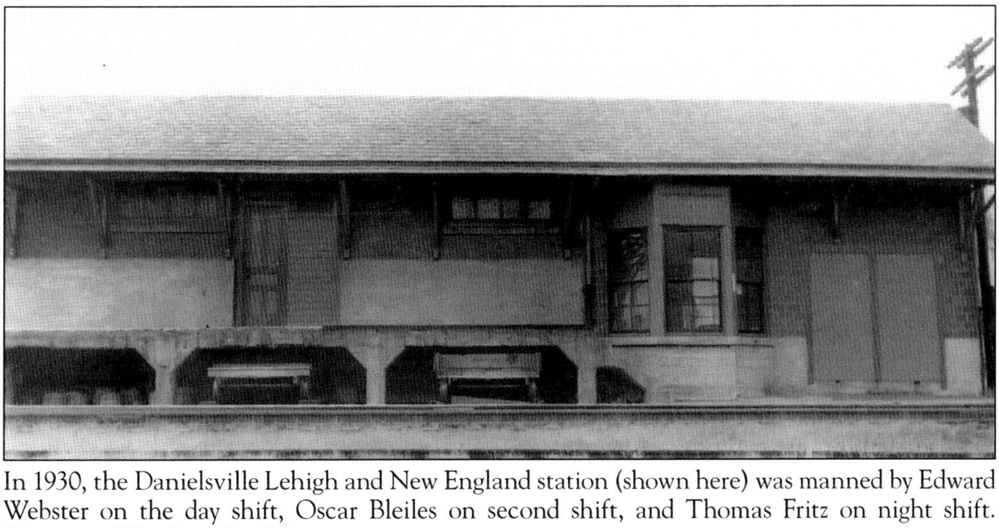

In 1930, the Danielsville Lehigh and New England station (shown here) was manned by Edward Webster on the day shift, Oscar Bleiles on second shift, and Thomas Fritz on night shift. (Courtesy Woodrow Reph.)

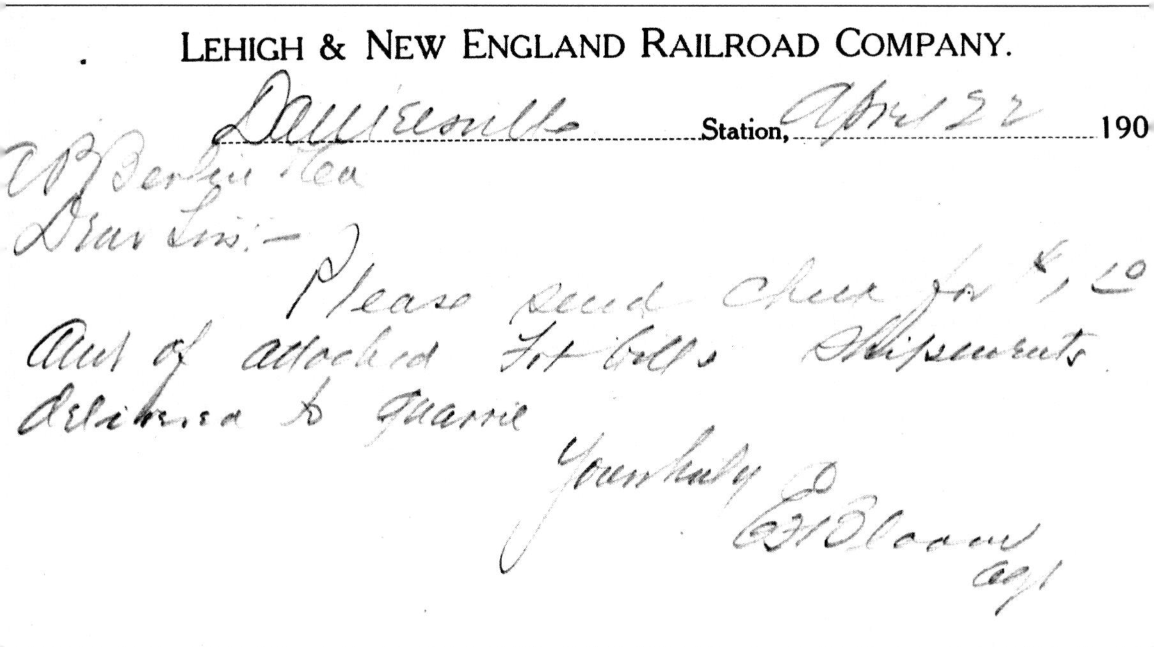

LEHIGH & NEW ENGLAND RAILROAD COMPANY.

Danielsville Station, Apr 22 190

Dear Sir:—

Please send check for

Amt of attached Frt bills Shipments

delivered to Quarrie

Yours truly

Agt

This letterhead was used at the Lehigh and New England Railroad station in Danielsville. The letter is addressed to the Atlas Slate Company. (Courtesy David Altrichter.)

BLUE RIDGE TRACTION COMPANY

In Effect June 7, 1910 | **TIME TABLE** | **Subject to Change without Notice**

LEAVE	1	3	5	7	9	11	13	15	17	19	21	23
	A. M.	A. M.	A. M.	A. M.	A. M.	P. M.	P. M.	P. M.	P. M.	P. M.	P. M.	P. M.
DANIELSVILLE ...	5 15	6 30	8 00	9 30	11 00	12 30	2 00	3 30	5 00	7 00	8 30	10 00
EDGEMONT PARK	5 32	6 48	8 18	9 48	11 18	12 48	2 18	3 48	5 18	7 18	8 48	10 18
BERLINSVILLE ...	5 38	6 55	8 25	9 55	11 25	12 55	2 25	3 55	5 25	7 25	8 55	10 25
WALNUTPORT	5 50	7 10	8 40	10 10	11 40	1 10	2 40	4 10	5 40	7 40	9 10	10 40
ARRIVE												

LEAVE	2	4	6	8	10	12	14	16	18	20	22	24
	A. M.	A. M.	A. M.	A. M.	A. M.	P. M.	P. M.	P. M.	P. M.	P. M.	P. M.	P. M.
WALNUTPORT	5 50	7 15	8 45	10 15	11 45	1 15	2 45	4 15	5 45	7 45	9 15	10 45
BERLINSVILLE ..	6 05	7 30	9 00	10 30	12 00	1 30	3 00	4 30	6 00	8 00	9 30	11 00
EDGEMONT PARK	6 12	7 37	9 07	10 37	12 07	1 37	3 07	4 37	6 07	8 07	9 37	11 07
DANIELSVILLE ...	6 30	7 55	9 25	10 55	12 25	1 55	3 25	4 55	6 25	8 25	9 55	11 25
ARRIVE												

Nos. 1, 2, 3 and 4 do not run on Sundays and Holidays
Nos. 7 and 8 run on Sundays only. Nos. 9 and 10 do not run on Sundays
Nos. 13 and 14 run on Saturdays and Sundays only
Nos. 23 and 24 run on Saturdays only. C. C. MARSH, Superintendent

(OVER) Danielsville, Pa.

This time table for the Blue Ridge Traction Company trolley dates from 1910. (Courtesy Larry Hillborn.)

Blue Ridge Traction Company

Corrected to December 1, 1914

WEEK-DAY SCHEDULE

Leave Danielsville	Leave Edgemont	Leave Berlinsville	Arrive Walnutport
5.15 A. M.	5.32 A. M.	5.38 A. M.	5.50 A. M.
6.30 A. M.	6.48 A. M.	6.55 A. M.	7.10 A. M.
8.00 A. M.	8.18 A. M.	8.25 A. M.	8.40 A. M.
11.00 A. M.	11.18 A. M.	11.25 A. M.	11.40 A. M.
12.30 P. M.	12.48 P. M.	12.55 P. M.	1.10 P. M.
*2.00 P. M.	2.18 P. M.	2.25 P. M.	2.40 P. M.
3.30 P. M.	3.48 P. M.	3.55 P. M.	4.10 P. M.
5.00 P. M.	5.18 P. M.	5.25 P. M.	5.40 P. M.
7.00 P. M.	7.18 P. M.	7.25 P. M.	7.40 P. M.
*8.30 P. M.	8.48 P. M.	8.55 P. M.	9.10 P. M.
*10.00 P.M.	10.18 P. M.	10.25 P. M.	10.40 P. M.

Leave Walnutport	Leave Berlinsville	Leave Edgemont	Arrive Danielsville
5.50 A. M.	6.00 A. M.	6.07 A. M.	6.25 A. M.
7.20 A. M.	7.30 A. M.	7.37 A. M.	7.55 A. M.
8.48 A. M.	9.00 A. M.	9.07 A. M.	9.25 A. M.
11.45 A. M.	12.00 M.	12.07 P. M.	12.25 P. M.
1.20 P. M.	1.30 P. M.	1.37 P. M.	1.55 P. M.
*2.45 P. M.	3.00 P. M.	3.07 P. M.	3.25 P. M.
4.20 P. M.	4.30 P. M.	4.37 P. M.	4.55 P. M.
5.45 P. M.	6.00 P. M.	6.07 P. M.	6.25 P. M.
!8.20 P. M.	8.25 P. M.	8.32 P. M.	9.00 P. M.
*9.20 P. M.	9.30 P. M.	9.37 P. M.	9.55 P. M.
*10.45 P.M.	11.00 P. M.	11.07 P. M.	11.25 P. M.

*Saturdays only.

!On Saturday this car leaves Walnutport at 7.45 P. M.

(Over)

A 1914 time table for the Blue Ridge Traction Company's trolley is pictured here. (Courtesy Larry Hillborn.)

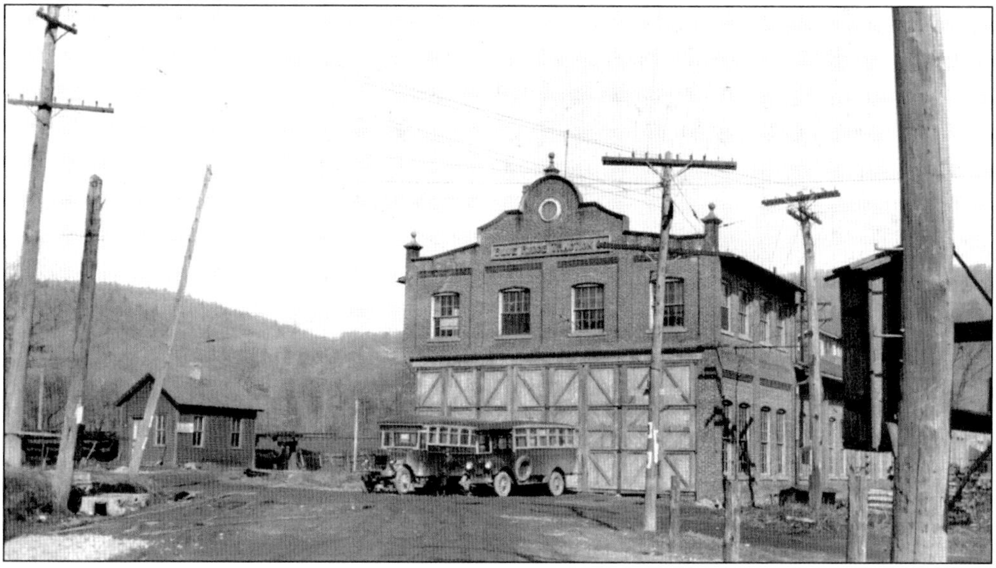

Buses are parked in front of the powerhouse of the Blue Ridge Traction Company. This photograph was taken soon after the trolley service was discontinued. A bus line started by the Solt brothers to run from Danielsville to Slatington lasted only two or three years. (Courtesy Larry Hillborn.)

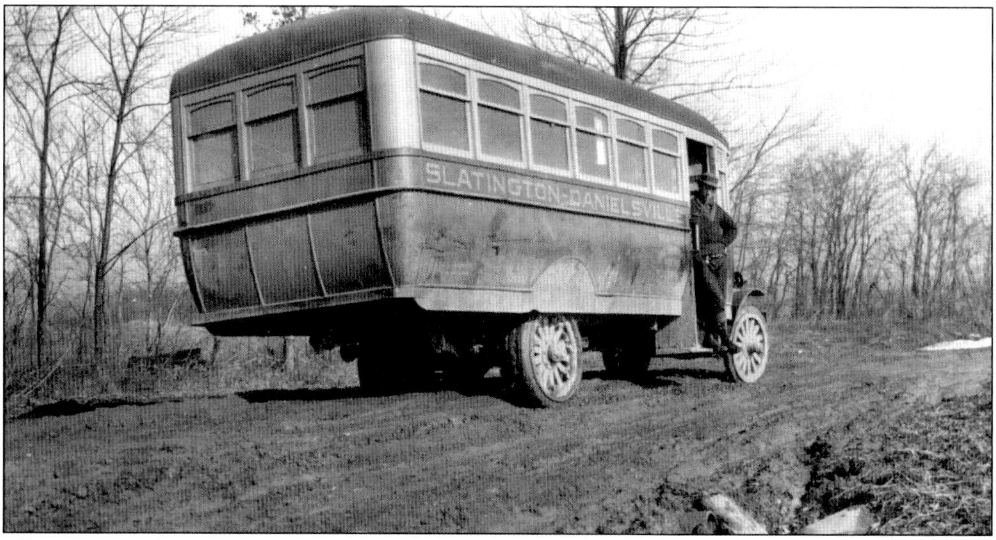

This close-up shows one of the buses used for the Danielsville-to-Slatington bus line. (Courtesy Larry Hillborn.)

Nine

INDUSTRY

Lehigh Township traces a lot of its history to slate—an important product used in the 1800s for roofing, school slates, and chalkboards. As the first local industry, slate brought many new people to the area.

The quarries changed owners (and names) numerous times over the years, making their history complex. The following information was taken from the 1883 geological survey of Lehigh and Northampton Counties. Although it is a partial list, it offers a glimpse into the condition of the quarries at that time. Notice that even by 1883, some of the quarries were already abandoned and full of water.

S. REPLE'S QUARRY. Located across the road from the Rockville Hotel. Abandoned and full of water. Dimensions: 100 by 200 feet.

HENRY'S QUARRY (OLD HARPER'S). Located one-half mile southeast of Danielsville.

J. Henry's Quarry. Located one-quarter mile south of Harper's quarry.

Eagle Slate Quarry. Owned by F.M. Hower. Located one-quarter mile south of Harper's.

MCCHUNK AND NATIONAL QUARRIES. Both located one-third mile east of the Eagle quarry. Dimensions: 100 by 150 feet and 250 by 250 feet. Both full of water.

UPLINGER & GRIFFITH'S QUARRY AND UPLINGER & HENRY'S QUARRY. Located 150 feet apart. Uplinger and Henry's full of water, located 500 feet south of Eagle quarry.

CONTINENTAL QUARRY. Located one and one-quarter miles south of Danielsville. Abandoned and full of water.

COL. B. MOURER'S SLATE FACTORY. Located one mile north of Poplar Grove. Produced some 2,000 school slates a day.

NEWVILLE SLATE COMPANY'S QUARRY. Located one mile north of Poplar Grove on the south side of Bertsch Creek.

NEW YORK AND PENNSYLVANIA QUARRY. Located one and one-quarter miles north of Poplar Grove. Abandoned and full of water.

KESTER'S MEADOW QUARRY. Leased by John Pauls and Peters. Dimensions: 150 by 100 feet, with 10 to 15 feet of loose slate on top.

DODDRIDGE QUARRY. Leased by Joseph Roberts. Located 500 yards north of the Kester Meadow Quarry.

HEINBACH'S QUARRY. Leased by Caskie & Emack. Located one and one-quarter miles northeast of Walnutport. The main cut originally 150 feet deep. Worked by two tunnels, one driving east and the other west. Used for making roofing slate. On-site factory produced school slate with a capacity of 10,000 cases a year.

OWEN WILLIAMS & COMPANY'S QUARRY. Located one-quarter mile west of Heinbacks. Used for roofing and school slates. David Williams opened a quarry 100 feet west of here.

BECH, BARGE & COMPANY'S QUARRY. Located one mile below Treichlers. Dimensions: 50 feet deep at the east side of the railroad.

Other slate quarries known to have been located in the township include the following: American Slateworks with factories in Walnutport and Slatington, school slates and blackboards (*c.* 1902); W.M. Benninger in Benningers, roofing slate and slate blackboards (*c.* 1908); the American Slate Company with quarries in Danielsville, roofing slate and slate products; the Atlas Slate Company in Walnutport (*c.* 1906); the Prudential Slate Company in Walnutport with quarries at Harpers, roofing slate, blackboard, and school slate (*c.* 1913); the Blue Ridge Slate Company with quarries and factory in Danielsville (1908); Harding, Jackson & Company, Danielsville (*c.* 1895); Granville Hahn in Walnutport, blackboards, roofing slate, urinals, sink tops, and grave covers (1912); Lobb, Parry & Company in Danielsville, roofing slate and other products; the Genuine Washington Slate Company in Berlinsville; and the Lehigh Slate Company in Walnutport (Samuel Caskie, superintendent).

The Amy Slate Company, in Danielsville, was founded on June 11, 1904, when the New Gem Slate Company was purchased at a receiver's sale. The president was Cotton Amy. Moses W. Amy served as secretary and treasurer. The name was changed to the Blue Ridge Slate Manufacturing Company, and offices were moved to Slatington on May 6, 1908.

The Northampton Slate Company, with a quarry in Berlinsville, was founded on September 9, 1946. It was discontinued on February 7, 1947. The partners were Hugh J. Roberts, John H. Roberts, and Michael J. Roberts.

Dieter's Foundry began in Cherryville in 1877 as a blacksmithing operation to service area farmers. It was founded by George Dieter and his son David, who owned it himself from 1904 to 1941. Among the foundry's products were hit-and-miss engines for use on farms and in sawmills. During World War II, the foundry ran 80 percent war production, including the manufacture of land mines. It was rebuilt following a 1943 fire that destroyed the building. It was then run by David Dieter's children Leon, Laird, Merritt, Roland, and Orpha until it ceased operation in 1981.

In 1936, David W. Dieter built a scale-model train, powered by a 1930 Model A Ford engine and a Model T Ford rear end, at the foundry in Cherryville. He took it to his Bowmanstown home to give train rides to children. This original train is located in Jacktown Park near Bangor, Pennsylvania, and is still in use. A second train was also built and used at Moser Park in Delps, in neighboring Moore Township. The number 55 on the engine is David Deiter's age when he built it.

This view shows the slate quarry located in Treichlers along the railroad to the south of the village.

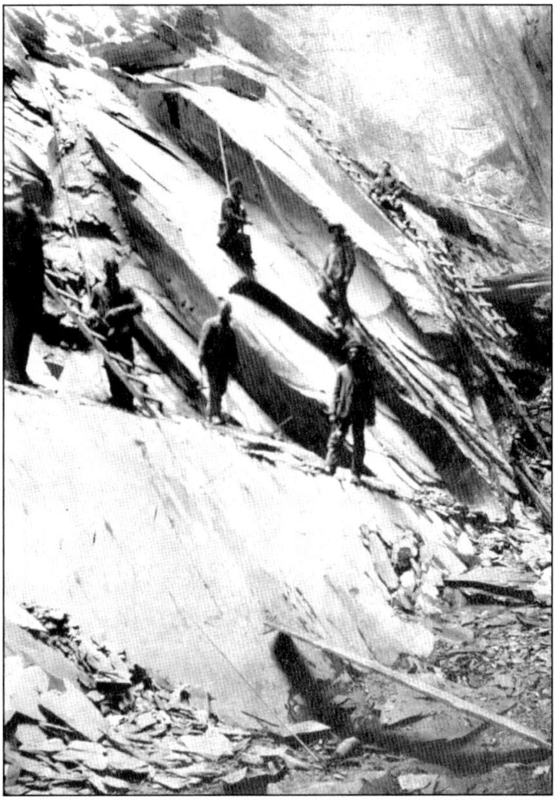

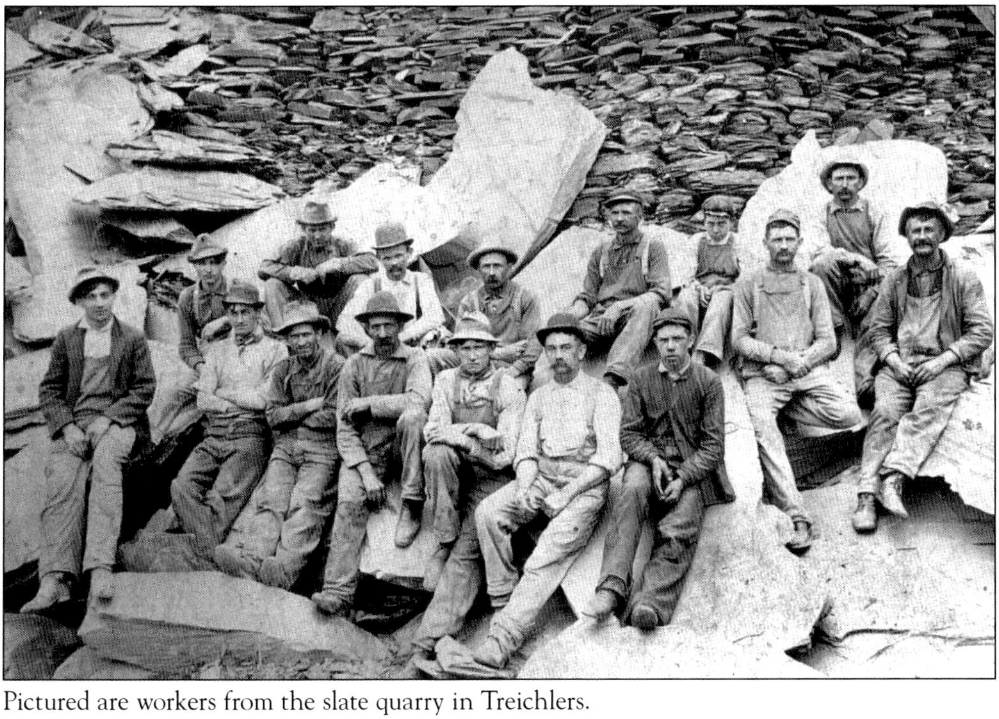

Pictured are workers from the slate quarry in Treichlers.

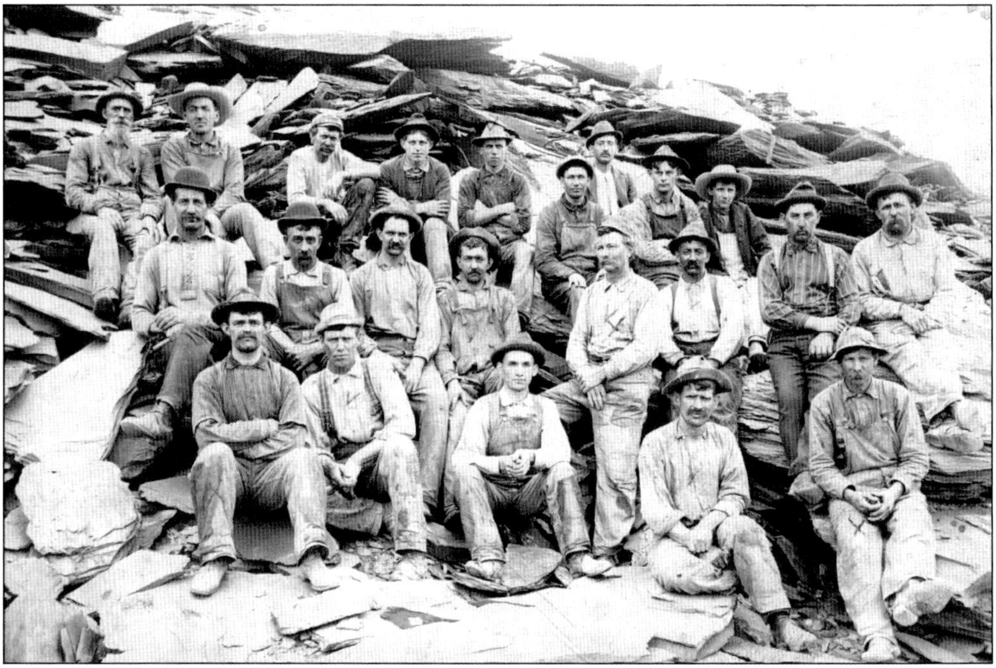

Slate workers pose at a quarry in Berlinsville. (Collection of the Lehigh Township Historical Society.)

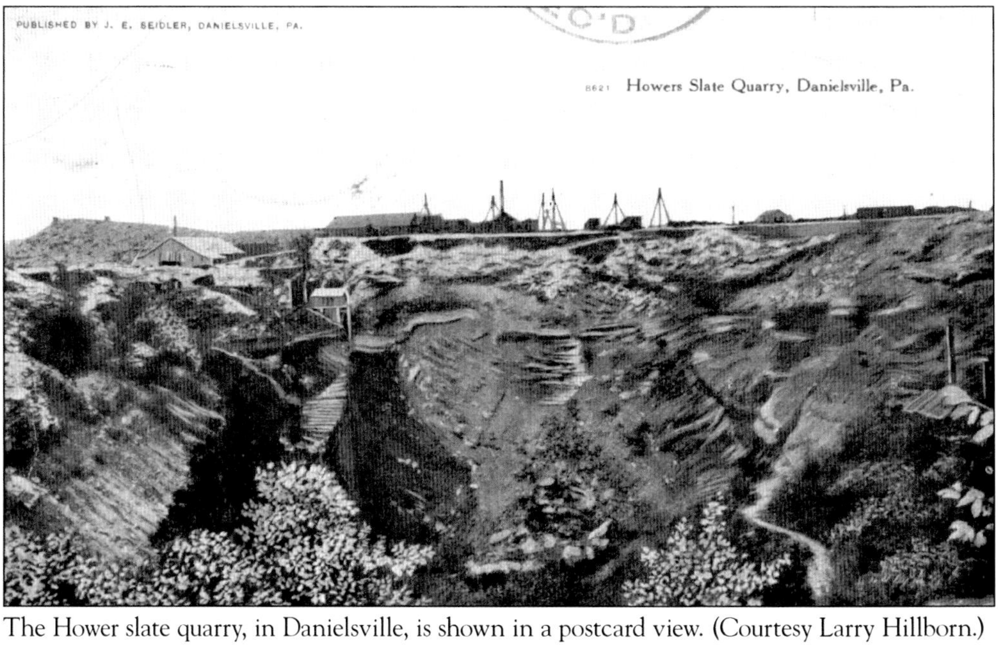

The Hower slate quarry, in Danielsville, is shown in a postcard view. (Courtesy Larry Hillborn.)

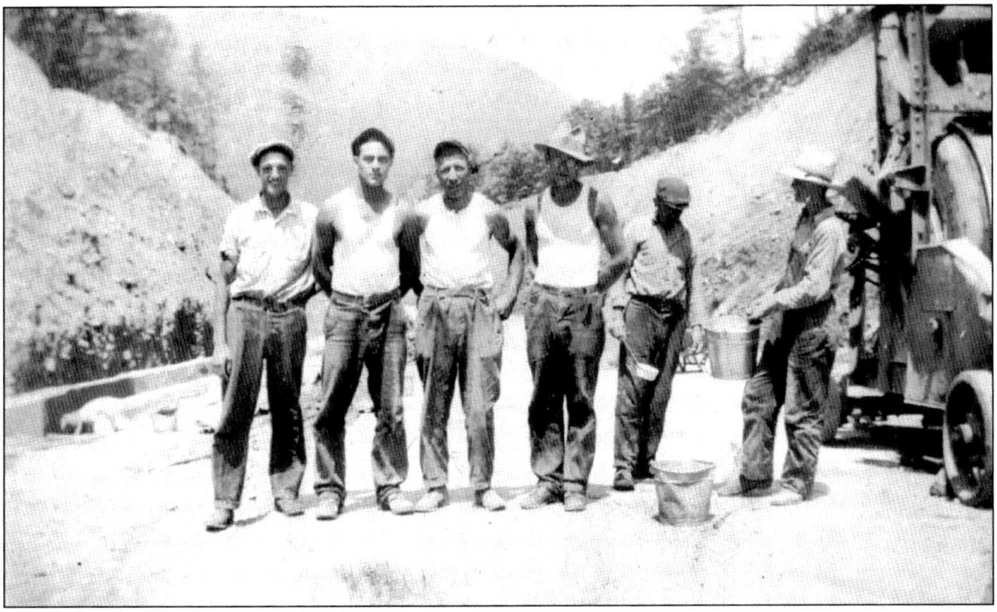

Shown c. 1930 are workers at the Edgemont slate quarry on Municipal Road. (Courtesy Alverta and Emily Jones.)

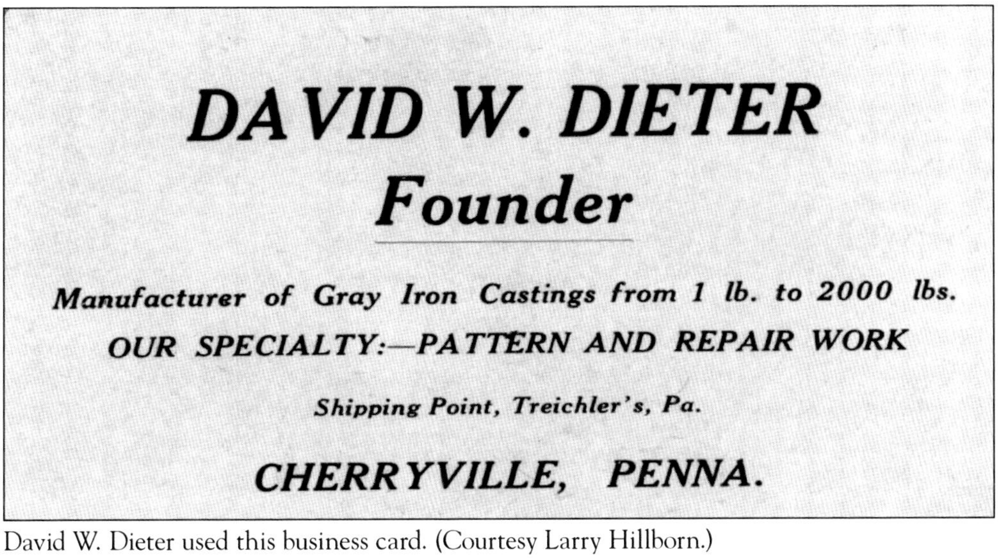

DAVID W. DIETER

Founder

Manufacturer of Gray Iron Castings from 1 lb. to 2000 lbs.

OUR SPECIALTY:—PATTERN AND REPAIR WORK

Shipping Point, Treichler's, Pa.

CHERRYVILLE, PENNA.

David W. Dieter used this business card. (Courtesy Larry Hillborn.)

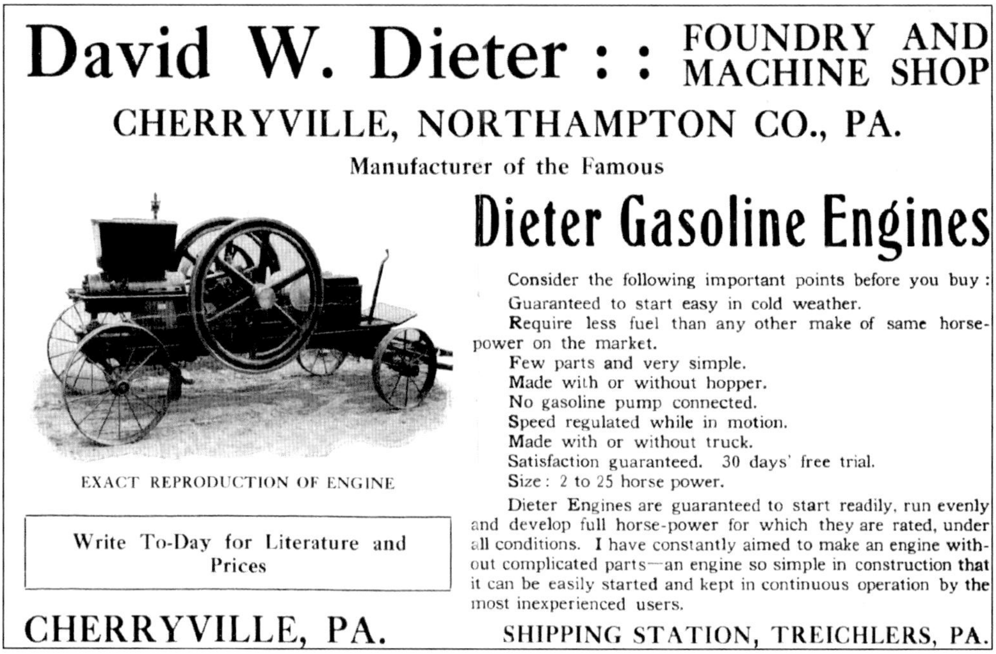

This early advertisement for Dieter's Foundry shows a hit-and-miss engine. (Courtesy Larry Hillborn.)

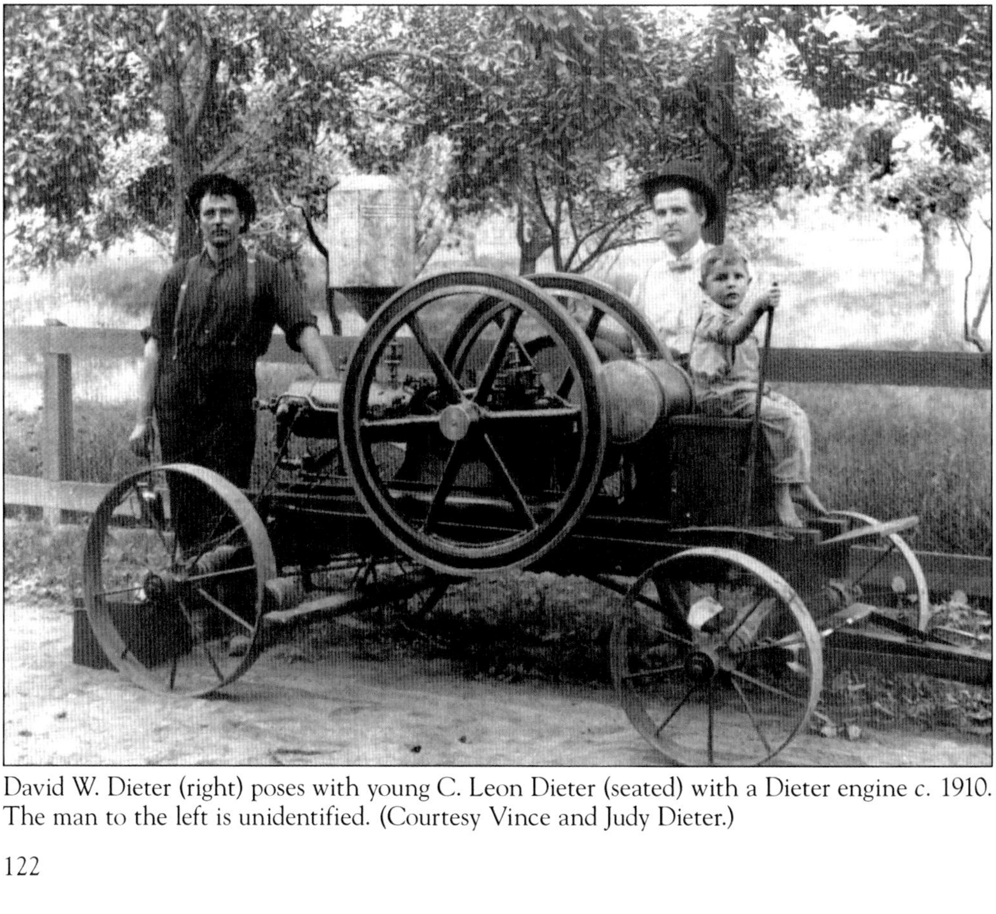
David W. Dieter (right) poses with young C. Leon Dieter (seated) with a Dieter engine *c.* 1910. The man to the left is unidentified. (Courtesy Vince and Judy Dieter.)

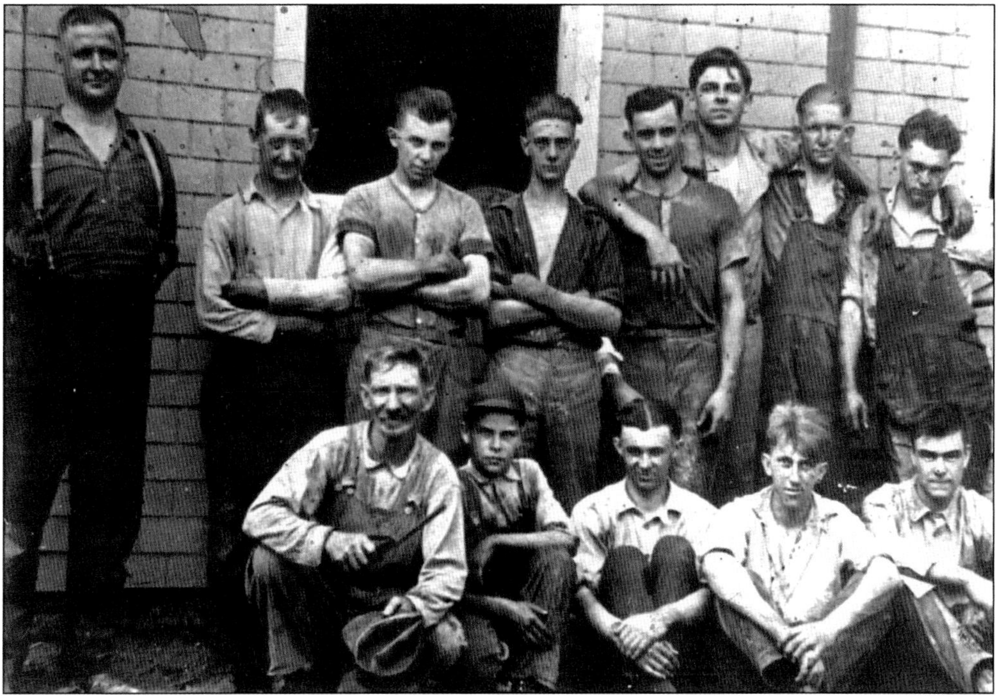

Posing in 1922, these Dieter's Foundry employees are, from left to right, as follows: (front row) Henry Huth, Ronald Dieter, Floyd Hall, Erwin Huth, and Clarence Reph; (back row) David Dieter, George Boucher, Albert Hall, Lester Kocher, Daniel Miller, C. Leon Dieter, Pete Huth, and Eddie Kramer. (Courtesy Vince and Judy Dieter.)

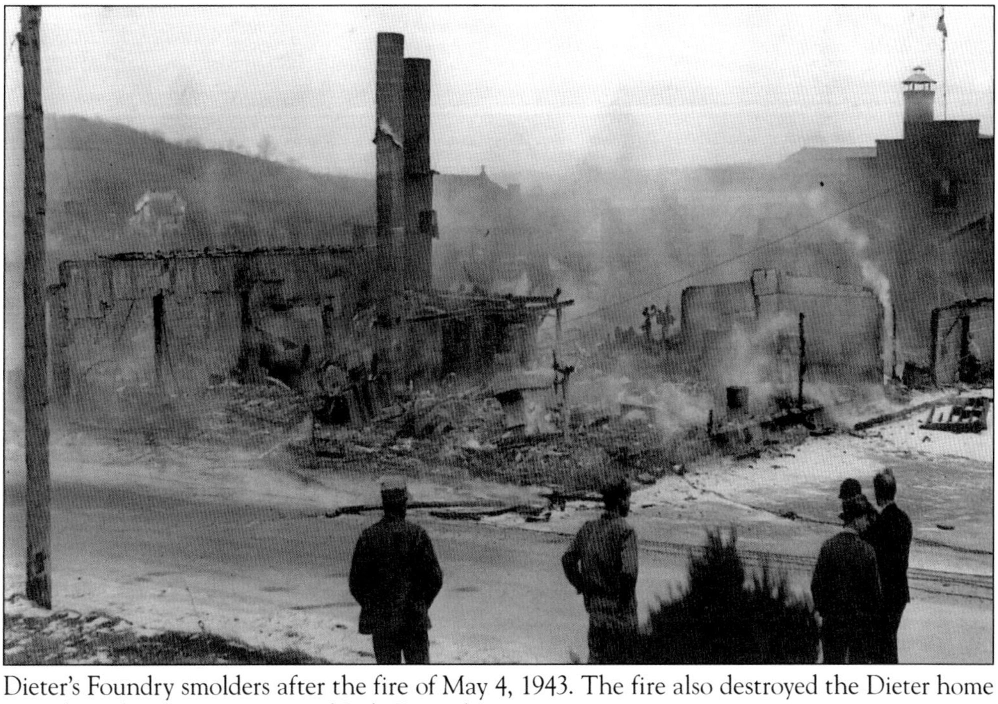

Dieter's Foundry smolders after the fire of May 4, 1943. The fire also destroyed the Dieter home next door. (Courtesy Vince and Judy Dieter.)

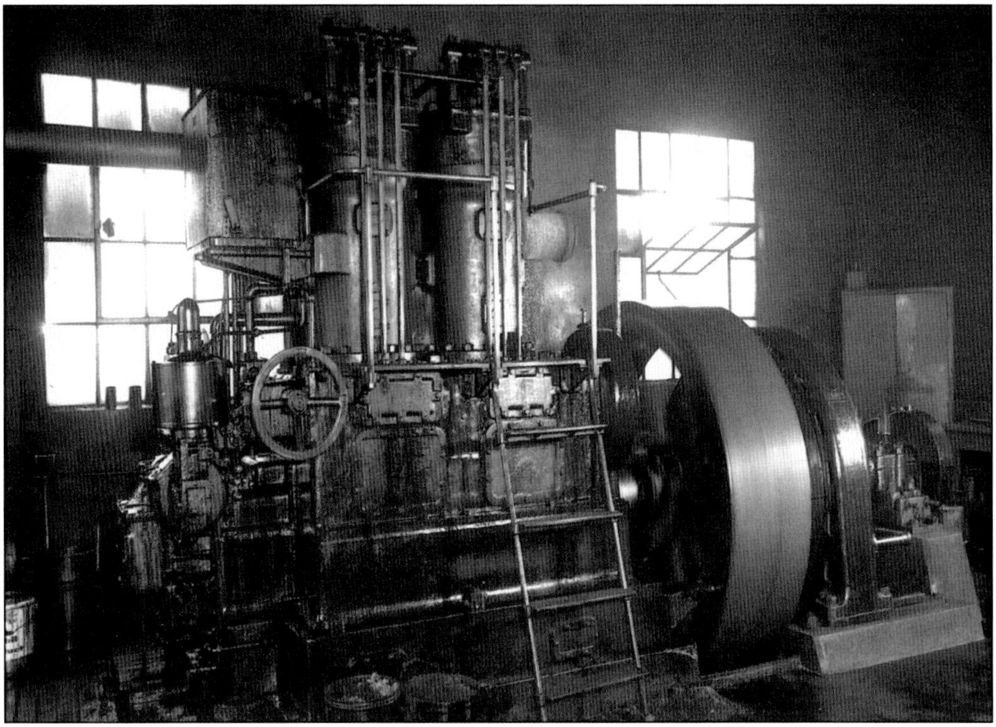

This diesel engine provided electricity for Dieter's Foundry. (Courtesy Vince and Judy Dieter.)

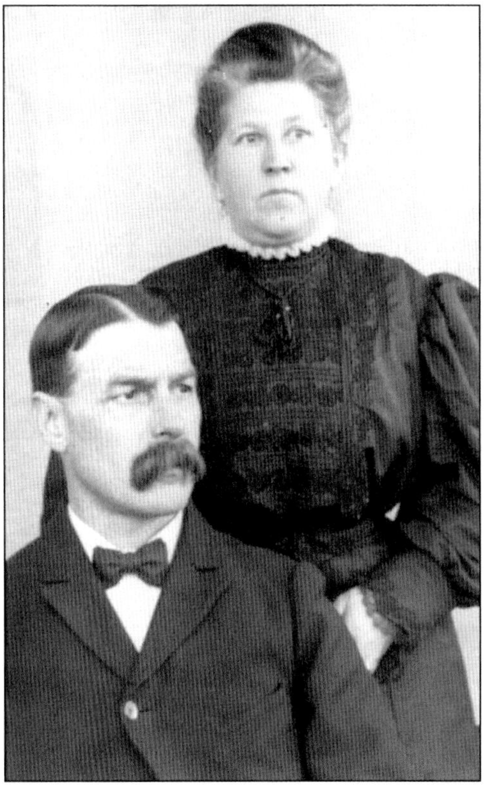

Rev. Hiram Frantz, shown here with his wife, was one of only three clergymen ever to build an automobile. From 1901 to 1902, he was the maker of the Frantz automobile and was a member of the clergy for St. Paul's Reformed Evangelical Church and Reformed United Church of Christ from 1900 to 1914. (Courtesy Larry Hillborn.)

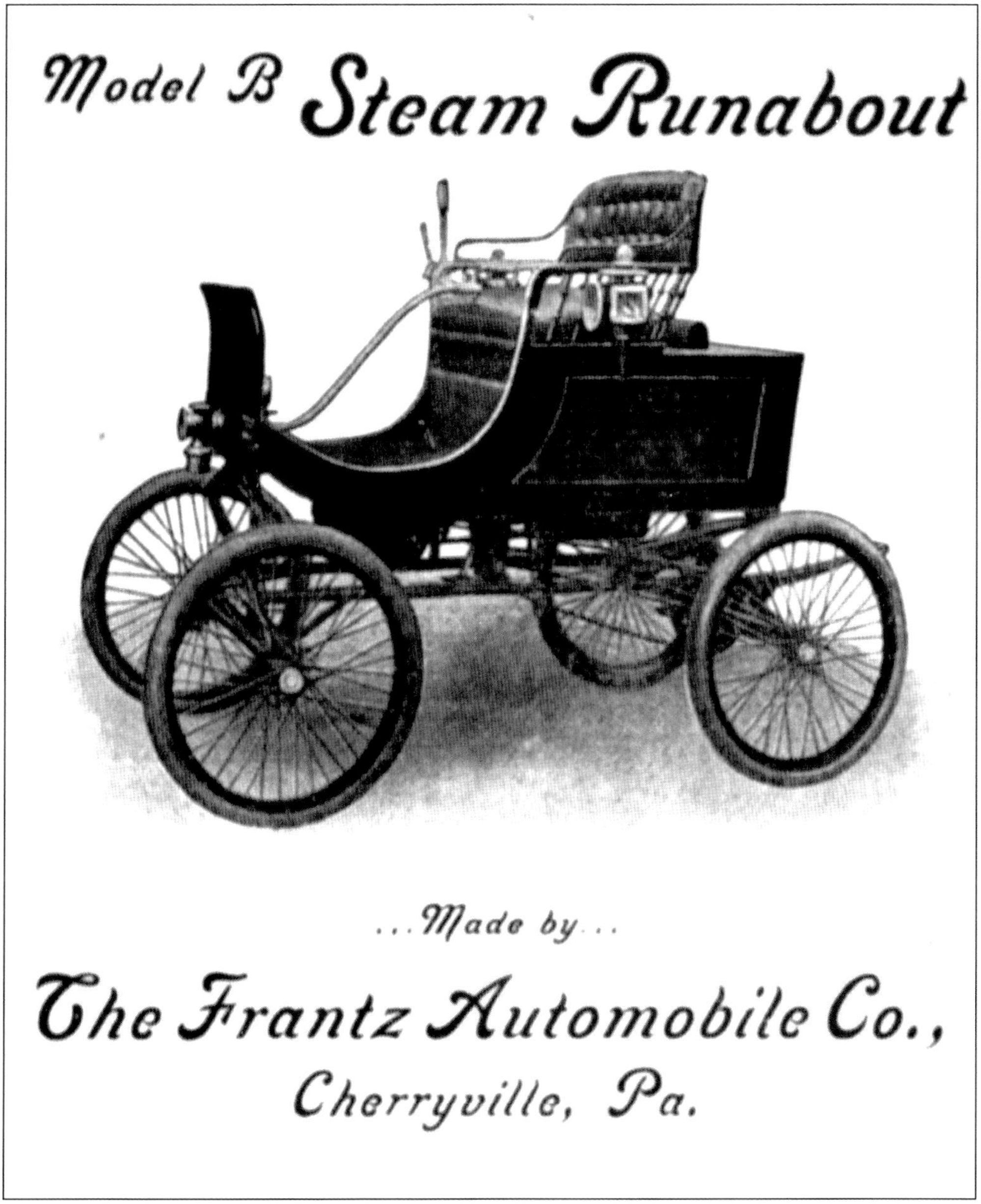

Pictured is the cover of an advertising brochure for the Frantz automobile. By 1901, Frantz had built four light steam cars that used his patented burner. The cars had tiller steering, wire wheels, and a single-chain drive. He announced that he would open a larger factory and build gasoline cars, but it appears he never did. (Courtesy David Bausch.)

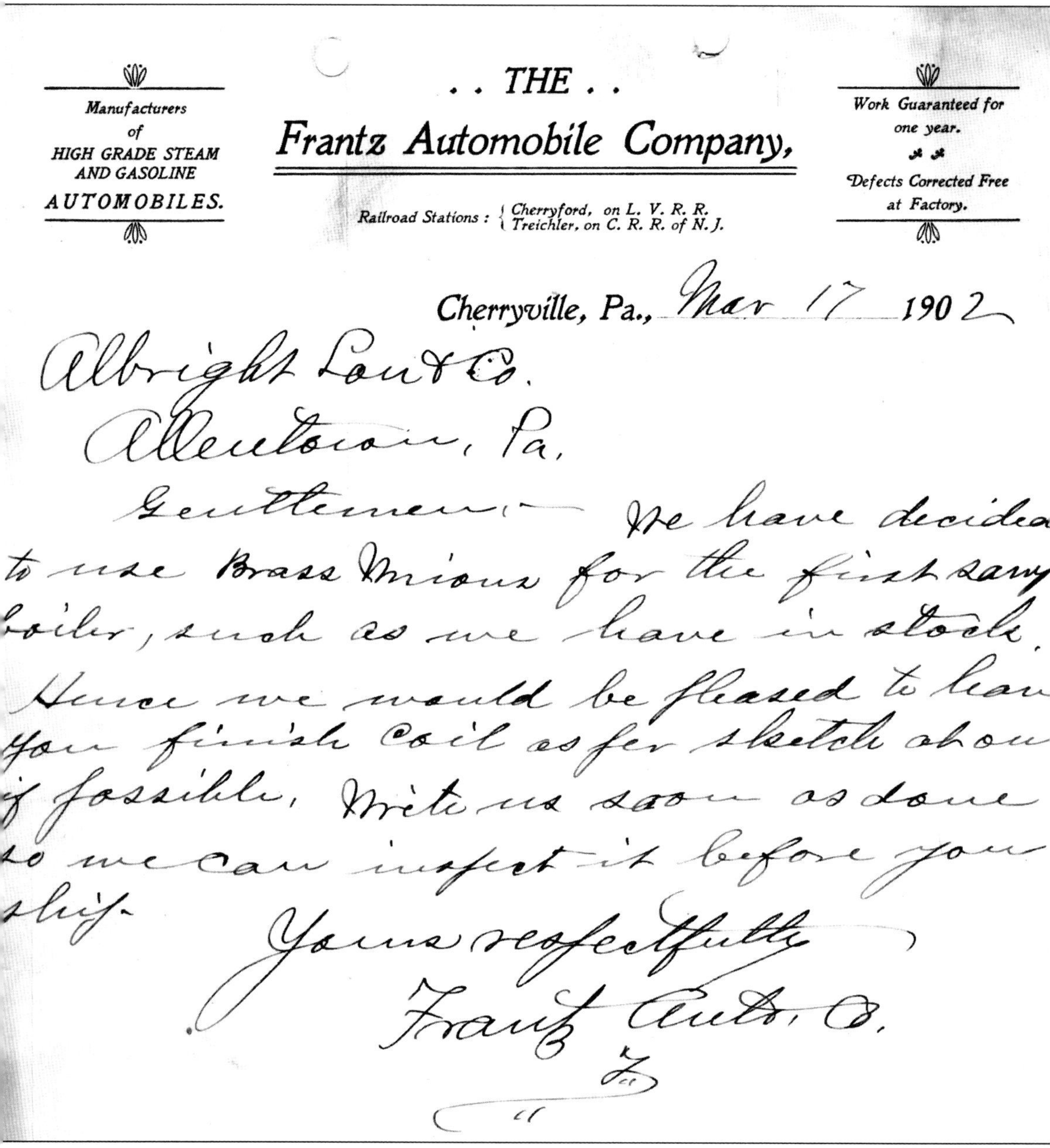

Manufacturers of HIGH GRADE STEAM AND GASOLINE AUTOMOBILES.

.. THE ..

Frantz Automobile Company,

Work Guaranteed for one year.

Defects Corrected Free at Factory.

Railroad Stations: Cherryford, on L. V. R. R. / Treichler, on C. R. R. of N. J.

Cherryville, Pa., Mar 17 1902

Albright Lau & Co.
Allentown, Pa.

Gentlemen:— We have decided to use Brass Unions for the first sam[ple] boiler, such as we have in stock. Hence we would be pleased to have you finish Coil as per sketch shown if possible. Write us soon as done so we can inspect it before you ship.

Yours respectfully
Frantz Auto. Co.
F.

The Frantz Automobile Company used this letterhead in 1902. (Courtesy Larry Hillborn.)

Ten

Lehigh Township Veterans

This chapter is dedicated to the men and women of all branches of the military who served their country, especially to those who made the supreme sacrifice. The names are categorized by war periods, but some do not fit neatly into these categories. They include Charles G. Arner, who served along the Mexican border; Reuben Hantz, who served in the Mexican War; Carl E. James, who served from October 1957 to September 1959 and was reactivated for the Berlin Crisis in October 1961; and Russell L. Miquel, who served from 1977 to 1981.

This listing has been compiled through information from people who answered our inquiry about those who served. Names are also taken from the honor roll in Treichlers and from Northampton County Veterans Affairs. Undoubtedly, there are many names missing.

The Revolutionary War. Frederick App, Frederich Eberhart, Conrad Herman, Jacob Kehs, Adam Kuntz, Frederich Kuntz, George Kuntz, Jacob Kuntz, Peter Kuntz, Abraham Leiengerger, Jacob Mummey, Issac Oplinger, Henrich Pest, and John Saeger.

The War of 1812. Peter Lynn and William Osterday.

The Civil War. Awra J. Andrews, Lewis Beer, John Deibert, William Fisher, Edward George, Stephen Green, Martin Habertorn, Paul Heffelfinger, Charles Hall, William Hawk, Michael F. Heiney, John Kester, Chester E. Kress, Samuel Kress, William Kuntz, Charles Leibenguth, Joseph Lentz, John Lever, John M. Link, William Lynn, Amandus Miller, John G. Moser, Robert Owens, John Person, David O. Pritchard, Robert Owens Pritchard, Henry Ravert, Moses Roth, Constantine Scherer, James M. Seip, Tilghman H. Seip, James Shaffer, Lewis H. Siegried, Josiah Snyder, Stephen Spengler, Carl A. Speth, Benneville F. Stahley, Edward F. Treichler, James B. Wagner, and Reuben Wagner.

The Spanish-American War. Elwood M. Beers and John W. Richardson.

World War I. Earl H. Anthony, Howard R. Beers, A. Lewey Benninger, Thomas F. Benninger, Raymond E. Bryfogle, Oscar L. Burbes, Howard F. Christman, Edward C. Davies, George Diehl, Carl Flickinger, Pasquale Freda, Howard J. Green, Harvey W. Griffith, Henry D. Haydt, Harry D. Jones, William A. Kromer, Franklin T. Kromer, Clarence Kuntz, Harry J. Kuntz, Leon C. Kuntz, John A. Lentz, Paul Lentz, Roland W. May, William W. McCray, Mary C. McElduff, William L. Miller, Floyd F. Oplinger, Earl E. Rodgers, Allen E. Roth, Charles F. Singer, DeForest E. Snyder, Fred W. Snyder, Raymond D. Snyder, Charles H. Stever, George F. Stever, Tilghman L. Vogel, and Ralph M. Wyatt.

World War II. Daniel R. Aldio, Fred Charles Allford, Edwin J. Andreas, Paul Andrews, Emma L. Anthony, Leonard M. Anthony, Merritt Anthony, Roy A. Anthony, William Anthony, Woodrow Anthony, Alexander Asbath Jr., Elwood J. Bachman, Thomas F. Becker, Carl R. Beil, Kenneth Beil, Gordon A. Benninger, Leslie G. Benninger, Vernon L. Benninger, Willard F. Benninger, Edward A. Binder, George Binder, Henry J. Binder, James N. Binder, Phyllis E. Binder, Robert Binder, Thomas H. Binder, John J. Bobal, Ernest W. Borger, Grant A. Bossard, Kenneth B. Bossard, Perry M. Bowman, Christian F. Braren, Raymond Brobst, Lewis R. Burbes,

Donald Burkhardt, Lester V. Burkhardt, Robert Burkhardt, George Cherry, Andrew Chimics, Charles Chimics, Frank Chimics, Michael Chimics, Peter Chimics, Kermit S. Christman, Frank Cihylik, Bernerd Clancy, Stanley Clark, John L. Clarke, Lincoln Coffin, Woodrow Coffin, Elias F. Crouthamel, Daniel D. Danner, Vance T. Deibert, Frank Dergosit, Owen O. Derhammer, Allen D. Diehl, George R. Diehl, Harold C. Distler, James W. Distler, Michael E. Downey, Kenneth Easterday, Walter D. Easterday, Willard Easterday, Gail Eisenhard, Lewis Eisenhard, Mahlon A. Eisenhard, Ralph T. Engle, August Erschen, Henry F. Fatzinger, Harold Finkbeinger, Floyd F. Fogle, George C. Fogle, Paul Frantz, Rev. Mark H. Frantz, Thomas J. Fritz, Harley R.J. Fritz Sr., Ralph F. Fritzinger, Carl Gabel, Paul Gabel, Vincent J.H. Gabel Sr., Floyd D. Geary Jr., Constantine T. Gerkovich, Alexander J. Glass Sr., Anna Glass, Calvin Gower, Clayton Gross, Paul K. Grube, Walter J. Gursky Sr., John J. Halko, Stephen M. Halko, Monroe Hall, Sherman P. Hall, Gordon Handwerk, Horace G. Harper Jr., Donald A. Hartzell, Arie V. Haydt, Leon C. Haydt, Herman J. Heatter, Laird K. Heckman, Clarence Heffelfinger Jr., George A. Heffelfinger, Robert P. Heffelfinger, Truman R. Heffelfinger, Stephen Heleva, George Hinkle, Henry Hinkle, William Hinkle, John Hoch, John Hohl, Homer W. Hontz, Neal R. Hontz, Joseph S. Horvath, Justin Howard, Robert Humphrey, Carlton E. Jones, Kenneth E. Jones, Quay G. Jones Jr., Claude F. Kern, Frank M. Kirchkesner, Glenn E. Kishline, Kermit K. Kleintop, Homer A. Kleppinger, Larue Kleppinger, Kenneth E. Kline, Wilbur Kline, John Klutzaritz, Stephen Konek, Alex Koran, William P. Kratzer, Louis J. Kremus, Walter W. Kroboth, Nevin J. Kuntz, Stephen A. Lacko, Emma Lentz, Palmer Lentz, Harold H. Lloyd, Llewellyn Logenbach, Warren R. Logenbach, Herbert A. Mack, Luther Mack, Vernon S. Mack, Malcom Mackenzie, William Mackenzie, Martin P. Manner, Delbert C. Marsh, Everet Marsh, Ray O. Marsh, Frank E. Marth, Joseph J. Marth, Frederick F. Mauer Jr., Arthur Meckes, Kenneth W. Mensinger, Frank J. Mesics, LaVerne T. Miguell, Clayton Miller, Luther Miller, Clarence D. Minnich, Darwin S. Minnich, Luther Minnich, Richard W. Morris Jr., Daniel T. Moyer, John A. Murray, Peter Myster, Dale Newhart, Charles Nicholas Jr., Jean Nicholas, Frank Nierer, Joseph Nikisher, Gizza J. Oncheck, Michael J. Papay, Arthur A. Parry Jr., Allen F. Reed, Hobart C. Reph, Theodore R. Reph, George Ritter, Leroy Ritter, Millard G. Ritter, Michael Roman, Stephen Royer, Joseph Ryno, Robert Santee, Russel P. Scheirer, Frank T. Schmidt, Stephen Schmidt, Peter M. Sedler, John Seidel, Curtis C. Shanfelt, J. Wayne Shoemaker, Paul Shoemaker, Richard M. Shoemaker, Frank S. Skrapits, John Skrapits, John F. Skrapits, Frank S. Slanina, Deibert Smale, Nevin C. Smith, William Walter Smith, Charles Snyder, Harold E. Snyder, Stanley J. Snyder, Ralph J. Solt, Daniel M. Stankovich, Carl Stever, Allen Strauss, Alex S. Szoke, Ralph M. Vogel, William P. Vogel, James Walker, Paul A. Weaver, Ralph E. Weaver, James E. Wehr, Raymond Weiss, Alton R. Weyer, Aaron P. Wildermuth, David Yale, James Yale, Richard Yale, Edward Zamadics, William Zamadics, Frank Zamadics Jr., Anthony Zangart, Joseph A. Zelinski, and George P. Zigo.

THE KOREAN WAR. Richard J. Adams, Mahlon T. Beers, Bert Beil, Harold Beil, Rudolph T. Benson, Paul Chimics, Steve Chimics, Luther L. Christman, Richard D. Eckhart, Sterling Gower, William Gower, Marlyn A. Hall, Roy W. Heckman, Albert J. Hofman, Andrew J. Jordan, Harold E. Kern, Stephen Kratzer, Michael L. Kurinec, Donald L. Miller, Cyrus A. Miquel, Jackson H. Neff, Theodore R. Potteiger Jr., Arthur A. Rehrig, John C. Rosenblatt, Donald D. Shoemaker, Joseph L. Steirer, William J. Stravinsky, Edward K. Unger, Lester G. Vogel, and Donald L. Wehr.

THE VIETNAM WAR. Edward Anderson, Roger Andrews, Glenn M. Anthony, Barry C. Beil, Jeffrey V. Beil, Joe Beil, Ray Beil, Dennis P. Briody, Jerry Bundra, Patricia I. Csencsits, Robert J. Drumheller, Sheldon Warren Endy Jr., Larry Frederick, James L. Gardner, Bradly Gasper, Jay N. Hontz, Gary L. Hummel, Harold D. Hunsicker, Patricia A. Jackson-James, David Jones, John B. Klutzaritz, Clark R. Latshaw, Brian D. Lloyd, Michael R. Madea, Dennis F. Mantz, Jeffrey C. Marsh, Larry Miquel, Larry Neff, Paul M. Newhard, John J. Roman, Carl P. Schoch, Brian Taras, and Russell W. Wieand.